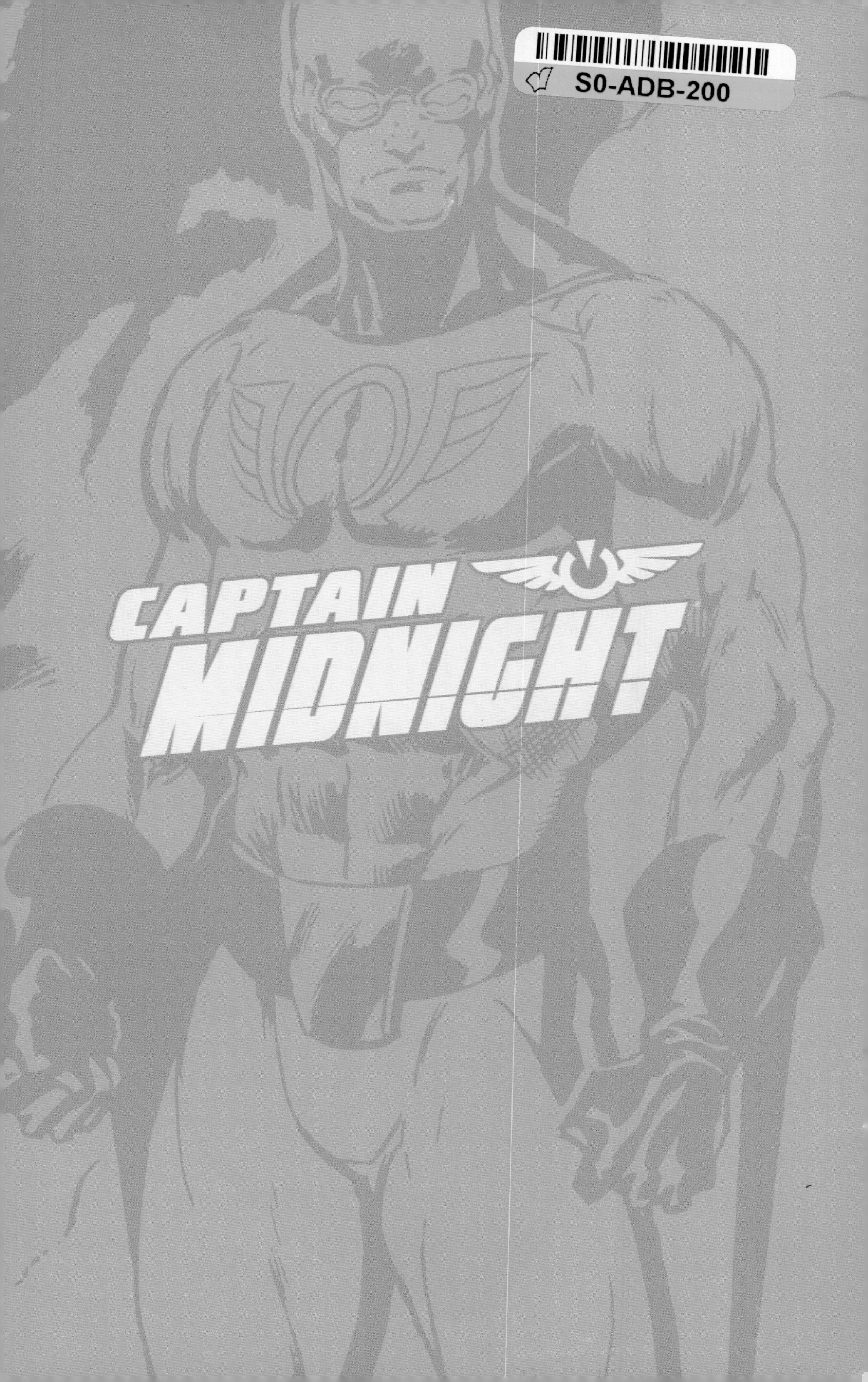
CAPTAIN
MIDNIGHT

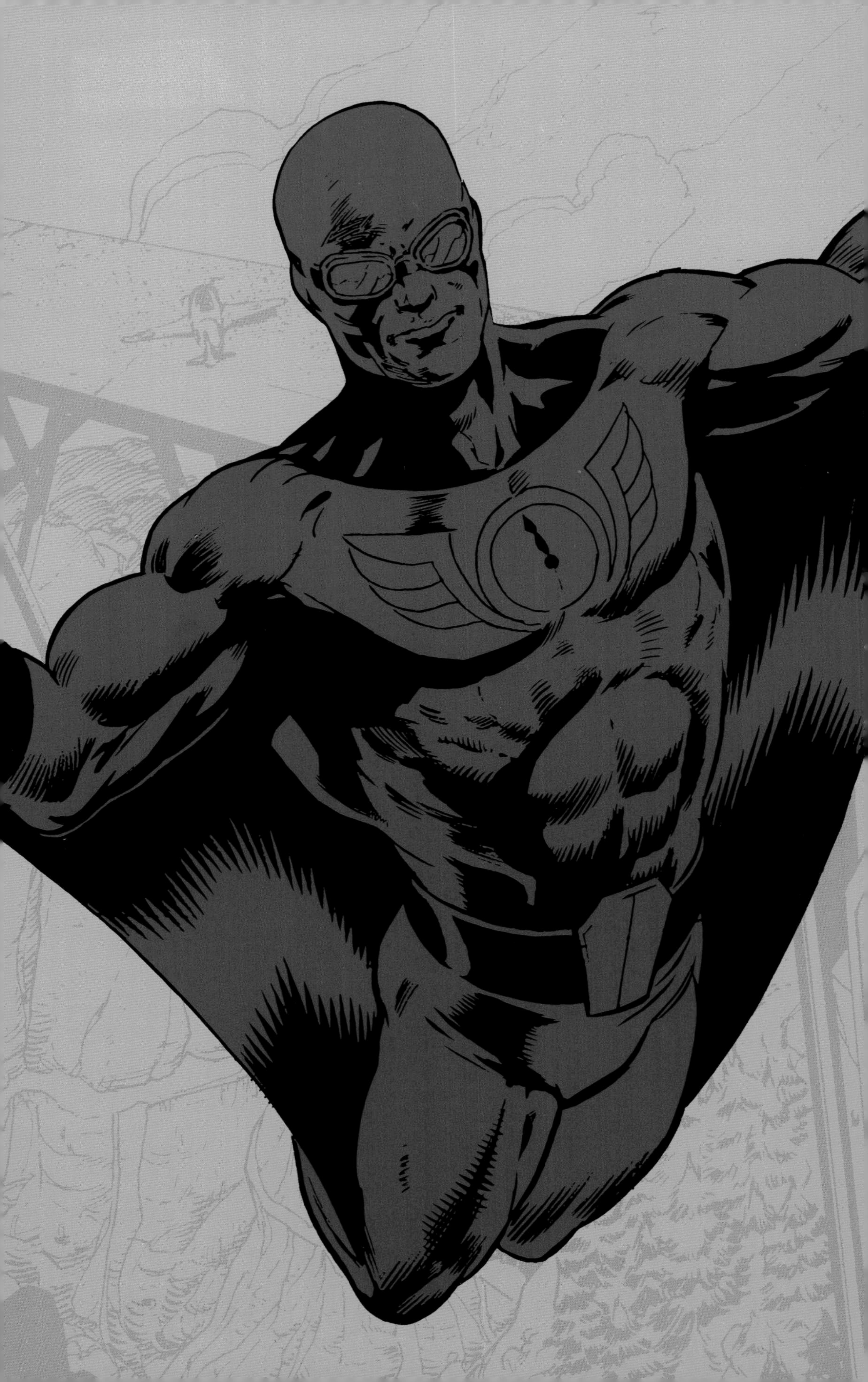

CAPTAIN MIDNIGHT

VOLUME 1 **ON THE RUN**

STORY BY
JOSHUA WILLIAMSON

ART BY
FERNANDO DAGNINO
(PAGES 41–110)
VICTOR IBÁÑEZ
(PAGES 7–22)
PERE PÉREZ
(PAGES 23–31, 38)
ROGER ROBINSON
(PAGES 32–37)

COLORS BY
EGO

LETTERS BY
NATE PIEKOS OF **BLAMBOT®**

COVER BY
FELIPE MASSAFERA

CHAPTER BREAK ART BY
FELIPE MASSAFERA
(CHAPTERS 1–3)
RAYMOND SWANLAND
(CHAPTER 0)
PAOLO RIVERA
(PIN-UP)

DARK HORSE BOOKS

PUBLISHER.................MIKE RICHARDSON
EDITOR.........................JIM GIBBONS
ASSISTANT EDITOR........SPENCER CUSHING
DIGITAL PRODUCTION........ALLYSON HALLER
COLLECTION DESIGNER............ADAM GRANO

Special thanks to Mike Richardson, Randy Stradley,
Scott Allie, and David Macho Gómez and Spanish Inq.

Mike Richardson, President and Publisher | Neil Hankerson, Executive Vice President | Tom Weddle, Chief Financial Officer | Randy Stradley, Vice President of Publishing | Michael Martens, Vice President of Book Trade Sales | Anita Nelson, Vice President of Business Affairs | Scott Allie, Editor in Chief | Matt Parkinson, Vice President of Marketing | David Scroggy, Vice President of Product Development | Dale LaFountain, Vice President of Information Technology | Darlene Vogel, Senior Director of Print, Design, and Production | Ken Lizzi, General Counsel | Davey Estrada, Editorial Director | Chris Warner, Senior Books Editor | Diana Schutz, Executive Editor | Cary Grazzini, Director of Print and Development | Lia Ribacchi, Art Director | Cara Niece, Director of Scheduling | Tim Wiesch, Director of International Licensing | Mark Bernardi, Director of Digital Publishing

Published by Dark Horse Books
A division of Dark Horse Comics, Inc.
10956 SE Main Street
Milwaukie, OR 97222

First edition: January 2014
ISBN 978-1-61655-229-9

3 5 7 9 10 8 6 4 2
Printed in China

International Licensing: (503) 905-2377
Comic Shop Locator Service: (888) 266-4226

CAPTAIN MIDNIGHT VOLUME 1: ON THE RUN

This volume collects the comic book Captain Midnight #0, the Free Comic Book Day 2013 story "Captain Midnight in 'Clues,'" and Captain Midnight #1–#3 from the ongoing comic series from Dark Horse Comics.

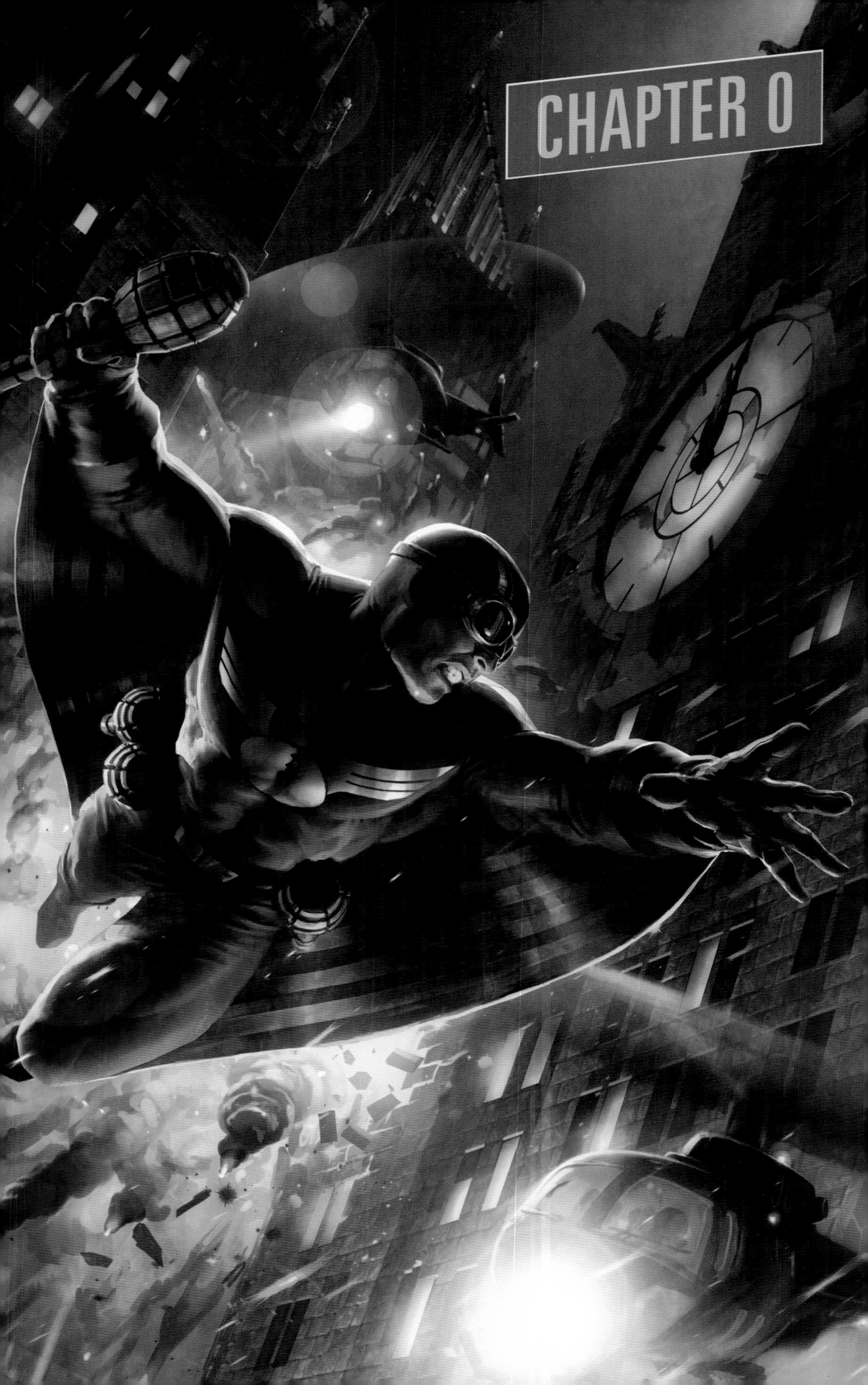
CHAPTER 0

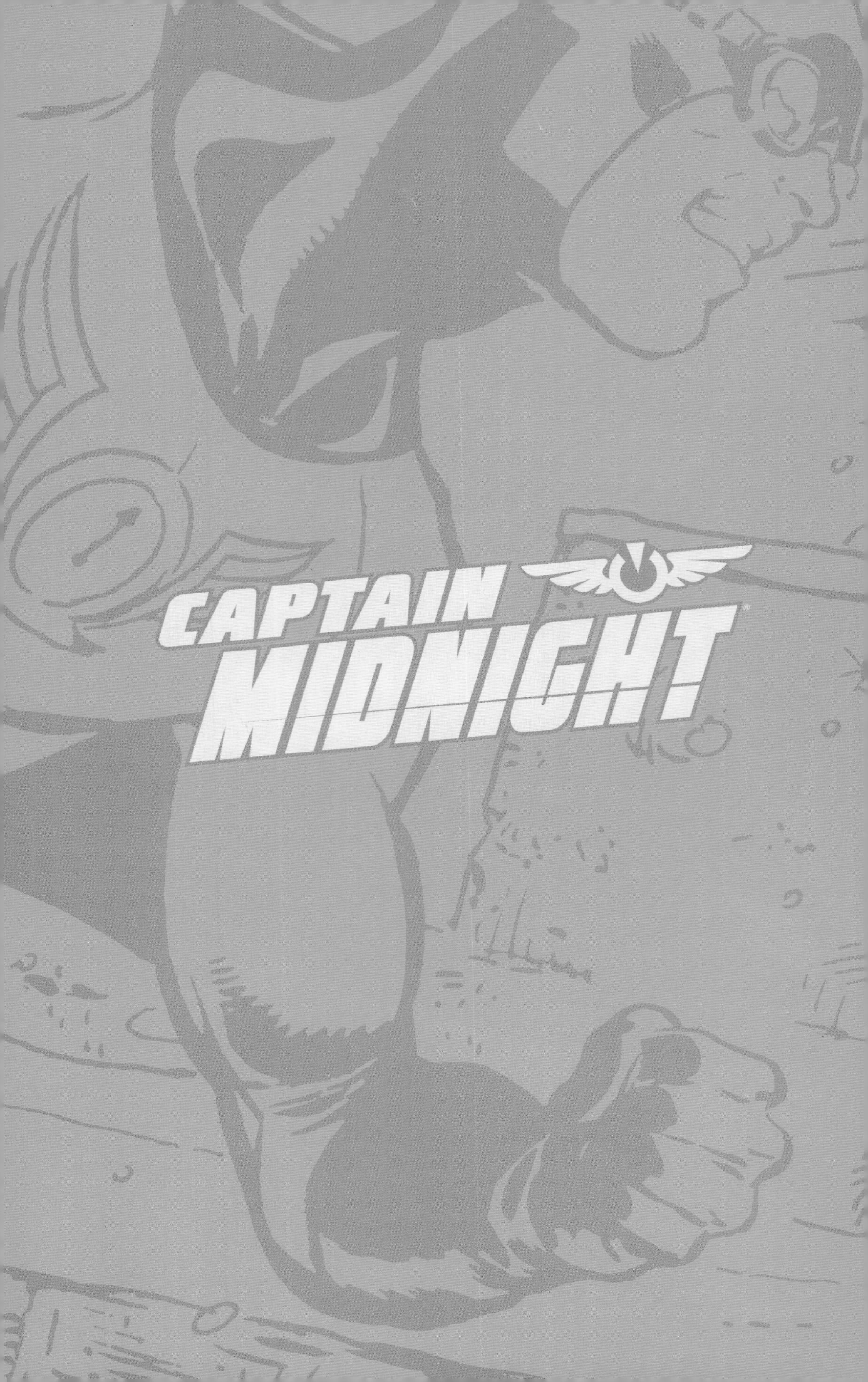
CAPTAIN
MIDNIGHT

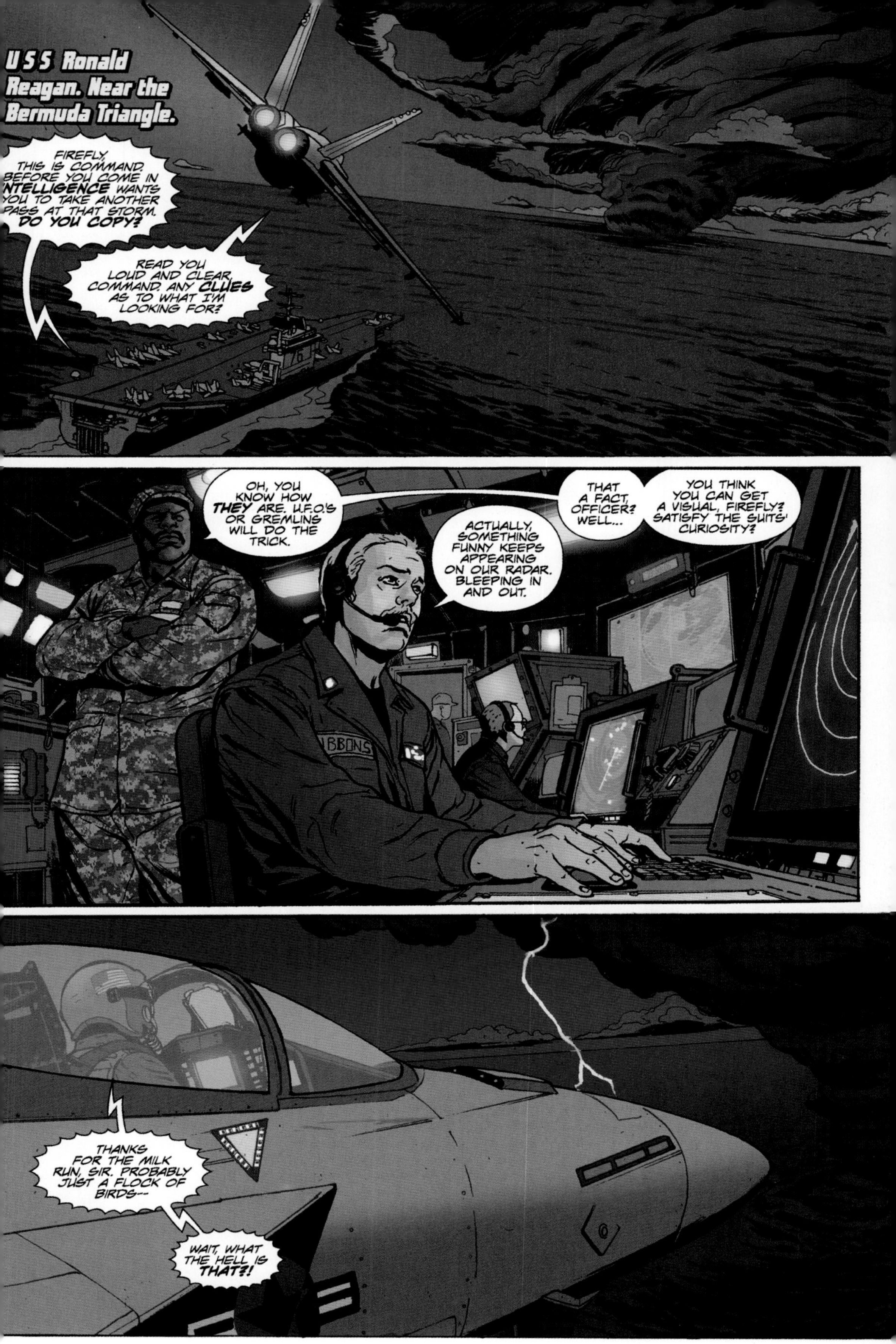
U S S Ronald Reagan. Near the Bermuda Triangle.
FIREFLY, THIS IS COMMAND. BEFORE YOU COME IN INTELLIGENCE WANTS YOU TO TAKE ANOTHER PASS AT THAT STORM. DO YOU COPY?
READ YOU LOUD AND CLEAR, COMMAND. ANY CLUES AS TO WHAT I'M LOOKING FOR?
OH, YOU KNOW HOW THEY ARE. U.F.O.'S OR GREMLINS WILL DO THE TRICK.
ACTUALLY, SOMETHING FUNNY KEEPS APPEARING ON OUR RADAR. BLEEPING IN AND OUT.
THAT A FACT, OFFICER? WELL...
YOU THINK YOU CAN GET A VISUAL, FIREFLY? SATISFY THE SUITS' CURIOSITY?
THANKS FOR THE MILK RUN, SIR. PROBABLY JUST A FLOCK OF BIRDS--
WAIT, WHAT THE HELL IS THAT?!

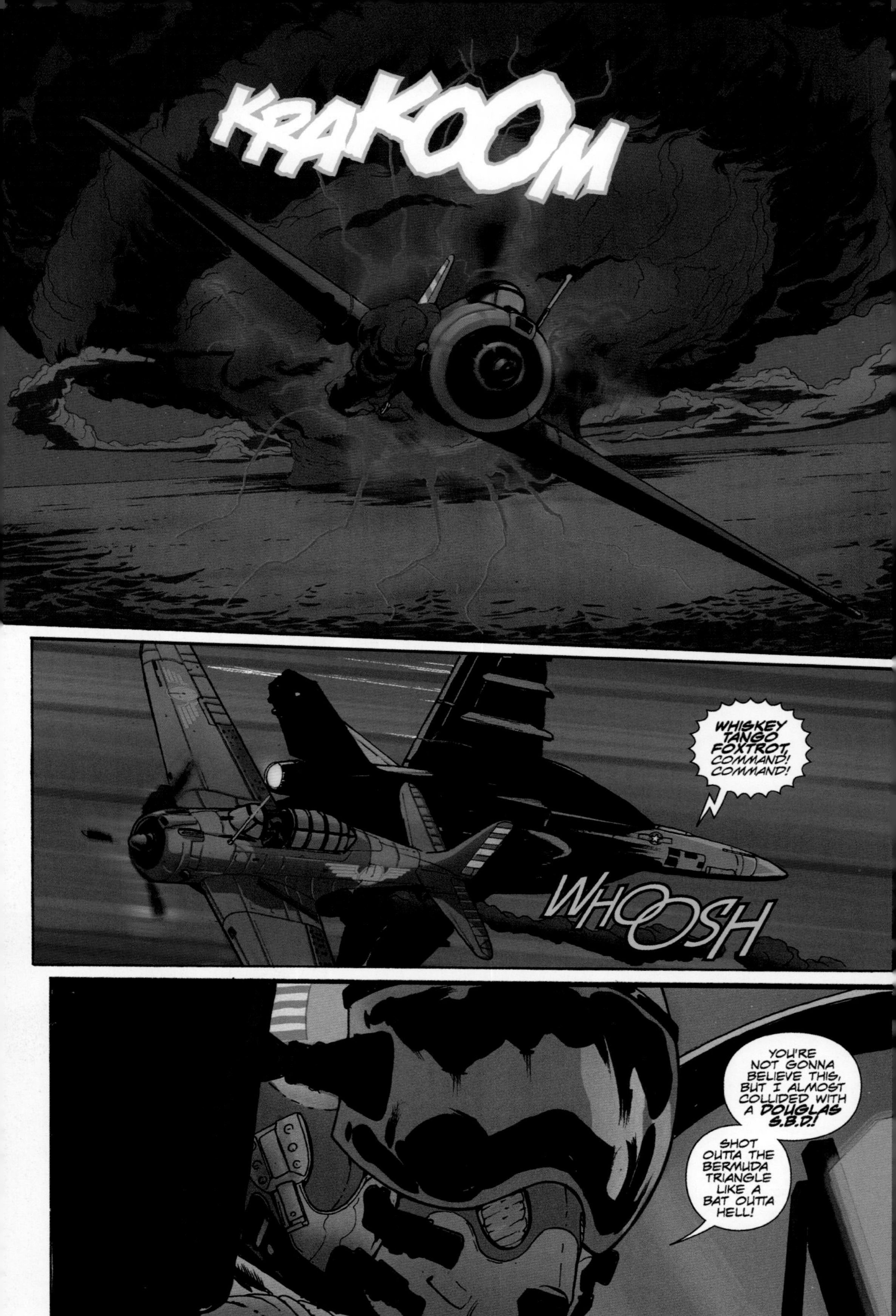
KRAKOOM
WHISKEY TANGO FOXTROT, COMMAND! COMMAND!
WHOOSH
YOU'RE NOT GONNA BELIEVE THIS, BUT I ALMOST COLLIDED WITH A DOUGLAS S.B.D.!
SHOT OUTTA THE BERMUDA TRIANGLE LIKE A BAT OUTTA HELL!

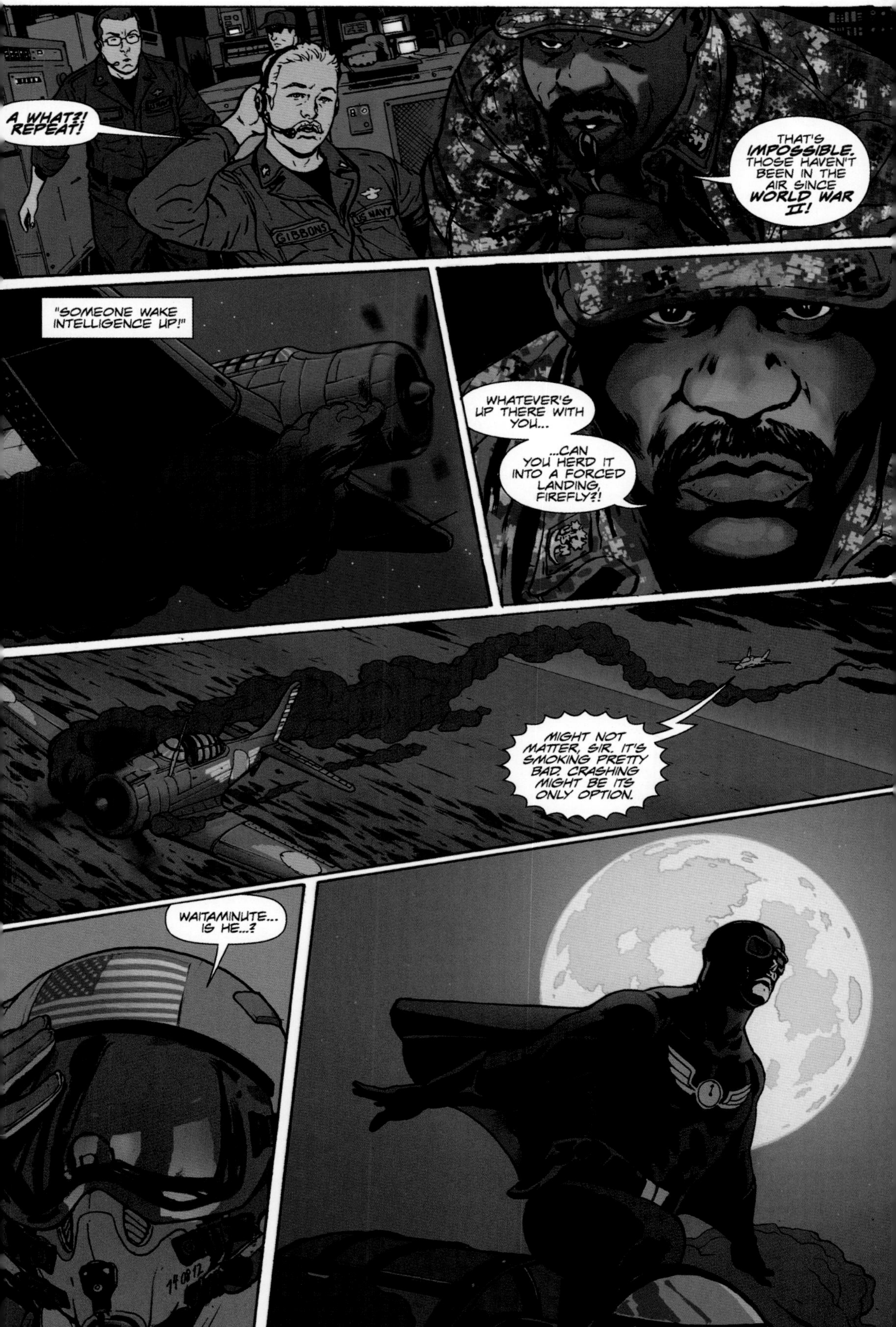
A WHAT?! REPEAT!
THAT'S IMPOSSIBLE. THOSE HAVEN'T BEEN IN THE AIR SINCE WORLD WAR II!
"SOMEONE WAKE INTELLIGENCE UP!"
WHATEVER'S UP THERE WITH YOU...
...CAN YOU HERD IT INTO A FORCED LANDING, FIREFLY?!
MIGHT NOT MATTER, SIR. IT'S SMOKING PRETTY BAD. CRASHING MIGHT BE ITS ONLY OPTION.
WAITAMINUTE... IS HE...?

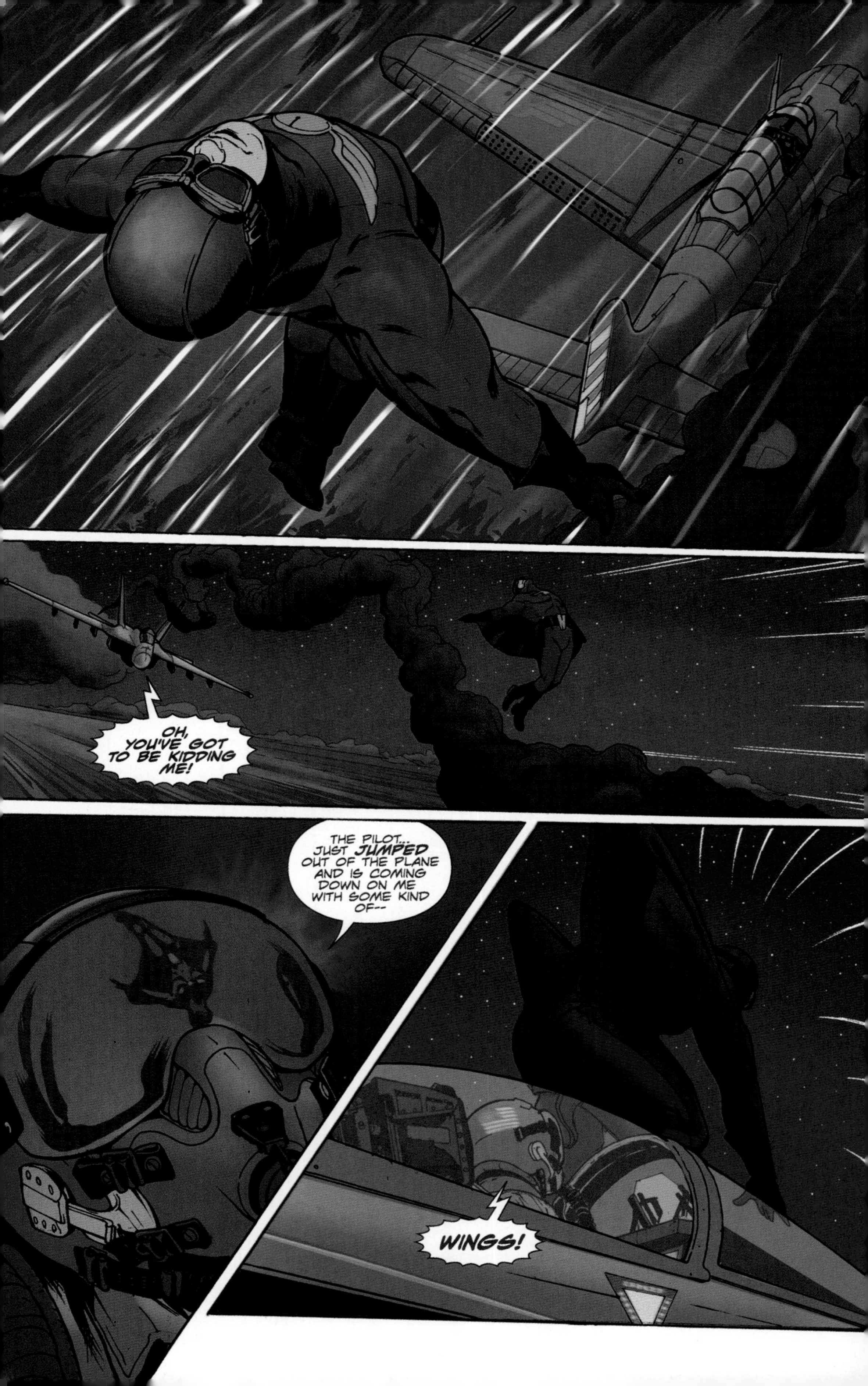
OH, YOU'VE GOT TO BE KIDDING ME!
THE PILOT... JUST JUMPED OUT OF THE PLANE AND IS COMING DOWN ON ME WITH SOME KIND OF--
WINGS!

"DID YOU SAY
WINGS, FIREFLY?!"
THOOM
YES! WINGS!
HE IS JUST HANGING ON TO MY CANOPY, SIR! I HAVE NO IDEA WHAT HE IS DOING!
IS THAT? NO--CAN'T BE.

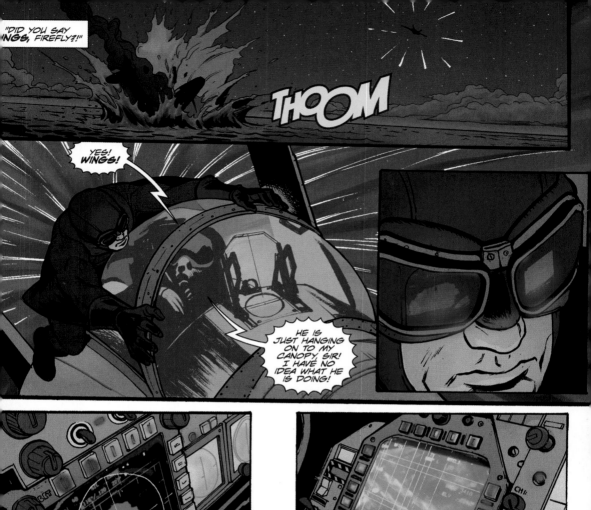

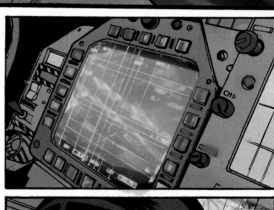

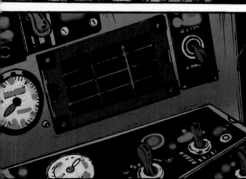

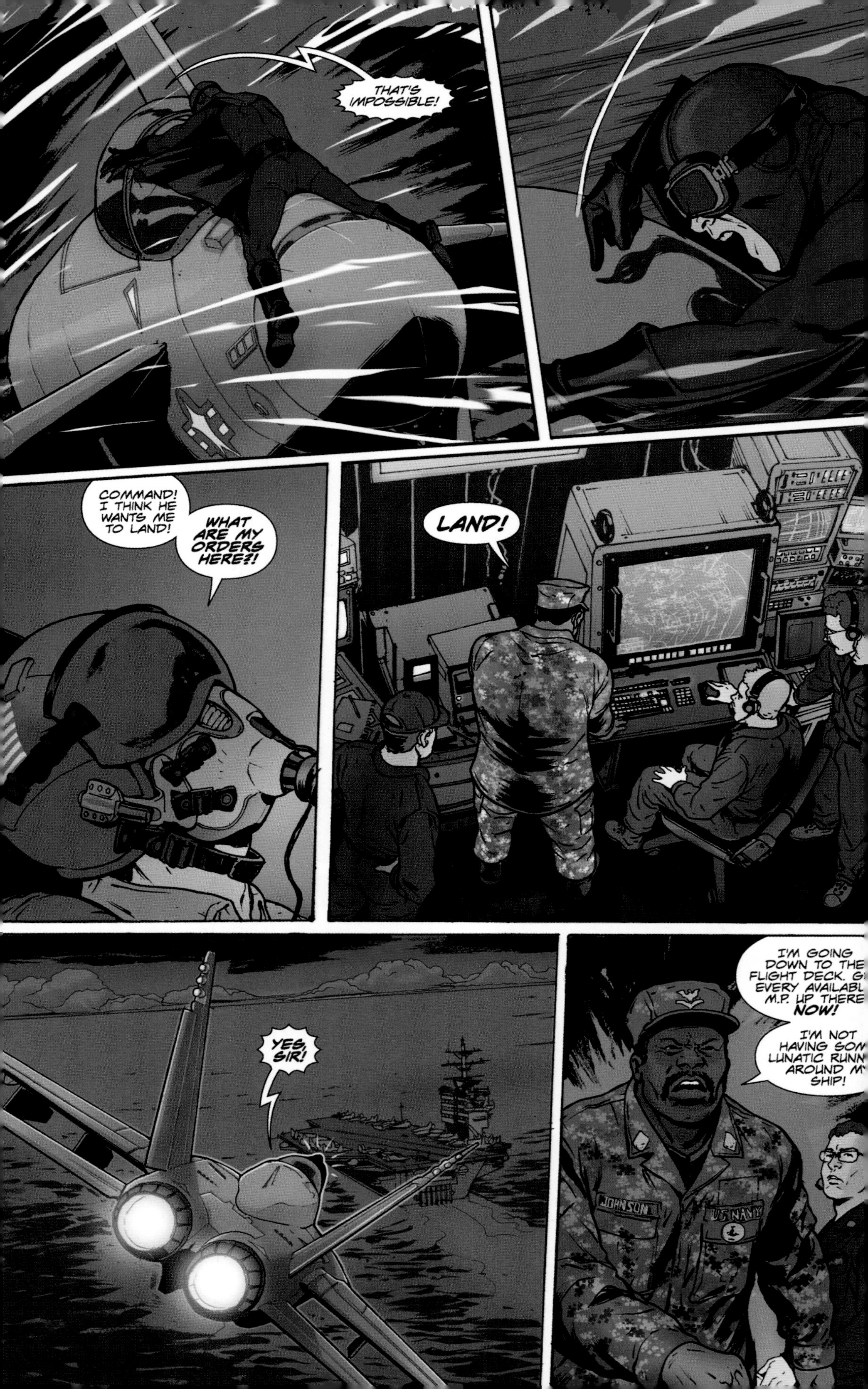
THAT'S IMPOSSIBLE!
COMMAND! I THINK HE WANTS ME TO LAND!
WHAT ARE MY ORDERS HERE?!
LAND!
YES, SIR!
I'M GOING DOWN TO THE FLIGHT DECK. G
EVERY AVAILABL
M.P. UP THERE
NOW!
I'M NOT HAVING SOM
LUNATIC RUNN
AROUND M
SHIP!
JOHNSON
U.S. NAVY

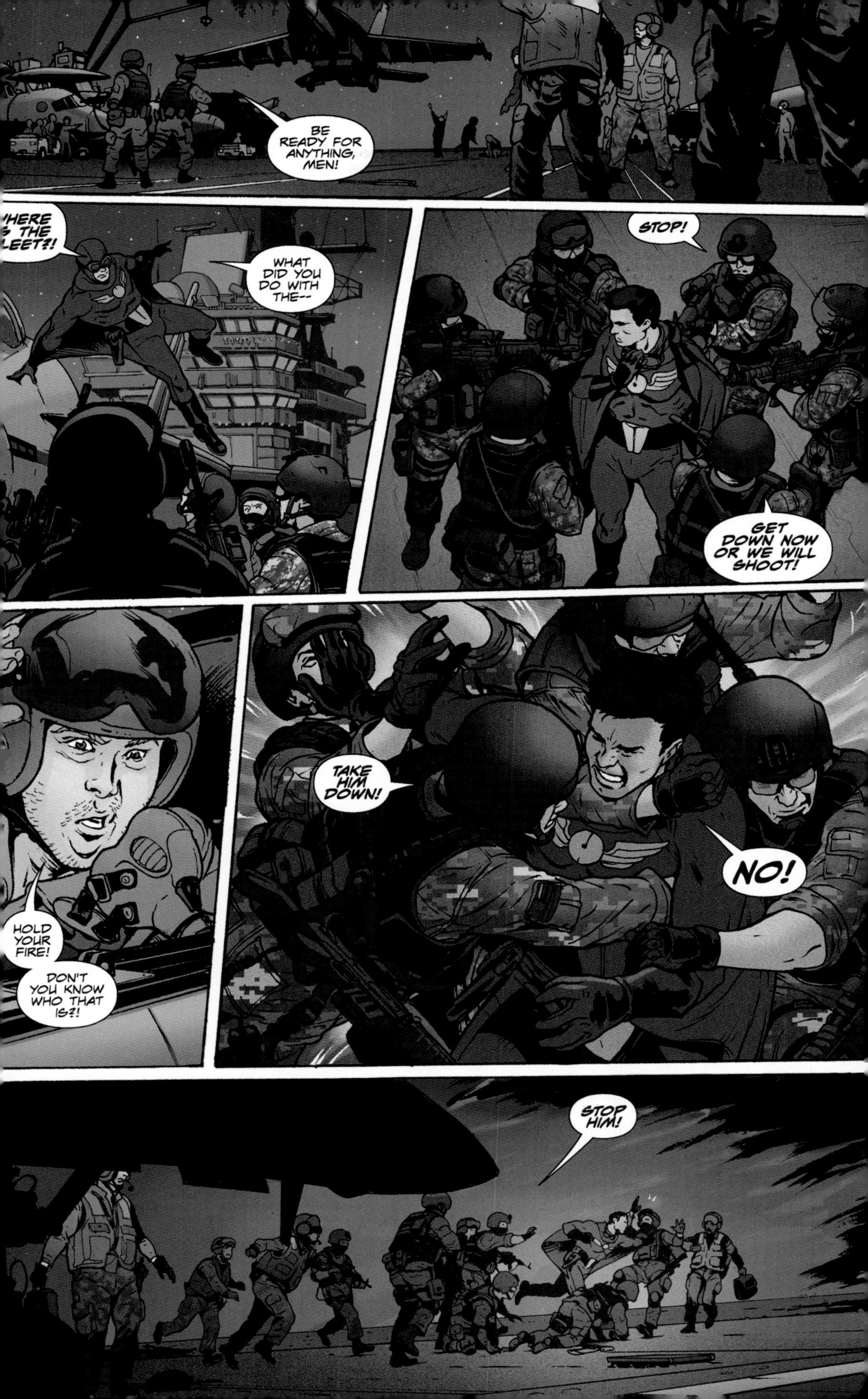
BE READY FOR ANYTHING, MEN!
WHERE IS THE FLEET?!
WHAT DID YOU DO WITH THE--
STOP!
GET DOWN NOW OR WE WILL SHOOT!
HOLD YOUR FIRE!
DON'T YOU KNOW WHO THAT IS?!
TAKE HIM DOWN!
NO!
STOP HIM!

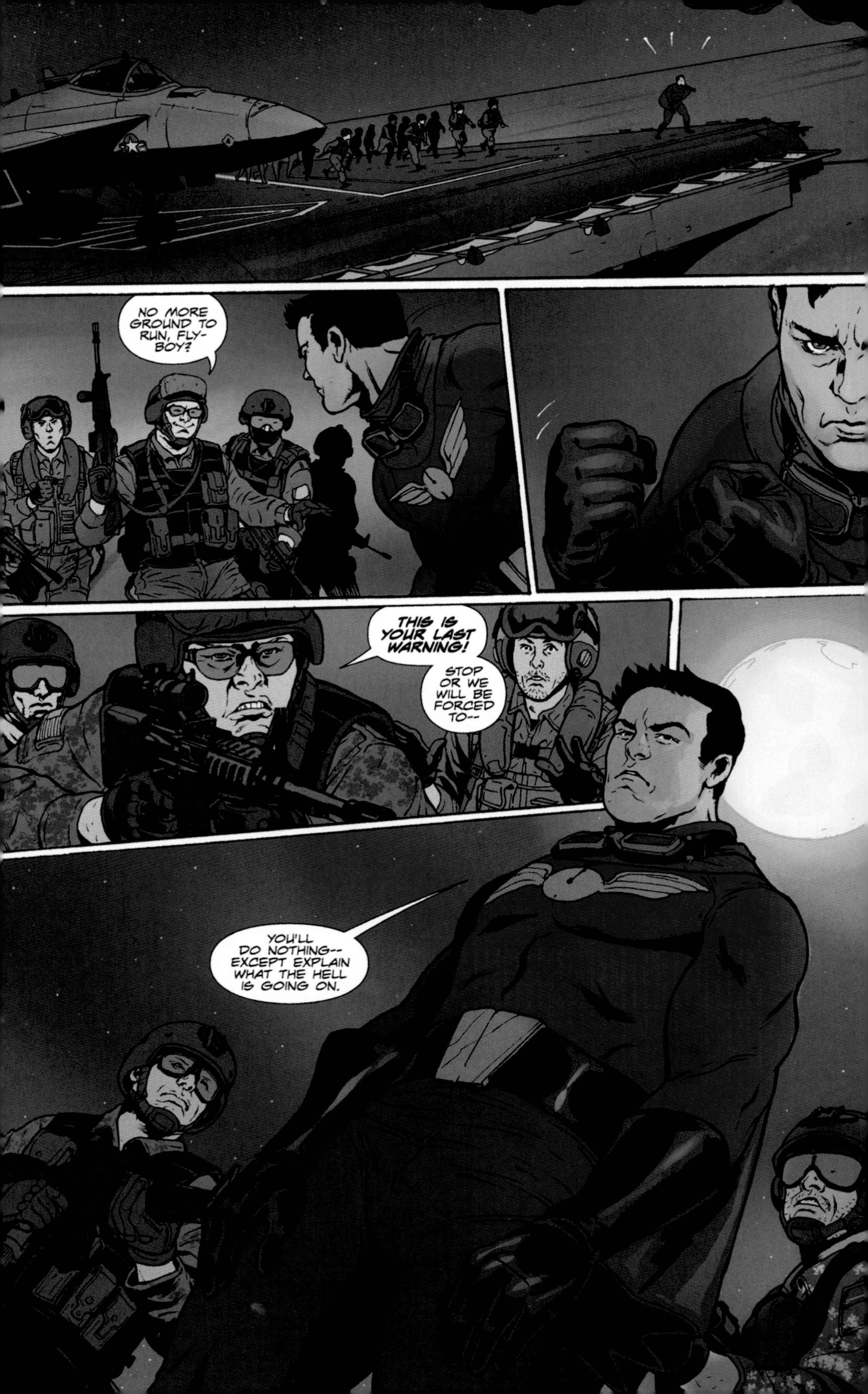
NO MORE GROUND TO RUN, FLY-BOY?
THIS IS YOUR LAST WARNING!
STOP OR WE WILL BE FORCED TO--
YOU'LL DO NOTHING-- EXCEPT EXPLAIN WHAT THE HELL IS GOING ON.

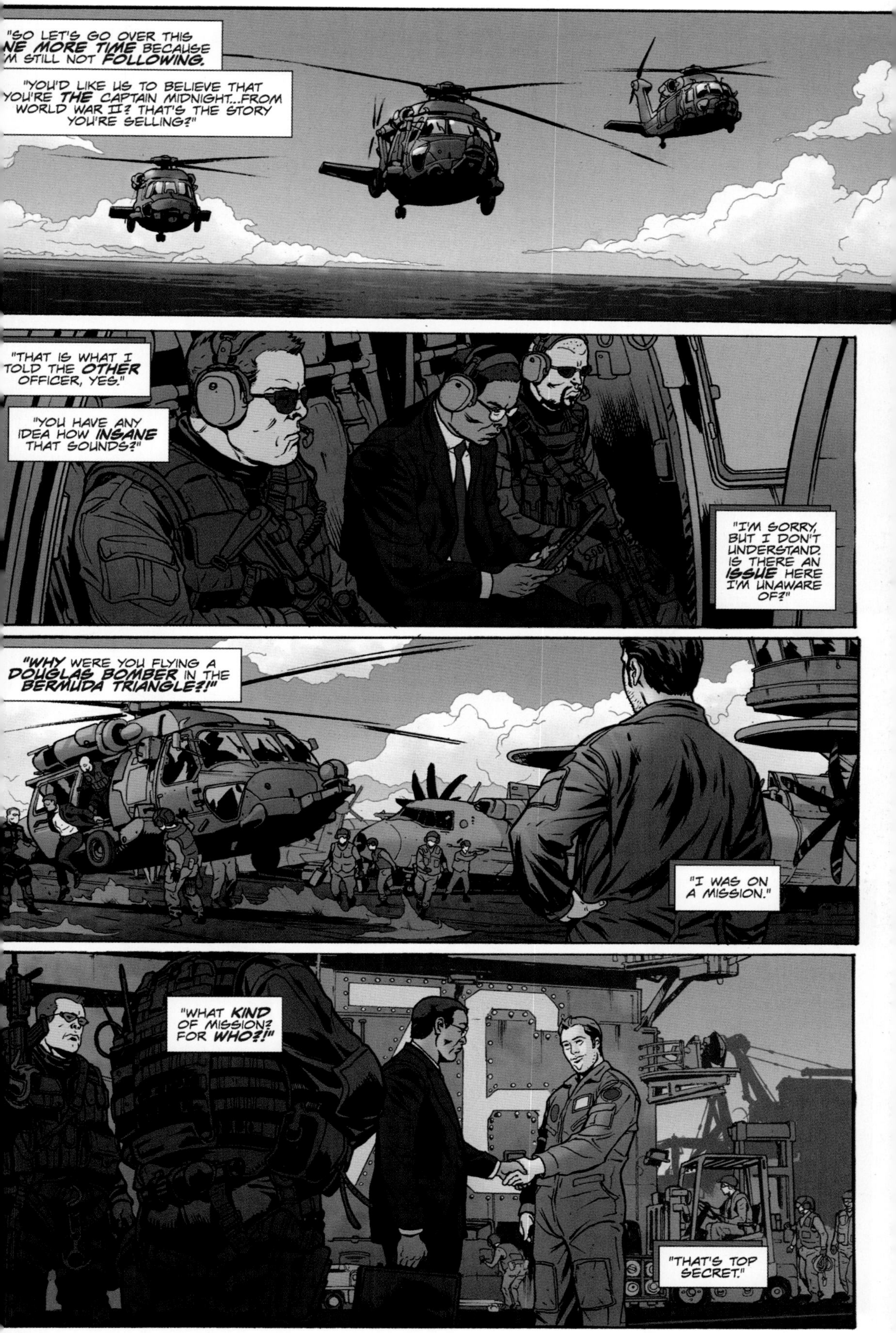
"SO LET'S GO OVER THIS NE MORE TIME BECAUSE M STILL NOT FOLLOWING.
"YOU'D LIKE US TO BELIEVE THAT YOU'RE THE CAPTAIN MIDNIGHT...FROM WORLD WAR II? THAT'S THE STORY YOU'RE SELLING?"
"THAT IS WHAT I TOLD THE OTHER OFFICER, YES."
"YOU HAVE ANY IDEA HOW INSANE THAT SOUNDS?"
"I'M SORRY, BUT I DON'T UNDERSTAND. IS THERE AN ISSUE HERE I'M UNAWARE OF?"
"WHY WERE YOU FLYING A DOUGLAS BOMBER IN THE BERMUDA TRIANGLE?!"
"I WAS ON A MISSION."
"WHAT KIND OF MISSION? FOR WHO?!"
"THAT'S TOP SECRET."

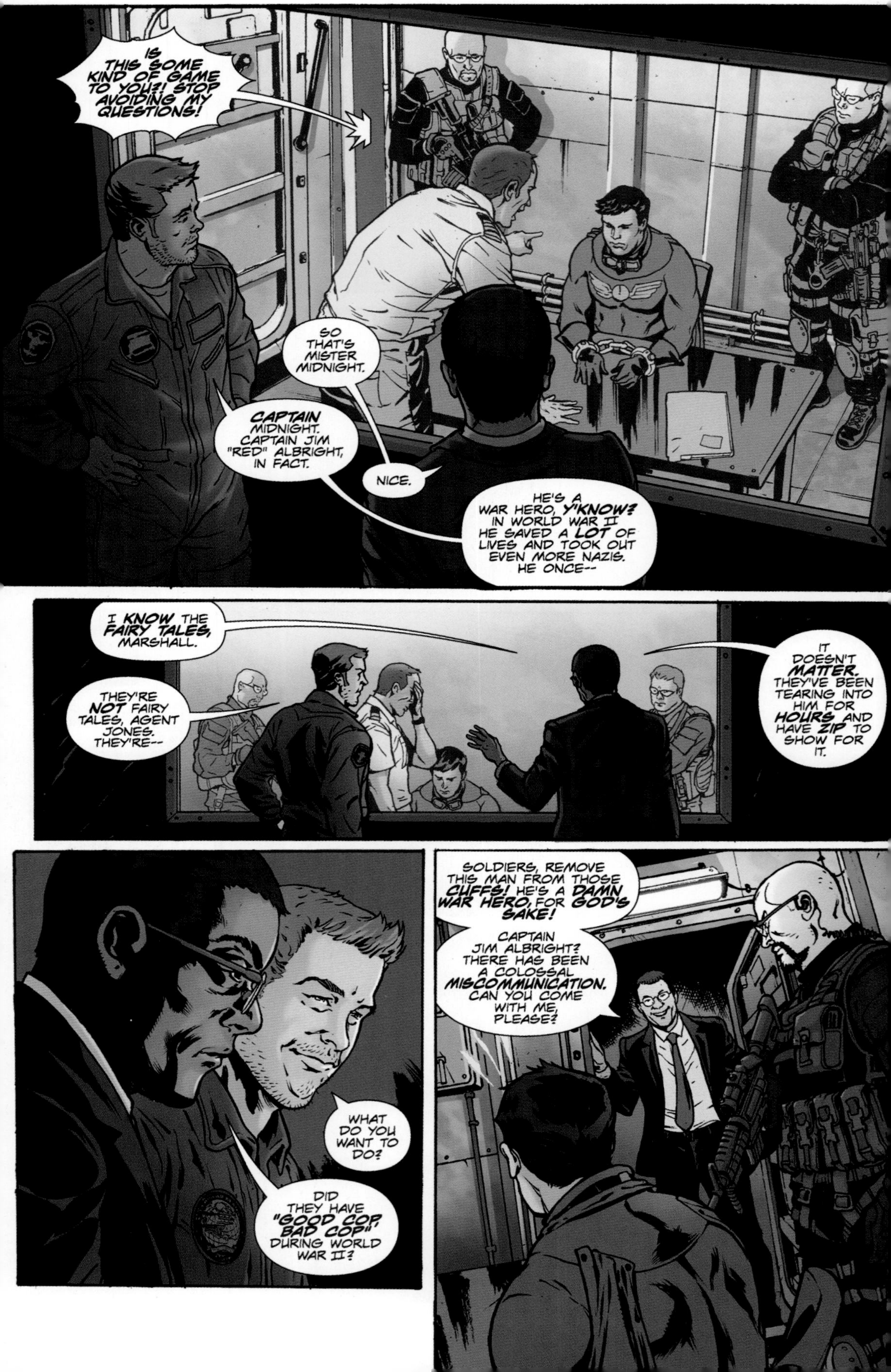
IS THIS SOME KIND OF GAME TO YOU?! STOP AVOIDING MY QUESTIONS!
SO THAT'S MISTER MIDNIGHT.
CAPTAIN MIDNIGHT. CAPTAIN JIM "RED" ALBRIGHT, IN FACT.
NICE.
HE'S A WAR HERO, Y'KNOW? IN WORLD WAR II HE SAVED A LOT OF LIVES AND TOOK OUT EVEN MORE NAZIS. HE ONCE--
I KNOW THE FAIRY TALES, MARSHALL.
THEY'RE NOT FAIRY TALES, AGENT JONES. THEY'RE--
IT DOESN'T MATTER. THEY'VE BEEN TEARING INTO HIM FOR HOURS AND HAVE ZIP TO SHOW FOR IT.
WHAT DO YOU WANT TO DO?
DID THEY HAVE "GOOD COP, BAD COP" DURING WORLD WAR II?
SOLDIERS, REMOVE THIS MAN FROM THOSE CUFFS! HE'S A DAMN WAR HERO, FOR GOD'S SAKE!
CAPTAIN JIM ALBRIGHT? THERE HAS BEEN A COLOSSAL MISCOMMUNICATION. CAN YOU COME WITH ME, PLEASE?

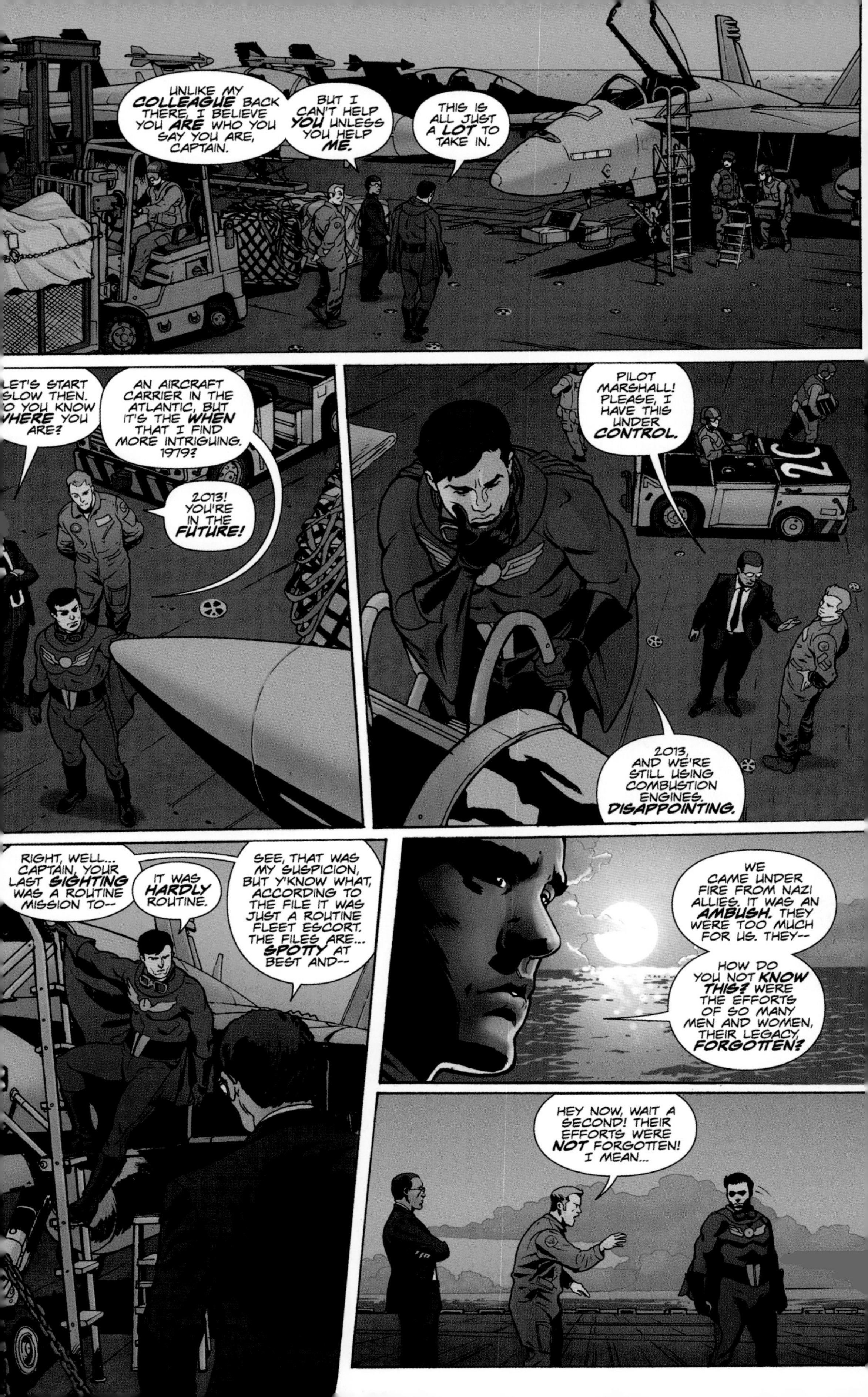
UNLIKE MY COLLEAGUE BACK THERE, I BELIEVE YOU ARE WHO YOU SAY YOU ARE, CAPTAIN.
BUT I CAN'T HELP YOU UNLESS YOU HELP ME.
THIS IS ALL JUST A LOT TO TAKE IN.
LET'S START SLOW THEN. DO YOU KNOW WHERE YOU ARE?
AN AIRCRAFT CARRIER IN THE ATLANTIC, BUT IT'S THE WHEN THAT I FIND MORE INTRIGUING. 1979?
2013! YOU'RE IN THE FUTURE!
PILOT MARSHALL! PLEASE, I HAVE THIS UNDER CONTROL.
2013, AND WE'RE STILL USING COMBUSTION ENGINES. DISAPPOINTING.
RIGHT, WELL... CAPTAIN, YOUR LAST SIGHTING WAS A ROUTINE MISSION TO--
IT WAS HARDLY ROUTINE.
SEE, THAT WAS MY SUSPICION, BUT Y'KNOW WHAT, ACCORDING TO THE FILE IT WAS JUST A ROUTINE FLEET ESCORT. THE FILES ARE... SPOTTY AT BEST AND--
WE CAME UNDER FIRE FROM NAZI ALLIES. IT WAS AN AMBUSH. THEY WERE TOO MUCH FOR US. THEY--
HOW DO YOU NOT KNOW THIS? WERE THE EFFORTS OF SO MANY MEN AND WOMEN, THEIR LEGACY, FORGOTTEN?
HEY NOW, WAIT A SECOND! THEIR EFFORTS WERE NOT FORGOTTEN! I MEAN...

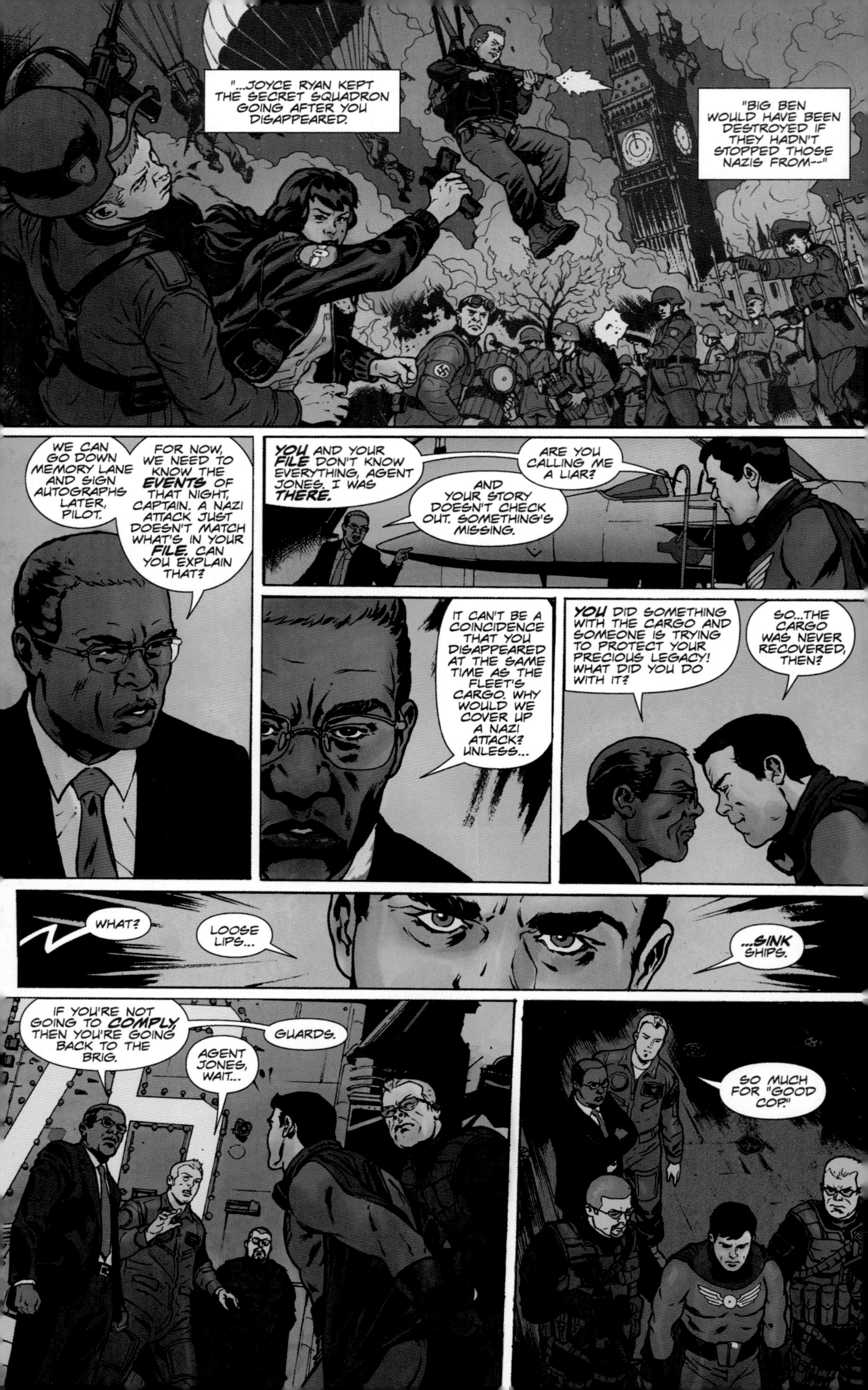
"...JOYCE RYAN KEPT THE SECRET SQUADRON GOING AFTER YOU DISAPPEARED.
"BIG BEN WOULD HAVE BEEN DESTROYED IF THEY HADN'T STOPPED THOSE NAZIS FROM--"
WE CAN GO DOWN MEMORY LANE AND SIGN AUTOGRAPHS LATER, PILOT.
FOR NOW, WE NEED TO KNOW THE EVENTS OF THAT NIGHT, CAPTAIN. A NAZI ATTACK JUST DOESN'T MATCH WHAT'S IN YOUR FILE. CAN YOU EXPLAIN THAT?
YOU AND YOUR FILE DON'T KNOW EVERYTHING, AGENT JONES. I WAS THERE.
ARE YOU CALLING ME A LIAR?
AND YOUR STORY DOESN'T CHECK OUT. SOMETHING'S MISSING.
IT CAN'T BE A COINCIDENCE THAT YOU DISAPPEARED AT THE SAME TIME AS THE FLEET'S CARGO. WHY WOULD WE COVER UP A NAZI ATTACK? UNLESS...
YOU DID SOMETHING WITH THE CARGO AND SOMEONE IS TRYING TO PROTECT YOUR PRECIOUS LEGACY! WHAT DID YOU DO WITH IT?
SO...THE CARGO WAS NEVER RECOVERED, THEN?
WHAT?
LOOSE LIPS...
...SINK SHIPS.
IF YOU'RE NOT GOING TO COMPLY, THEN YOU'RE GOING BACK TO THE BRIG.
GUARDS.
AGENT JONES, WAIT...
SO MUCH FOR "GOOD COP."

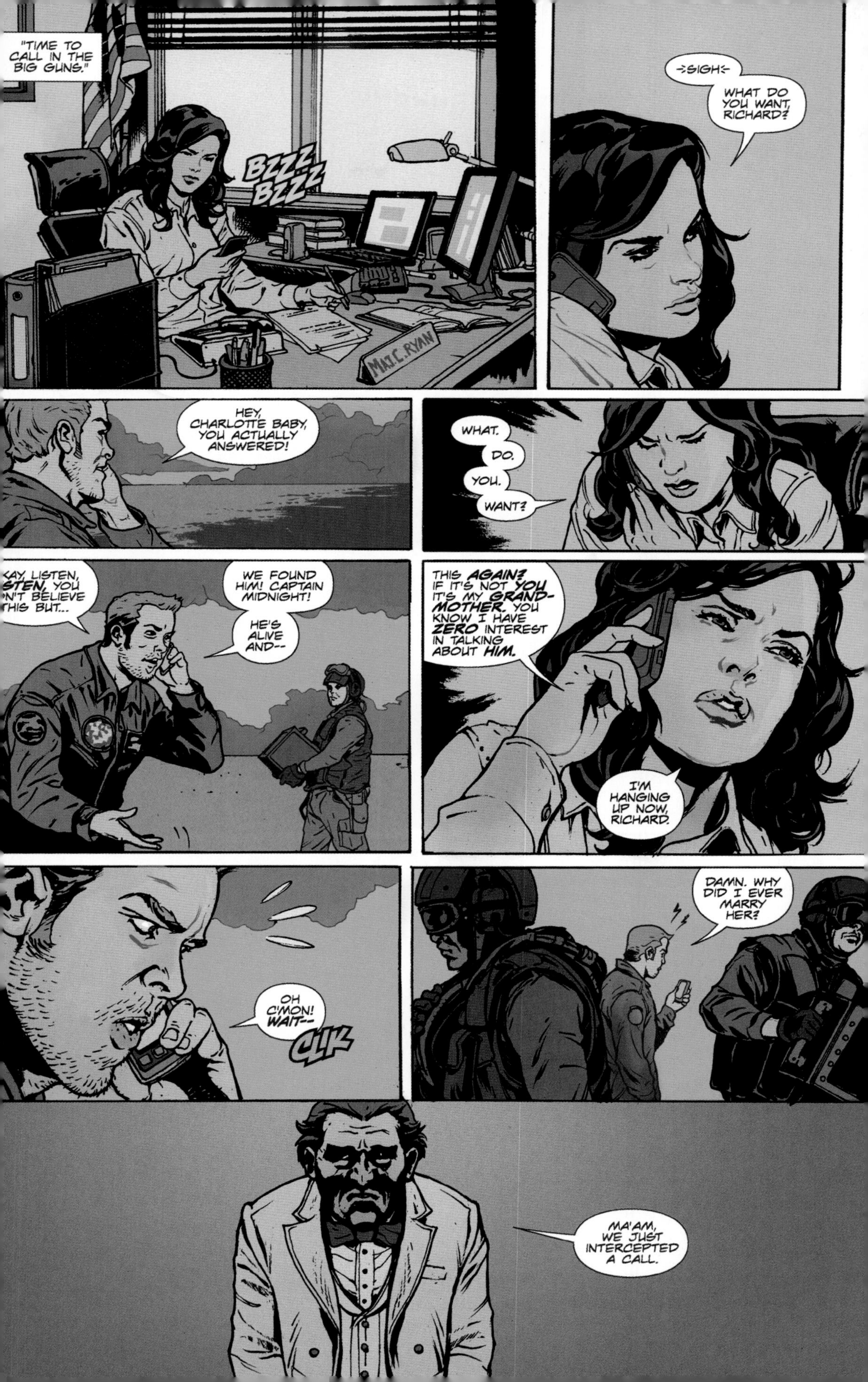
"TIME TO CALL IN THE BIG GUNS."
BZZZ BZZZ
MAJ. C. RYAN
-SIGH-
WHAT DO YOU WANT, RICHARD?
HEY, CHARLOTTE BABY, YOU ACTUALLY ANSWERED!
WHAT.
DO.
YOU.
WANT?
KAY, LISTEN, STEN, YOU N'T BELIEVE THIS BUT...
WE FOUND HIM! CAPTAIN MIDNIGHT!
HE'S ALIVE AND--
THIS AGAIN? IF IT'S NOT YOU IT'S MY GRAND-MOTHER. YOU KNOW I HAVE ZERO INTEREST IN TALKING ABOUT HIM.
I'M HANGING UP NOW, RICHARD.
OH C'MON! WAIT--
CLIK
DAMN. WHY DID I EVER MARRY HER?
MA'AM, WE JUST INTERCEPTED A CALL.

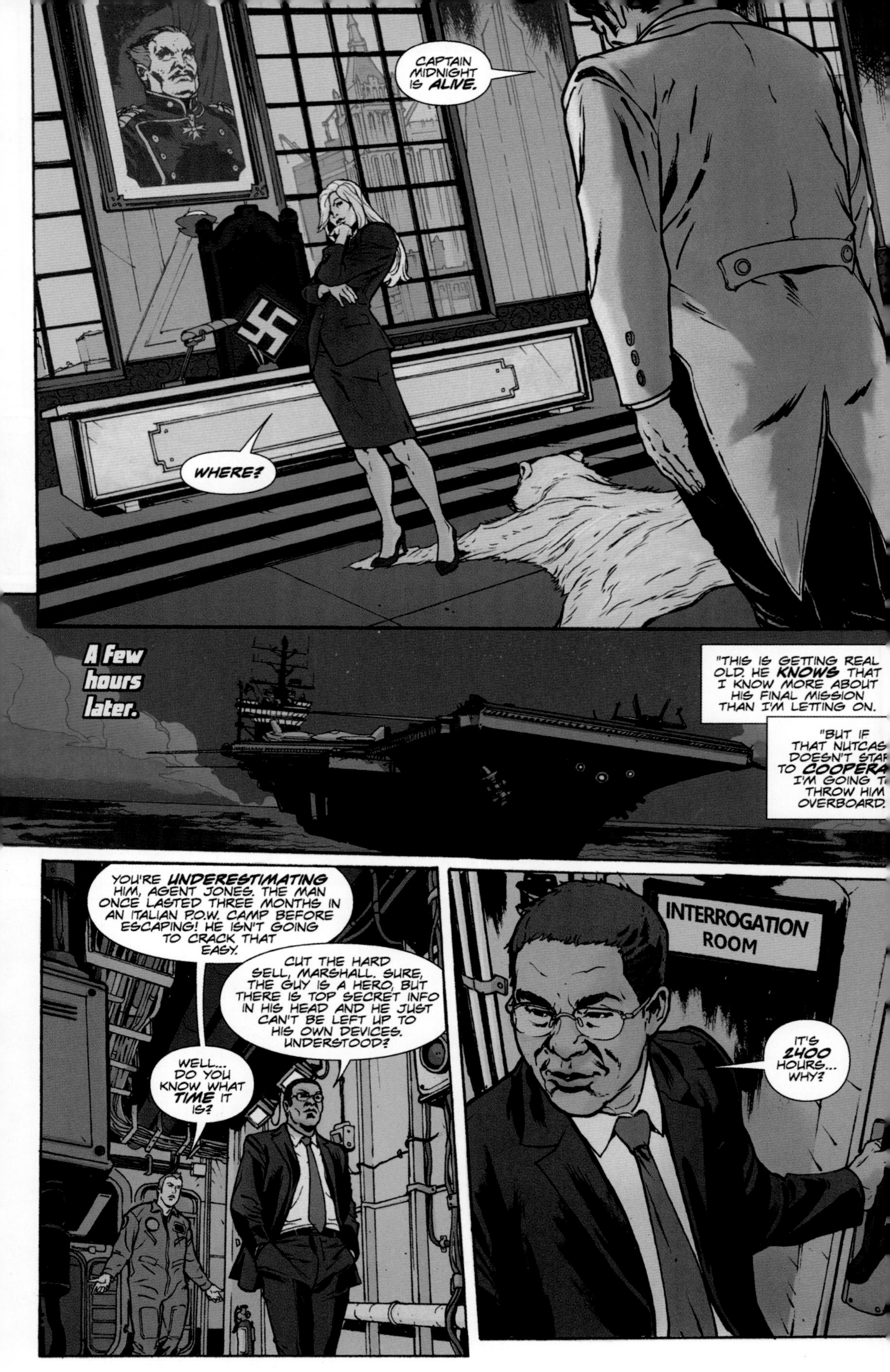
CAPTAIN MIDNIGHT IS ALIVE.
WHERE?
A few hours later.
"THIS IS GETTING REAL OLD. HE KNOWS THAT I KNOW MORE ABOUT HIS FINAL MISSION THAN I'M LETTING ON.
"BUT IF THAT NUTCAS DOESN'T STAR TO COOPERA I'M GOING T THROW HIM OVERBOARD.
YOU'RE UNDERESTIMATING HIM, AGENT JONES. THE MAN ONCE LASTED THREE MONTHS IN AN ITALIAN P.O.W. CAMP BEFORE ESCAPING! HE ISN'T GOING TO CRACK THAT EASY.
CUT THE HARD SELL, MARSHALL. SURE, THE GUY IS A HERO, BUT THERE IS TOP SECRET INFO IN HIS HEAD AND HE JUST CAN'T BE LEFT UP TO HIS OWN DEVICES. UNDERSTOOD?
WELL... DO YOU KNOW WHAT TIME IT IS?
INTERROGATION ROOM
IT'S 2400 HOURS... WHY?

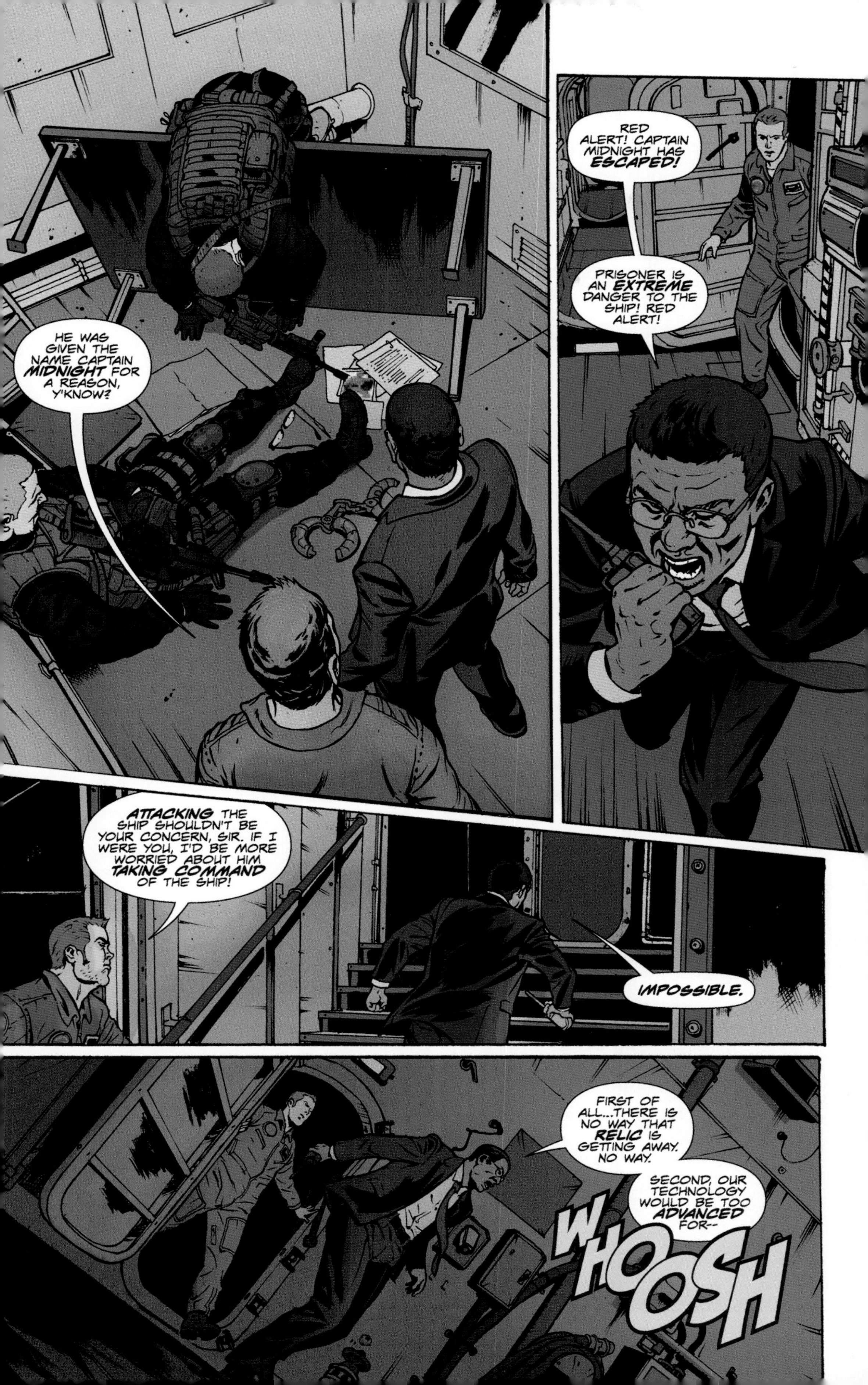
HE WAS GIVEN THE NAME CAPTAIN MIDNIGHT FOR A REASON, Y'KNOW?
RED ALERT! CAPTAIN MIDNIGHT HAS ESCAPED!
PRISONER IS AN EXTREME DANGER TO THE SHIP! RED ALERT!
ATTACKING THE SHIP SHOULDN'T BE YOUR CONCERN, SIR. IF I WERE YOU, I'D BE MORE WORRIED ABOUT HIM TAKING COMMAND OF THE SHIP!
IMPOSSIBLE.
FIRST OF ALL...THERE IS NO WAY THAT RELIC IS GETTING AWAY. NO WAY.
SECOND, OUR TECHNOLOGY WOULD BE TOO ADVANCED FOR--
WHOOSH

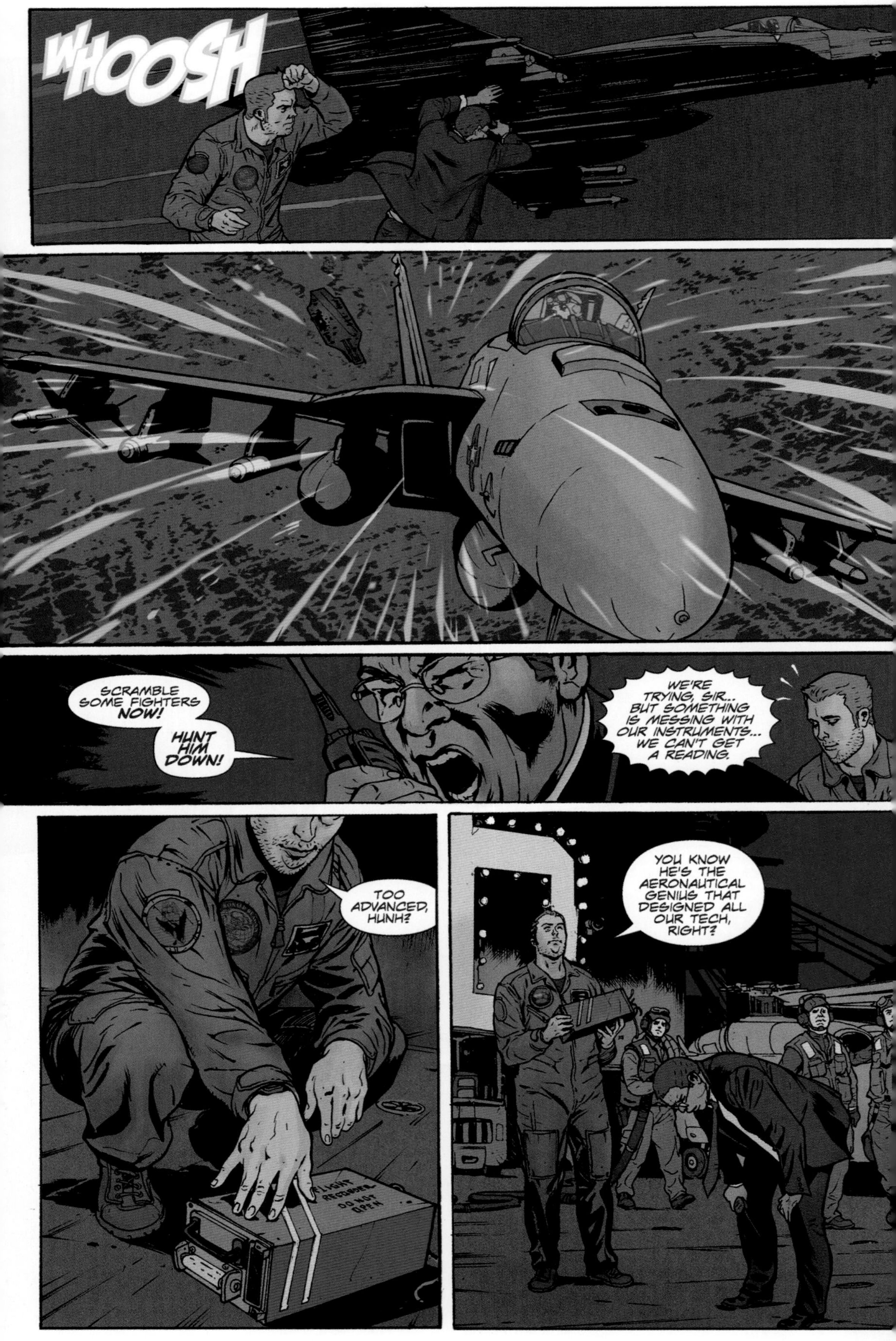
WHOOSH
SCRAMBLE SOME FIGHTERS NOW!
HUNT HIM DOWN!
WE'RE TRYING, SIR... BUT SOMETHING IS MESSING WITH OUR INSTRUMENTS... WE CAN'T GET A READING.
TOO ADVANCED, HUNH?
FLIGHT RECORDER DO NOT OPEN
YOU KNOW HE'S THE AERONAUTICAL GENIUS THAT DESIGNED ALL OUR TECH, RIGHT?

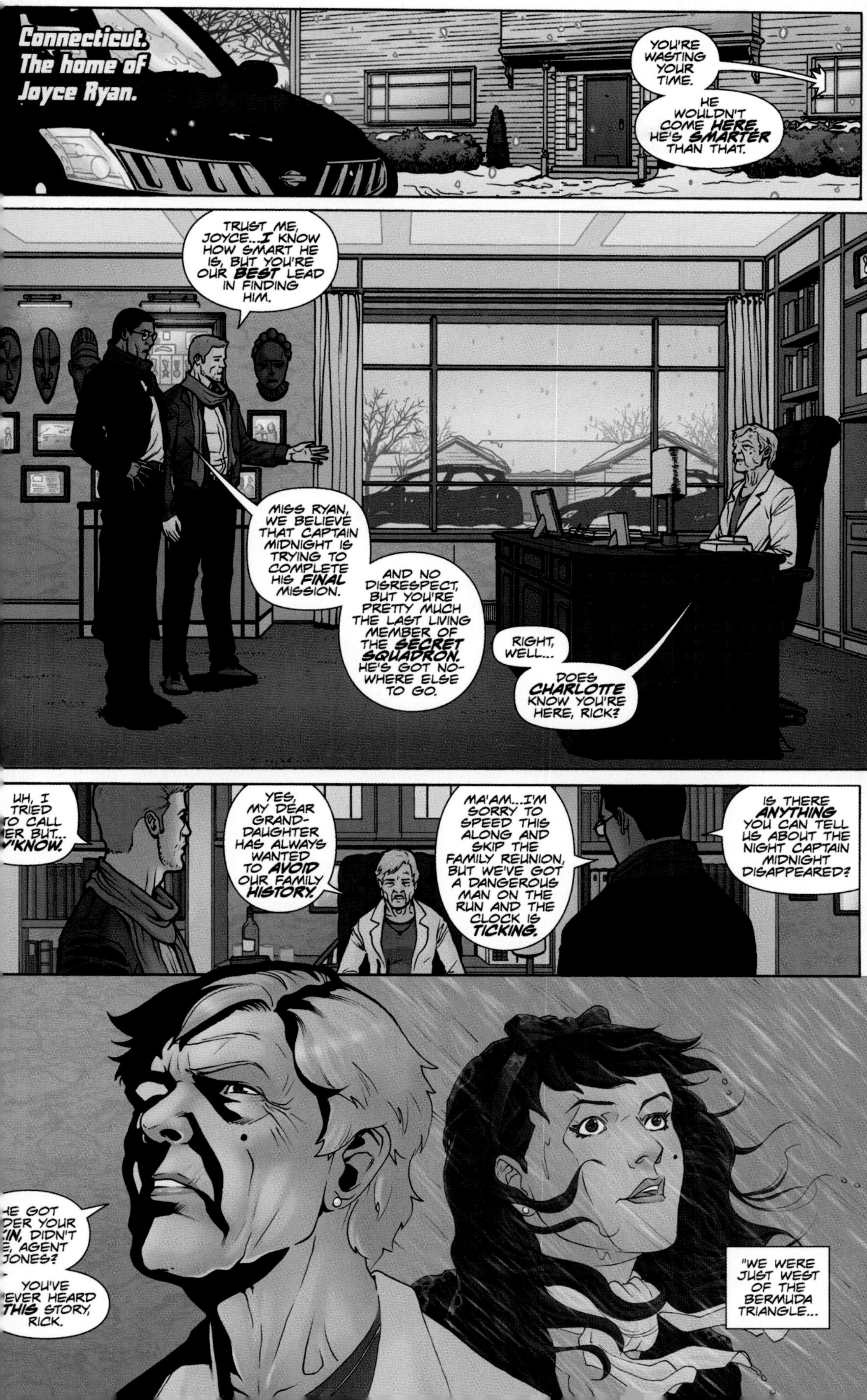
Connecticut. The home of Joyce Ryan.
YOU'RE WASTING YOUR TIME.
HE WOULDN'T COME HERE. HE'S SMARTER THAN THAT.
TRUST ME, JOYCE... I KNOW HOW SMART HE IS, BUT YOU'RE OUR BEST LEAD IN FINDING HIM.
MISS RYAN, WE BELIEVE THAT CAPTAIN MIDNIGHT IS TRYING TO COMPLETE HIS FINAL MISSION.
AND NO DISRESPECT, BUT YOU'RE PRETTY MUCH THE LAST LIVING MEMBER OF THE SECRET SQUADRON. HE'S GOT NO-WHERE ELSE TO GO.
RIGHT, WELL...
DOES CHARLOTTE KNOW YOU'RE HERE, RICK?
UH, I TRIED TO CALL ER BUT... 'KNOW.
YES, MY DEAR GRAND-DAUGHTER HAS ALWAYS WANTED TO AVOID OUR FAMILY HISTORY.
MA'AM... I'M SORRY TO SPEED THIS ALONG AND SKIP THE FAMILY REUNION, BUT WE'VE GOT A DANGEROUS MAN ON THE RUN AND THE CLOCK IS TICKING.
IS THERE ANYTHING YOU CAN TELL US ABOUT THE NIGHT CAPTAIN MIDNIGHT DISAPPEARED?
HE GOT DER YOUR KIN, DIDN'T E, AGENT JONES?
YOU'VE EVER HEARD THIS STORY, RICK.
"WE WERE JUST WEST OF THE BERMUDA TRIANGLE...

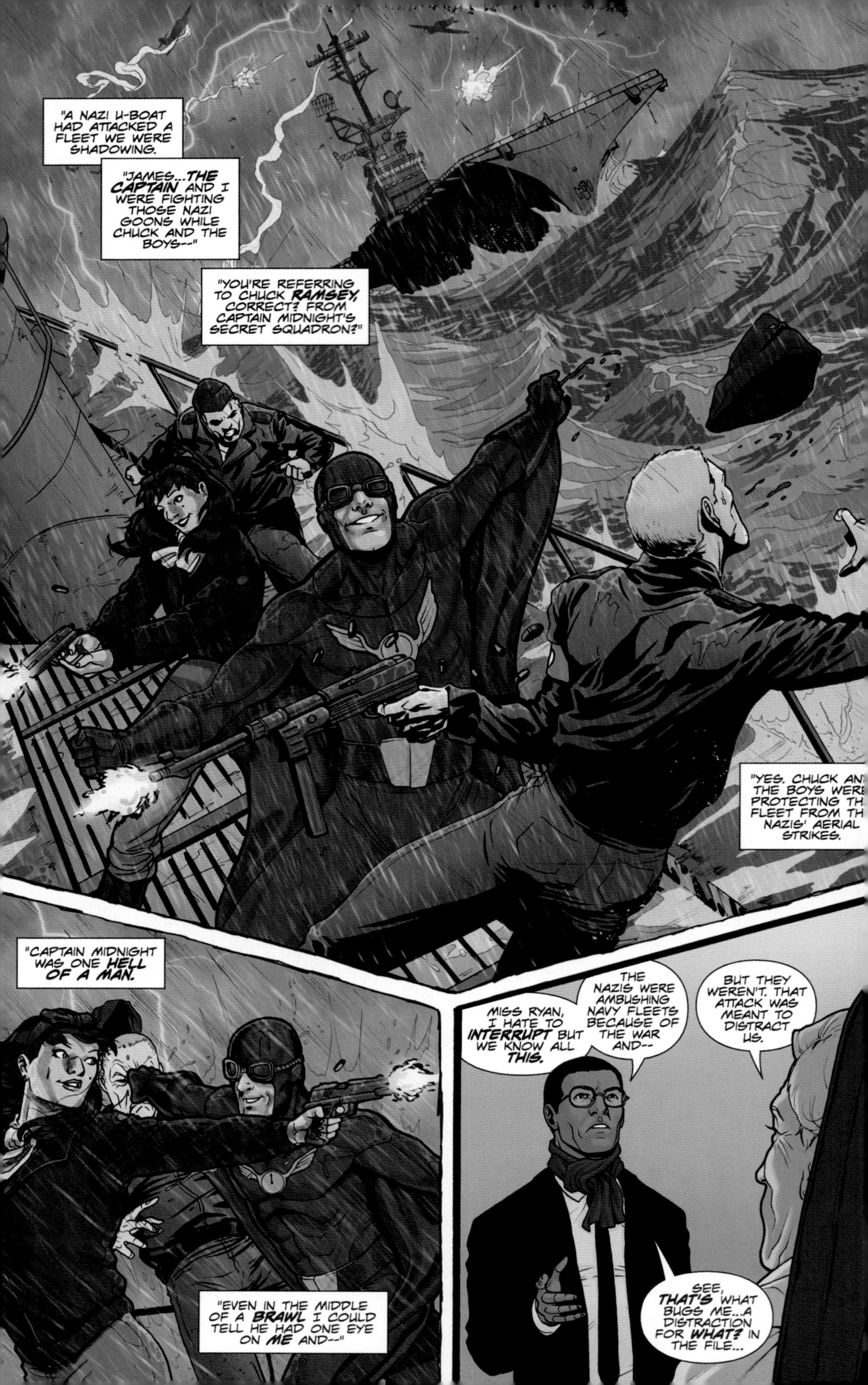
"A NAZI U-BOAT HAD ATTACKED A FLEET WE WERE SHADOWING.
"JAMES... THE CAPTAIN AND I WERE FIGHTING THOSE NAZI GOONS WHILE CHUCK AND THE BOYS--"
"YOU'RE REFERRING TO CHUCK RAMSEY, CORRECT? FROM CAPTAIN MIDNIGHT'S SECRET SQUADRON?"
"YES. CHUCK AN THE BOYS WERE PROTECTING TH FLEET FROM TH NAZIS' AERIAL STRIKES.
"CAPTAIN MIDNIGHT WAS ONE HELL OF A MAN.
"EVEN IN THE MIDDLE OF A BRAWL I COULD TELL HE HAD ONE EYE ON ME AND--"
MISS RYAN, I HATE TO INTERRUPT BUT WE KNOW ALL THIS.
THE NAZIS WERE AMBUSHING NAVY FLEETS BECAUSE OF THE WAR AND--
BUT THEY WEREN'T. THAT ATTACK WAS MEANT TO DISTRACT US.
SEE, THAT'S WHAT BUGS ME... A DISTRACTION FOR WHAT? IN THE FILE...

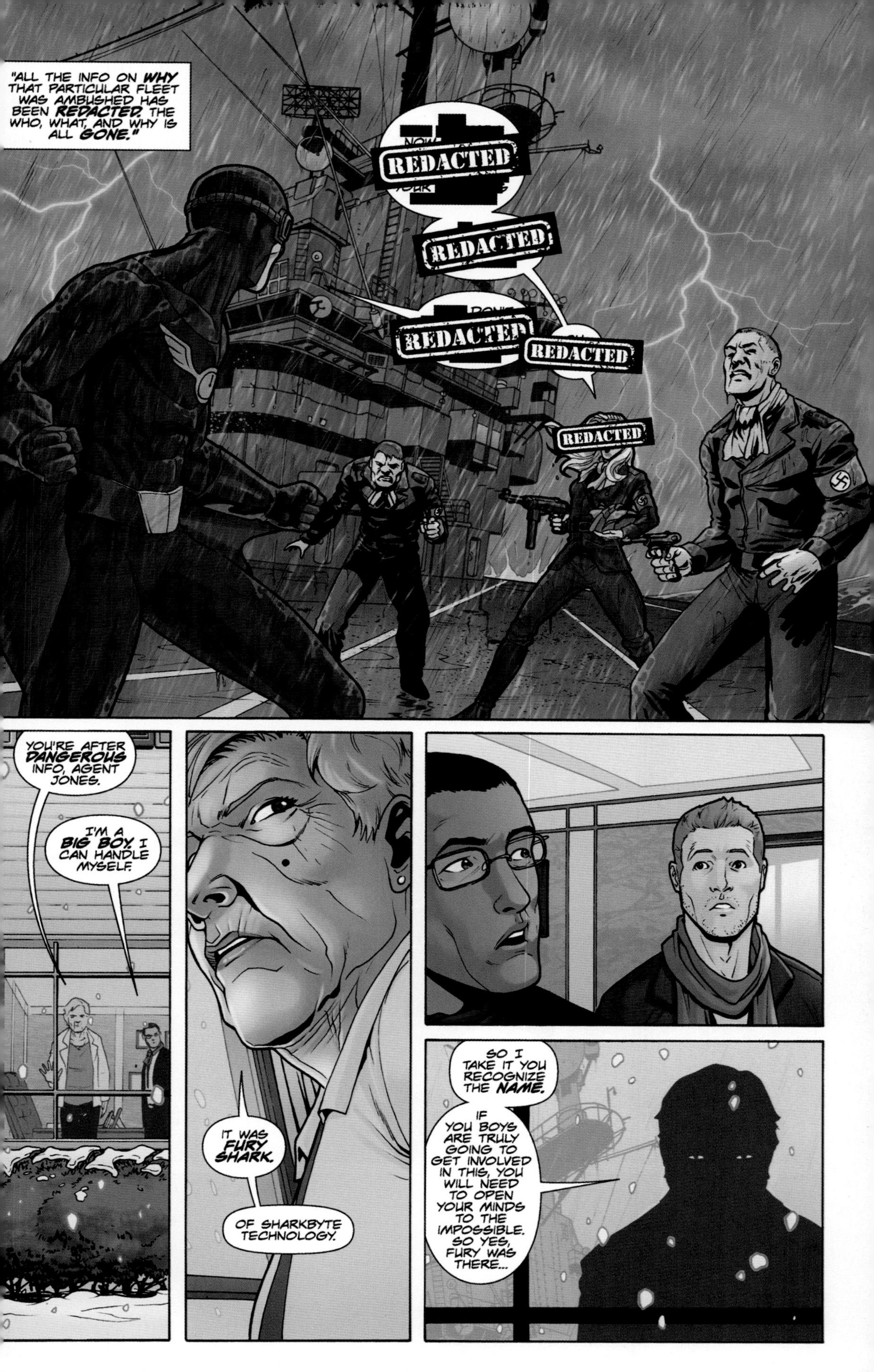
"ALL THE INFO ON WHY THAT PARTICULAR FLEET WAS AMBUSHED HAS BEEN REDACTED. THE WHO, WHAT, AND WHY IS ALL GONE."
[redacted] REDACTED [redacted]
[redacted] REDACTED
[redacted] REDACTED [redacted]
[redacted] REDACTED
REDACTED
YOU'RE AFTER DANGEROUS INFO, AGENT JONES.
I'M A BIG BOY. I CAN HANDLE MYSELF.
IT WAS FURY SHARK.
OF SHARKBYTE TECHNOLOGY.
SO I TAKE IT YOU RECOGNIZE THE NAME.
IF YOU BOYS ARE TRULY GOING TO GET INVOLVED IN THIS, YOU WILL NEED TO OPEN YOUR MINDS TO THE IMPOSSIBLE. SO YES, FURY WAS THERE...

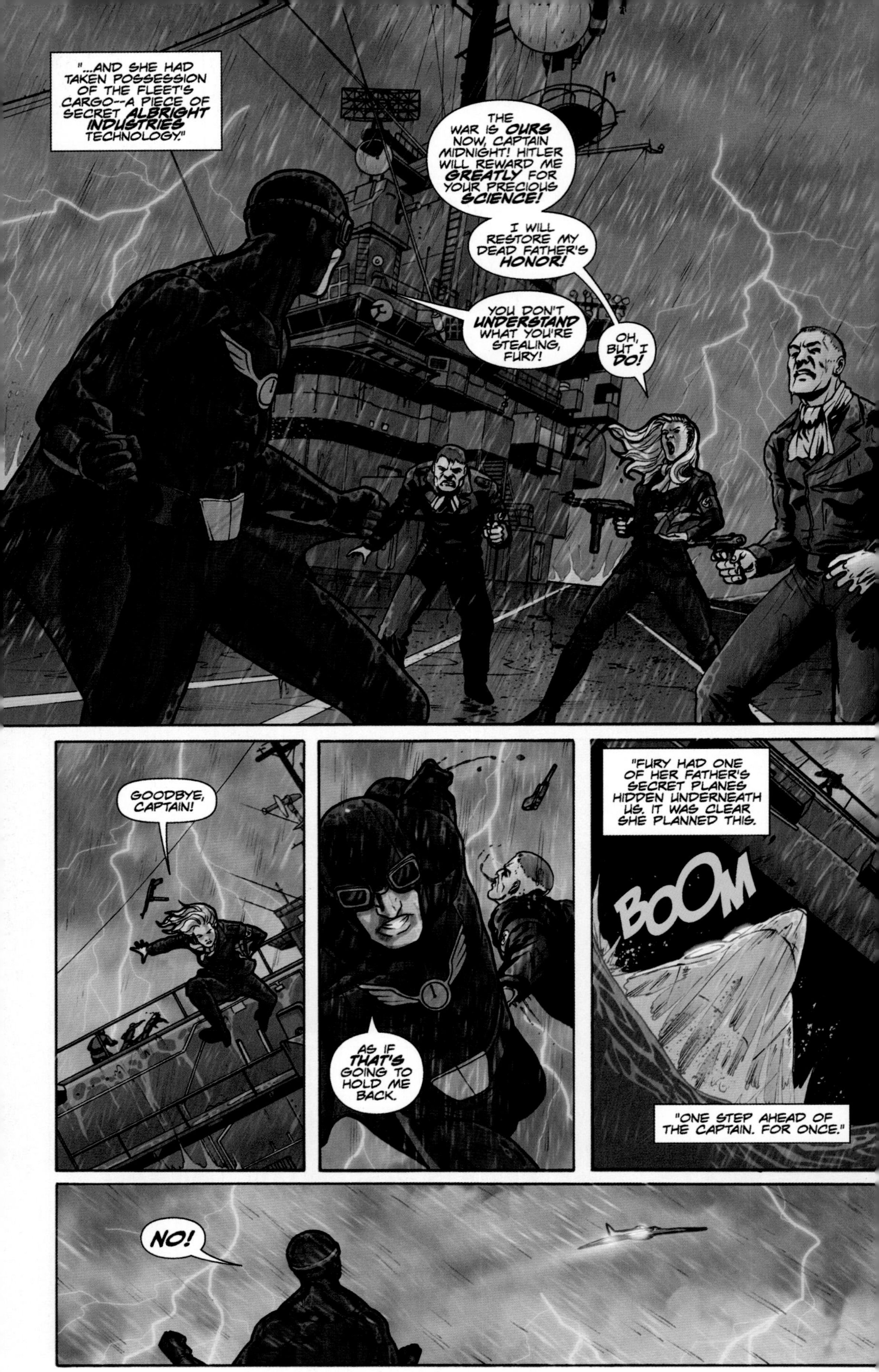
"...AND SHE HAD TAKEN POSSESSION OF THE FLEET'S CARGO--A PIECE OF SECRET ALBRIGHT INDUSTRIES TECHNOLOGY."
THE WAR IS OURS NOW, CAPTAIN MIDNIGHT! HITLER WILL REWARD ME GREATLY FOR YOUR PRECIOUS SCIENCE!
I WILL RESTORE MY DEAD FATHER'S HONOR!
YOU DON'T UNDERSTAND WHAT YOU'RE STEALING, FURY!
OH, BUT I DO!
GOODBYE, CAPTAIN!
AS IF THAT'S GOING TO HOLD ME BACK.
"FURY HAD ONE OF HER FATHER'S SECRET PLANES HIDDEN UNDERNEATH US. IT WAS CLEAR SHE PLANNED THIS.
BOOM
"ONE STEP AHEAD OF THE CAPTAIN. FOR ONCE."
NO!

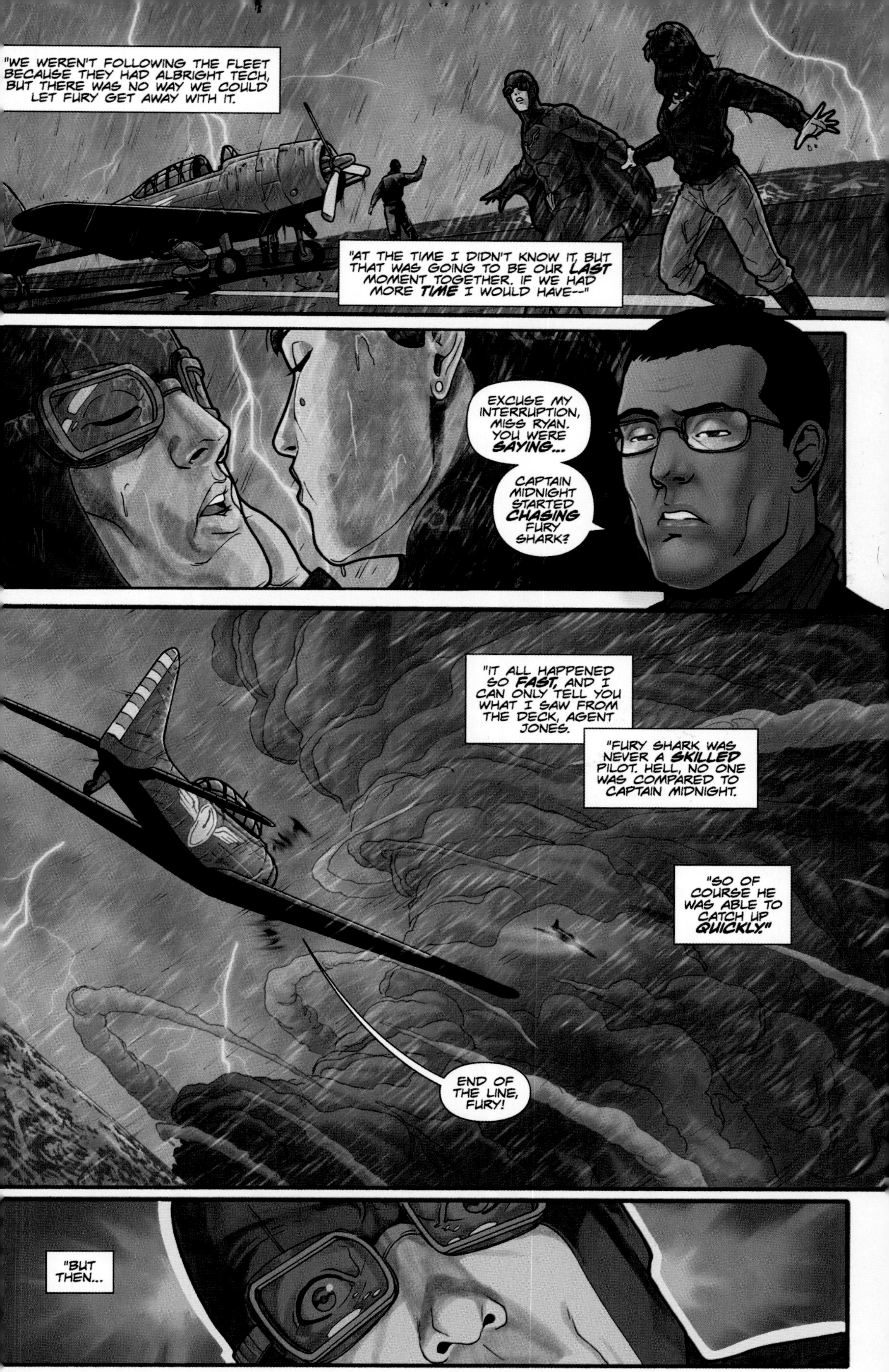
"WE WEREN'T FOLLOWING THE FLEET BECAUSE THEY HAD ALBRIGHT TECH, BUT THERE WAS NO WAY WE COULD LET FURY GET AWAY WITH IT.
"AT THE TIME I DIDN'T KNOW IT, BUT THAT WAS GOING TO BE OUR LAST MOMENT TOGETHER. IF WE HAD MORE TIME I WOULD HAVE--"
EXCUSE MY INTERRUPTION, MISS RYAN. YOU WERE SAYING...
CAPTAIN MIDNIGHT STARTED CHASING FURY SHARK?
"IT ALL HAPPENED SO FAST, AND I CAN ONLY TELL YOU WHAT I SAW FROM THE DECK, AGENT JONES.
"FURY SHARK WAS NEVER A SKILLED PILOT. HELL, NO ONE WAS COMPARED TO CAPTAIN MIDNIGHT.
"SO OF COURSE HE WAS ABLE TO CATCH UP QUICKLY."
END OF THE LINE, FURY!
"BUT THEN...

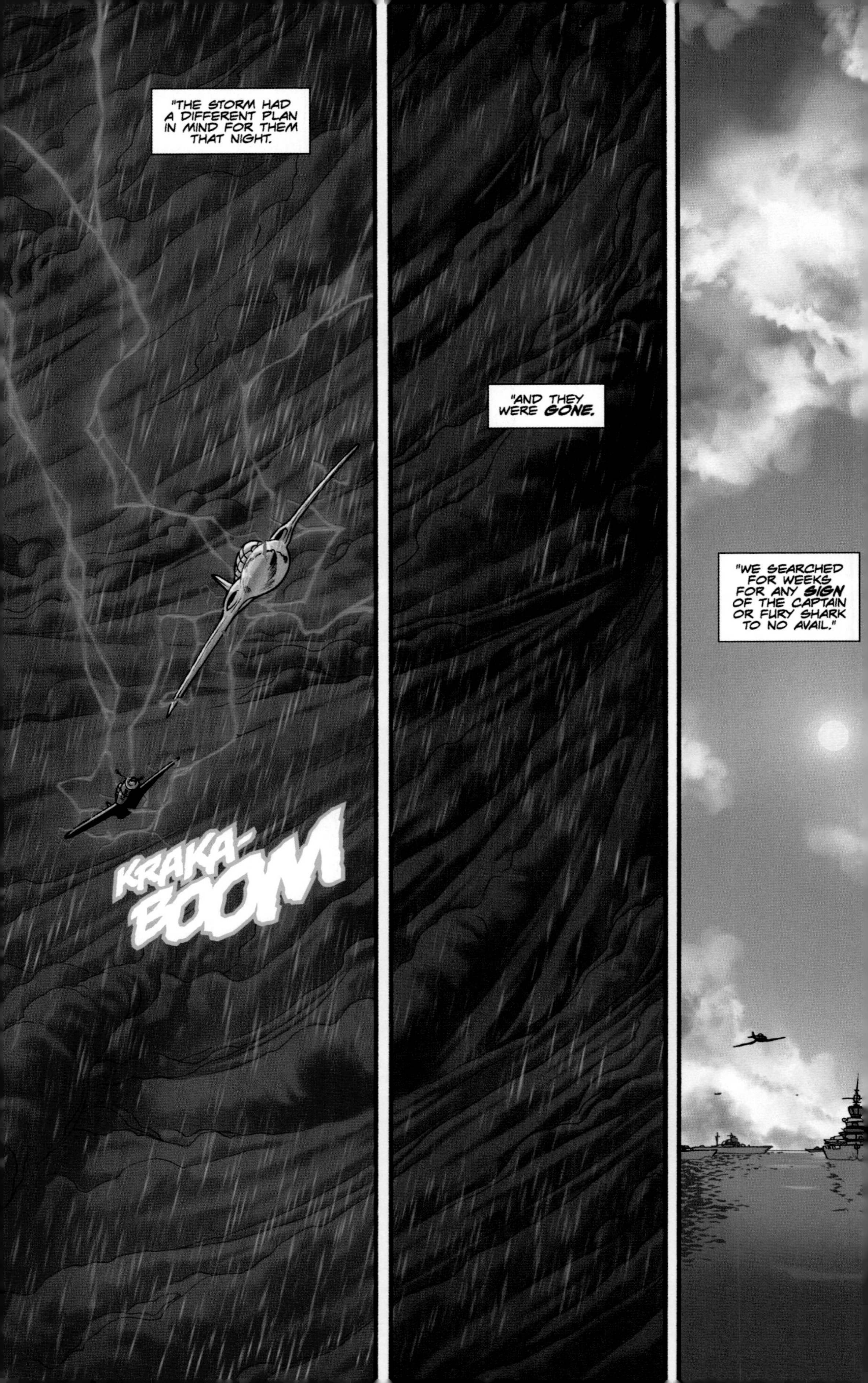
"THE STORM HAD A DIFFERENT PLAN IN MIND FOR THEM THAT NIGHT.
KRAKA-BOOM
"AND THEY WERE GONE.
"WE SEARCHED FOR WEEKS FOR ANY SIGN OF THE CAPTAIN OR FURY SHARK TO NO AVAIL."

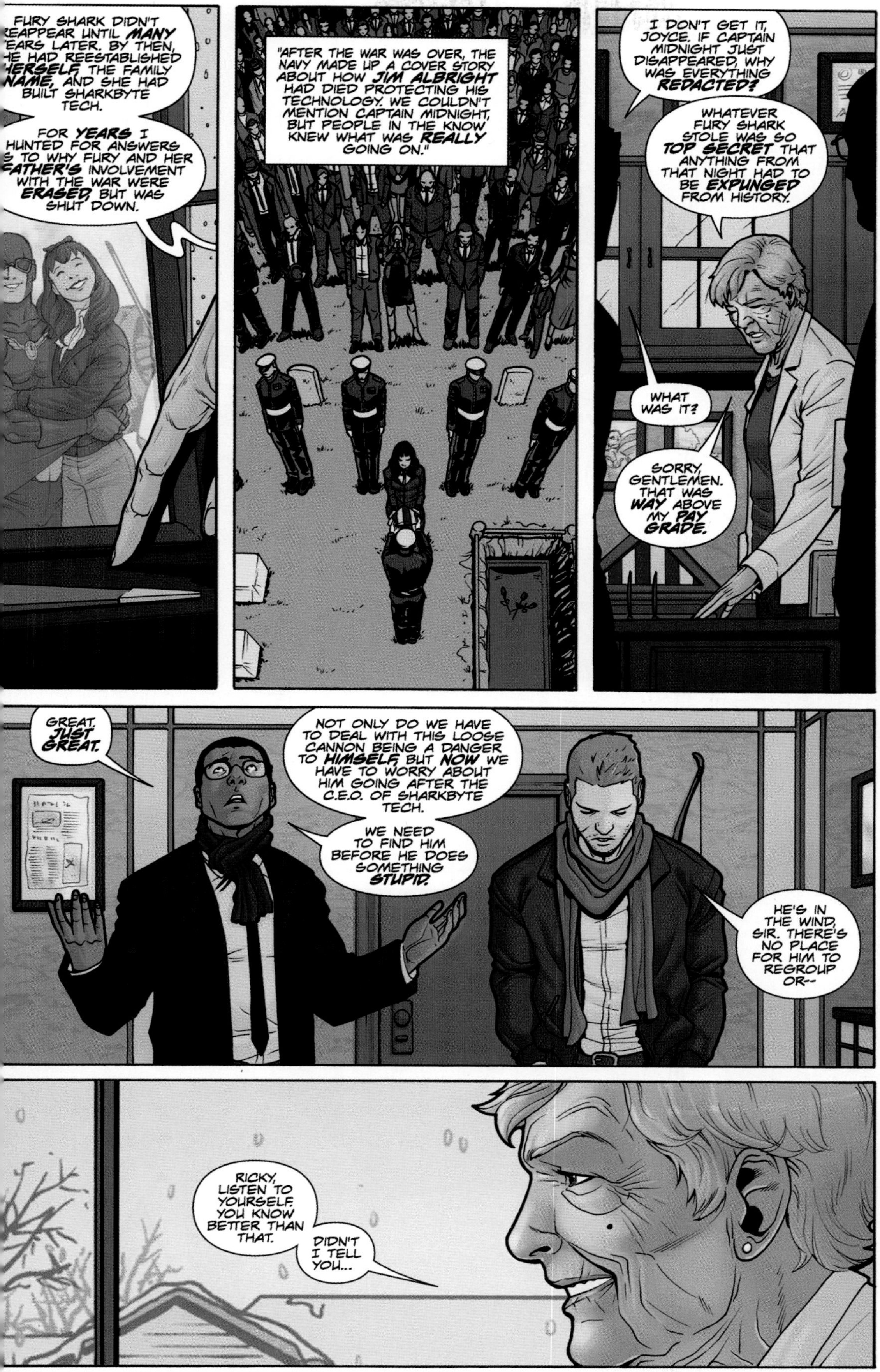
FURY SHARK DIDN'T REAPPEAR UNTIL MANY YEARS LATER. BY THEN, SHE HAD REESTABLISHED HERSELF, THE FAMILY NAME, AND SHE HAD BUILT SHARKBYTE TECH.
FOR YEARS I HUNTED FOR ANSWERS AS TO WHY FURY AND HER FATHER'S INVOLVEMENT WITH THE WAR WERE ERASED, BUT WAS SHUT DOWN.
"AFTER THE WAR WAS OVER, THE NAVY MADE UP A COVER STORY ABOUT HOW JIM ALBRIGHT HAD DIED PROTECTING HIS TECHNOLOGY. WE COULDN'T MENTION CAPTAIN MIDNIGHT, BUT PEOPLE IN THE KNOW KNEW WHAT WAS REALLY GOING ON."
I DON'T GET IT, JOYCE. IF CAPTAIN MIDNIGHT JUST DISAPPEARED, WHY WAS EVERYTHING REDACTED?
WHATEVER FURY SHARK STOLE WAS SO TOP SECRET THAT ANYTHING FROM THAT NIGHT HAD TO BE EXPUNGED FROM HISTORY.
WHAT WAS IT?
SORRY, GENTLEMEN. THAT WAS WAY ABOVE MY PAY GRADE.
GREAT. JUST GREAT.
NOT ONLY DO WE HAVE TO DEAL WITH THIS LOOSE CANNON BEING A DANGER TO HIMSELF, BUT NOW WE HAVE TO WORRY ABOUT HIM GOING AFTER THE C.E.O. OF SHARKBYTE TECH.
WE NEED TO FIND HIM BEFORE HE DOES SOMETHING STUPID.
HE'S IN THE WIND, SIR. THERE'S NO PLACE FOR HIM TO REGROUP OR--
RICKY, LISTEN TO YOURSELF. YOU KNOW BETTER THAN THAT.
DIDN'T I TELL YOU...

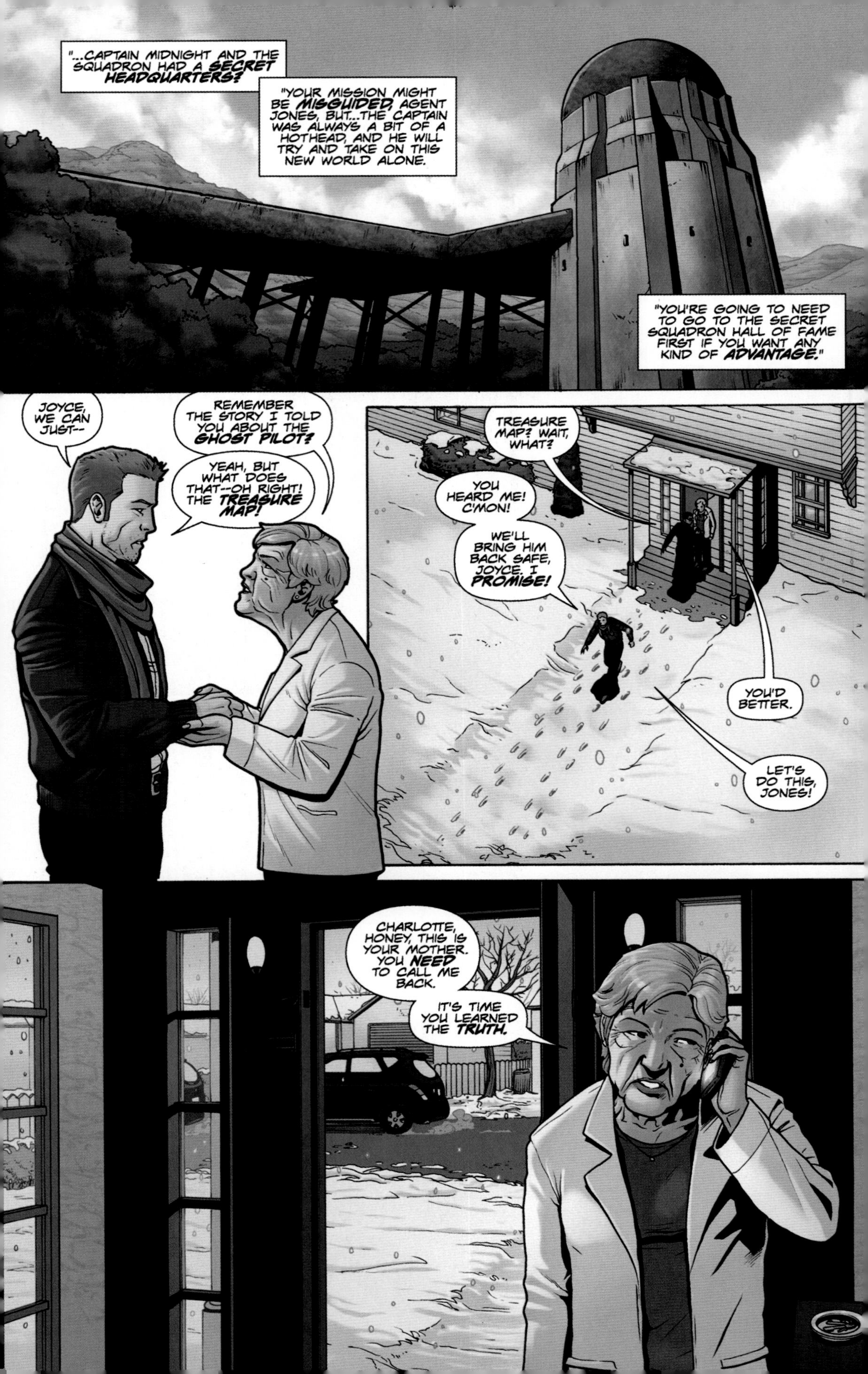
"...CAPTAIN MIDNIGHT AND THE SQUADRON HAD A SECRET HEADQUARTERS?
"YOUR MISSION MIGHT BE MISGUIDED, AGENT JONES, BUT...THE CAPTAIN WAS ALWAYS A BIT OF A HOTHEAD, AND HE WILL TRY AND TAKE ON THIS NEW WORLD ALONE.
"YOU'RE GOING TO NEED TO GO TO THE SECRET SQUADRON HALL OF FAME FIRST IF YOU WANT ANY KIND OF ADVANTAGE."
JOYCE, WE CAN JUST--
REMEMBER THE STORY I TOLD YOU ABOUT THE GHOST PILOT?
YEAH, BUT WHAT DOES THAT--OH RIGHT! THE TREASURE MAP!
TREASURE MAP? WAIT, WHAT?
YOU HEARD ME! C'MON!
WE'LL BRING HIM BACK SAFE, JOYCE. I PROMISE!
YOU'D BETTER.
LET'S DO THIS, JONES!
CHARLOTTE, HONEY, THIS IS YOUR MOTHER. YOU NEED TO CALL ME BACK.
IT'S TIME YOU LEARNED THE TRUTH.

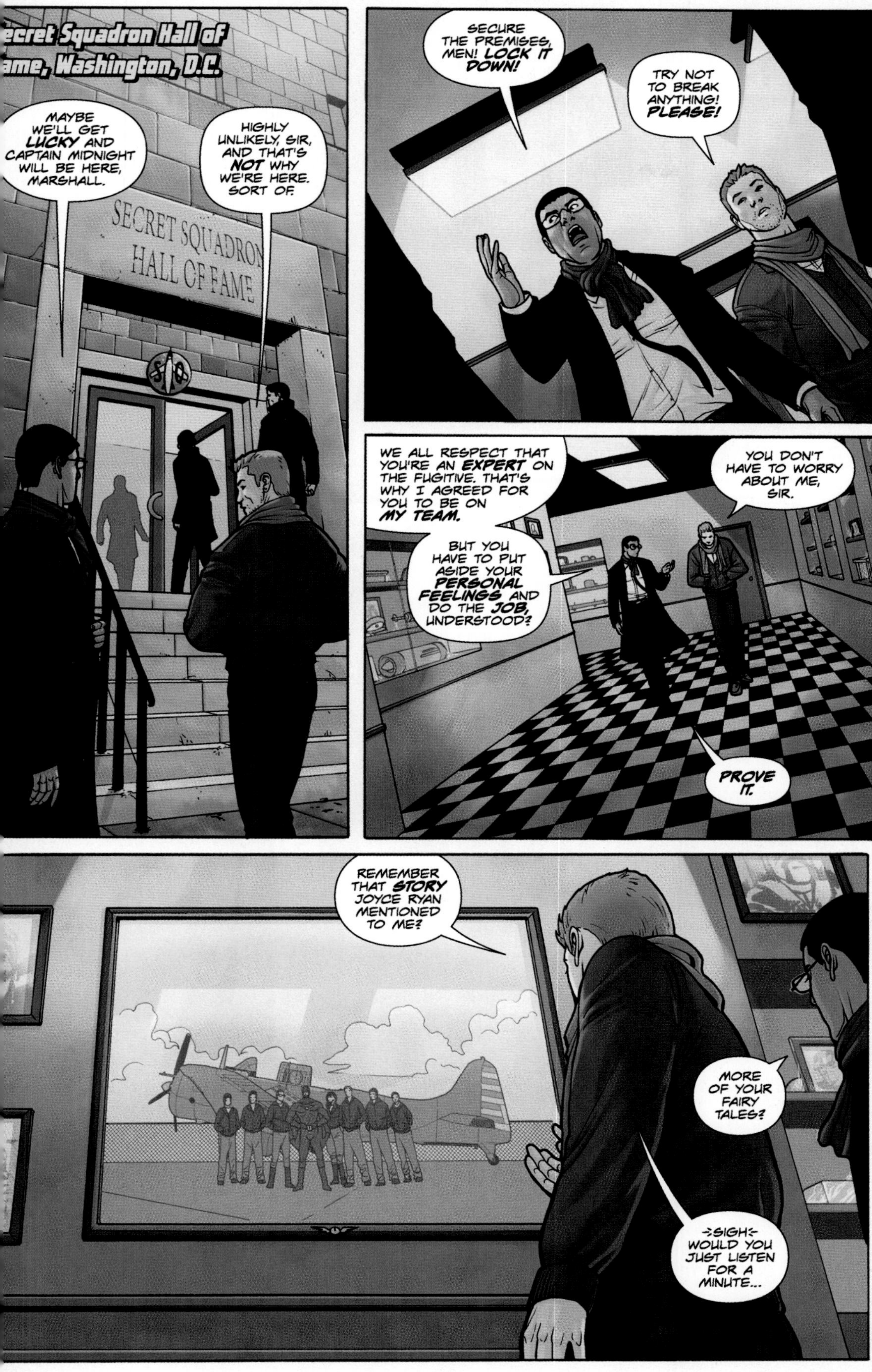
ecret Squadron Hall of
ame, Washington, D.C.
MAYBE WE'LL GET LUCKY AND CAPTAIN MIDNIGHT WILL BE HERE, MARSHALL.
HIGHLY UNLIKELY, SIR, AND THAT'S NOT WHY WE'RE HERE. SORT OF.
SECRET SQUADRON HALL OF FAME
SECURE THE PREMISES, MEN! LOCK IT DOWN!
TRY NOT TO BREAK ANYTHING! PLEASE!
WE ALL RESPECT THAT YOU'RE AN EXPERT ON THE FUGITIVE. THAT'S WHY I AGREED FOR YOU TO BE ON MY TEAM.
BUT YOU HAVE TO PUT ASIDE YOUR PERSONAL FEELINGS AND DO THE JOB, UNDERSTOOD?
YOU DON'T HAVE TO WORRY ABOUT ME, SIR.
PROVE IT.
REMEMBER THAT STORY JOYCE RYAN MENTIONED TO ME?
MORE OF YOUR FAIRY TALES?
-SIGH- WOULD YOU JUST LISTEN FOR A MINUTE...

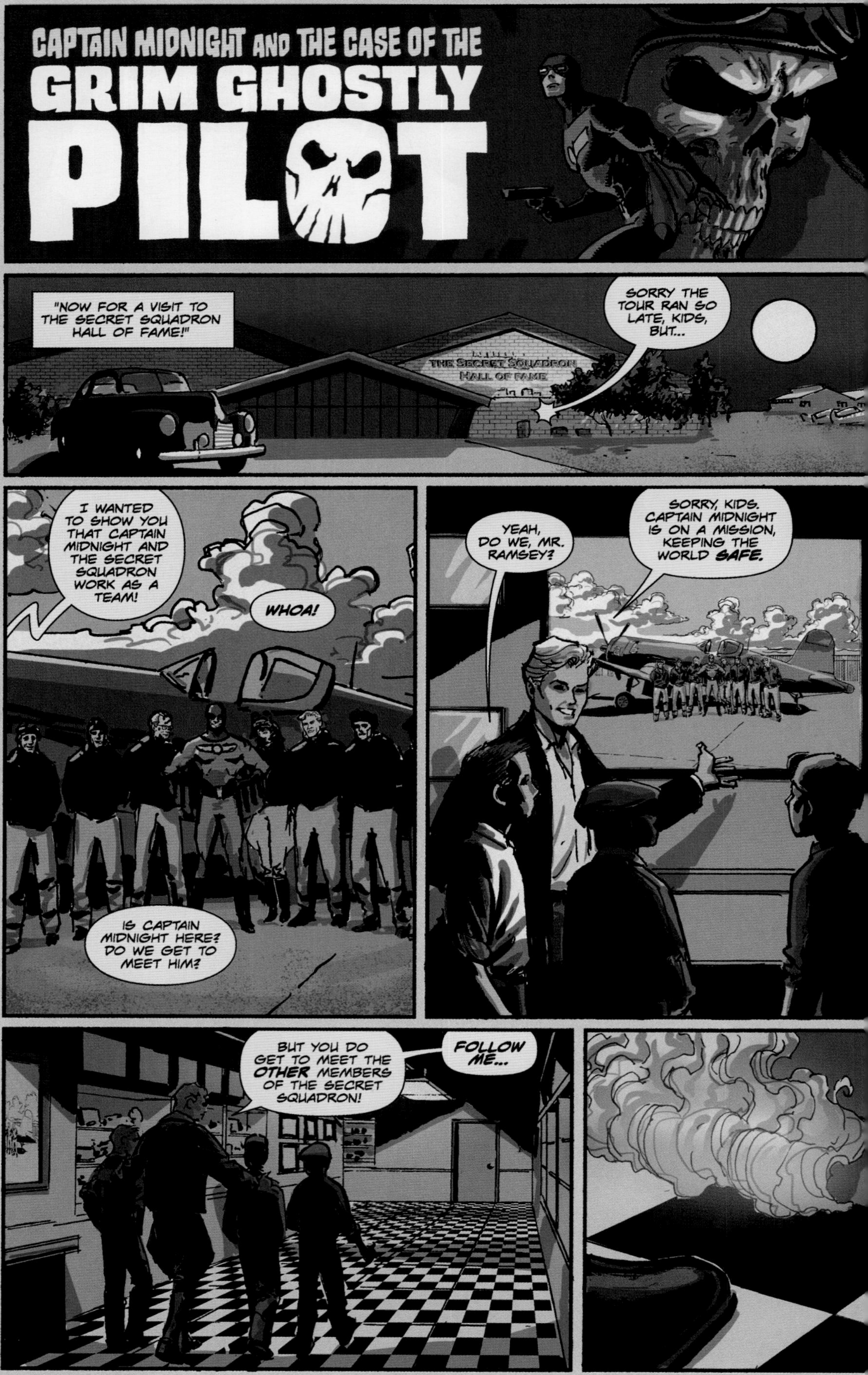
CAPTAIN MIDNIGHT AND THE CASE OF THE
GRIM GHOSTLY PILOT
"NOW FOR A VISIT TO THE SECRET SQUADRON HALL OF FAME!"
THE SECRET SQUADRON HALL OF FAME
SORRY THE TOUR RAN SO LATE, KIDS, BUT...
I WANTED TO SHOW YOU THAT CAPTAIN MIDNIGHT AND THE SECRET SQUADRON WORK AS A TEAM!
WHOA!
IS CAPTAIN MIDNIGHT HERE? DO WE GET TO MEET HIM?
YEAH, DO WE, MR. RAMSEY?
SORRY, KIDS. CAPTAIN MIDNIGHT IS ON A MISSION, KEEPING THE WORLD SAFE.
BUT YOU DO GET TO MEET THE OTHER MEMBERS OF THE SECRET SQUADRON!
FOLLOW ME...

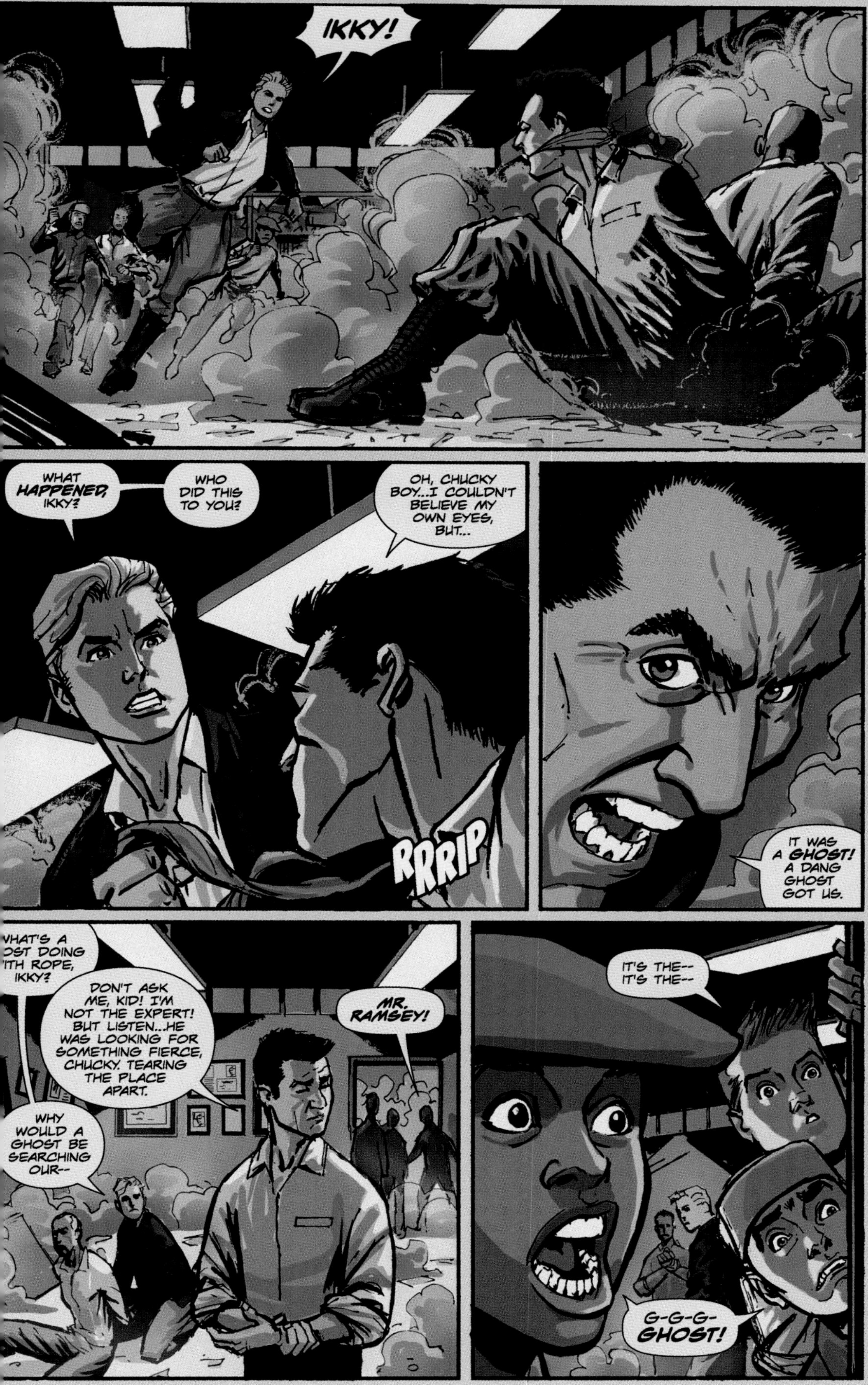
IKKY!
WHAT HAPPENED, IKKY?
WHO DID THIS TO YOU?
OH, CHUCKY BOY...I COULDN'T BELIEVE MY OWN EYES, BUT...
RRRIP
IT WAS A GHOST! A DANG GHOST GOT US.
WHAT'S A OST DOING ITH ROPE, IKKY?
DON'T ASK ME, KID! I'M NOT THE EXPERT! BUT LISTEN...HE WAS LOOKING FOR SOMETHING FIERCE, CHUCKY. TEARING THE PLACE APART.
WHY WOULD A GHOST BE SEARCHING OUR--
MR. RAMSEY!
IT'S THE-- IT'S THE--
G-G-G-GHOST!

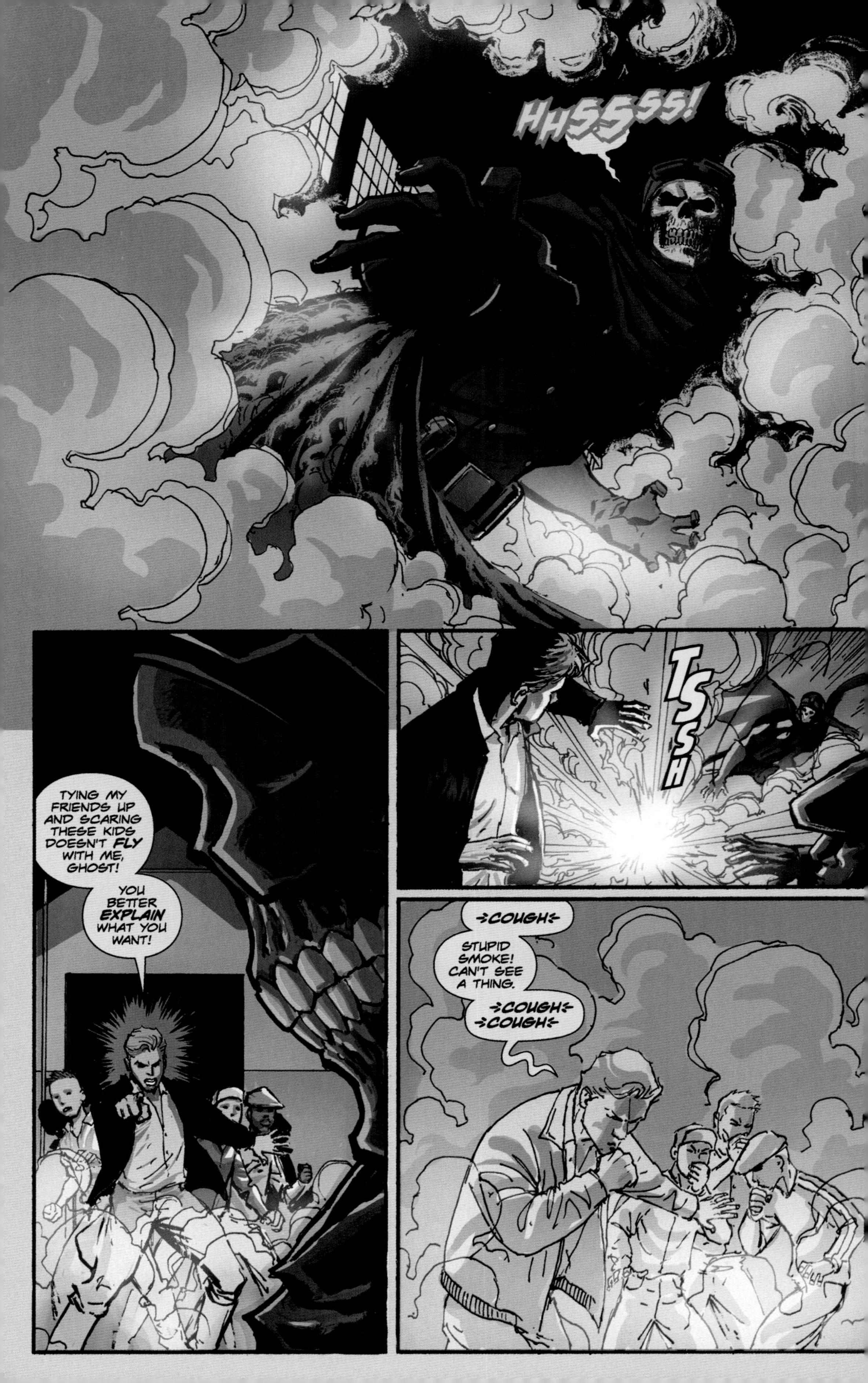
HHSSSSS!
TYING MY FRIENDS UP AND SCARING THESE KIDS DOESN'T FLY WITH ME, GHOST!
YOU BETTER EXPLAIN WHAT YOU WANT!
TSSSH
-COUGH-
STUPID SMOKE! CAN'T SEE A THING.
-COUGH- -COUGH-

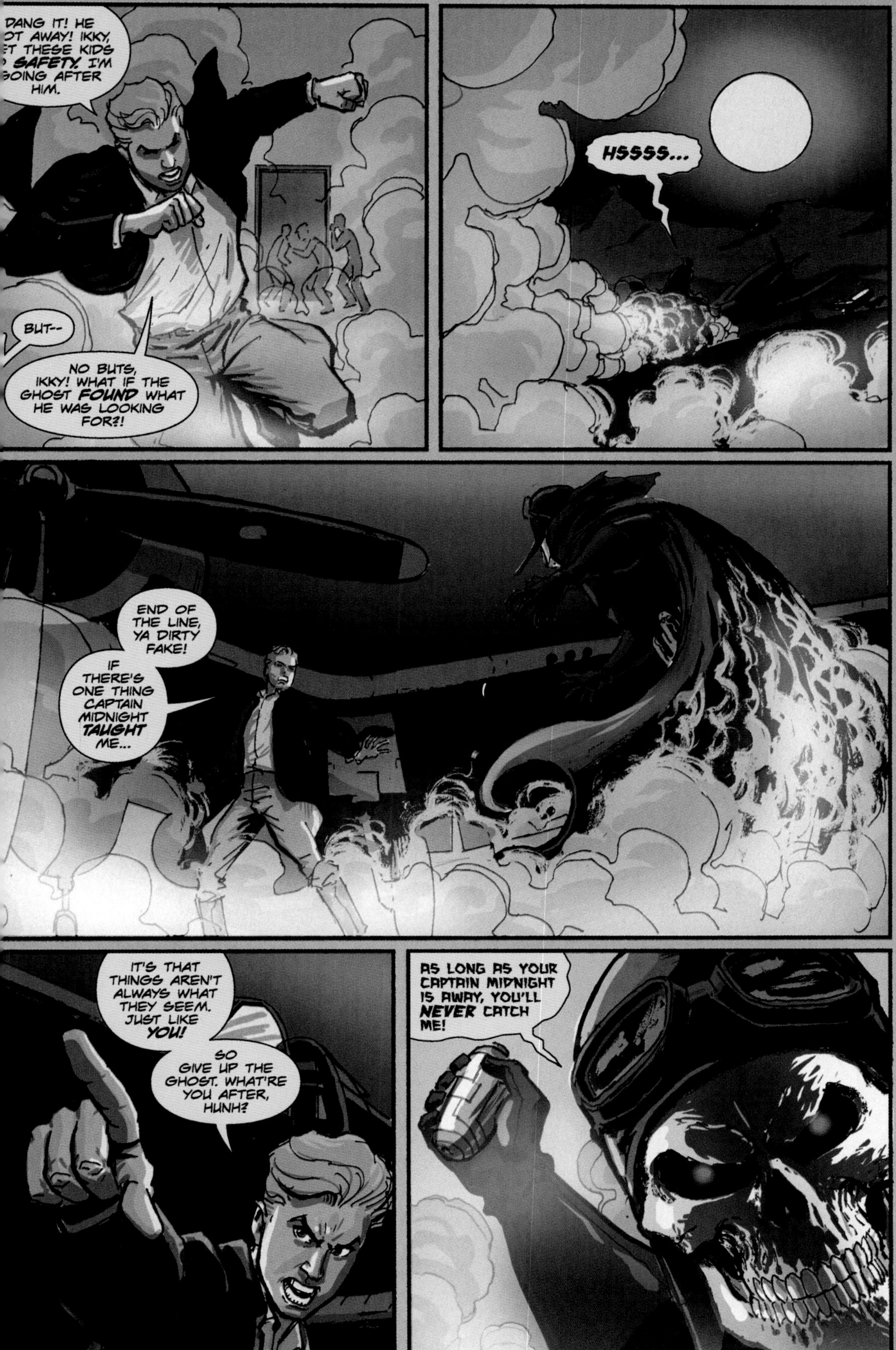
DANG IT! HE GOT AWAY! IKKY, GET THESE KIDS TO SAFETY. I'M GOING AFTER HIM.
BUT--
NO BUTS, IKKY! WHAT IF THE GHOST FOUND WHAT HE WAS LOOKING FOR?!
HSSSS...
END OF THE LINE, YA DIRTY FAKE!
IF THERE'S ONE THING CAPTAIN MIDNIGHT TAUGHT ME...
IT'S THAT THINGS AREN'T ALWAYS WHAT THEY SEEM. JUST LIKE YOU!
SO GIVE UP THE GHOST. WHAT'RE YOU AFTER, HUNH?
AS LONG AS YOUR CAPTAIN MIDNIGHT IS AWAY, YOU'LL NEVER CATCH ME!

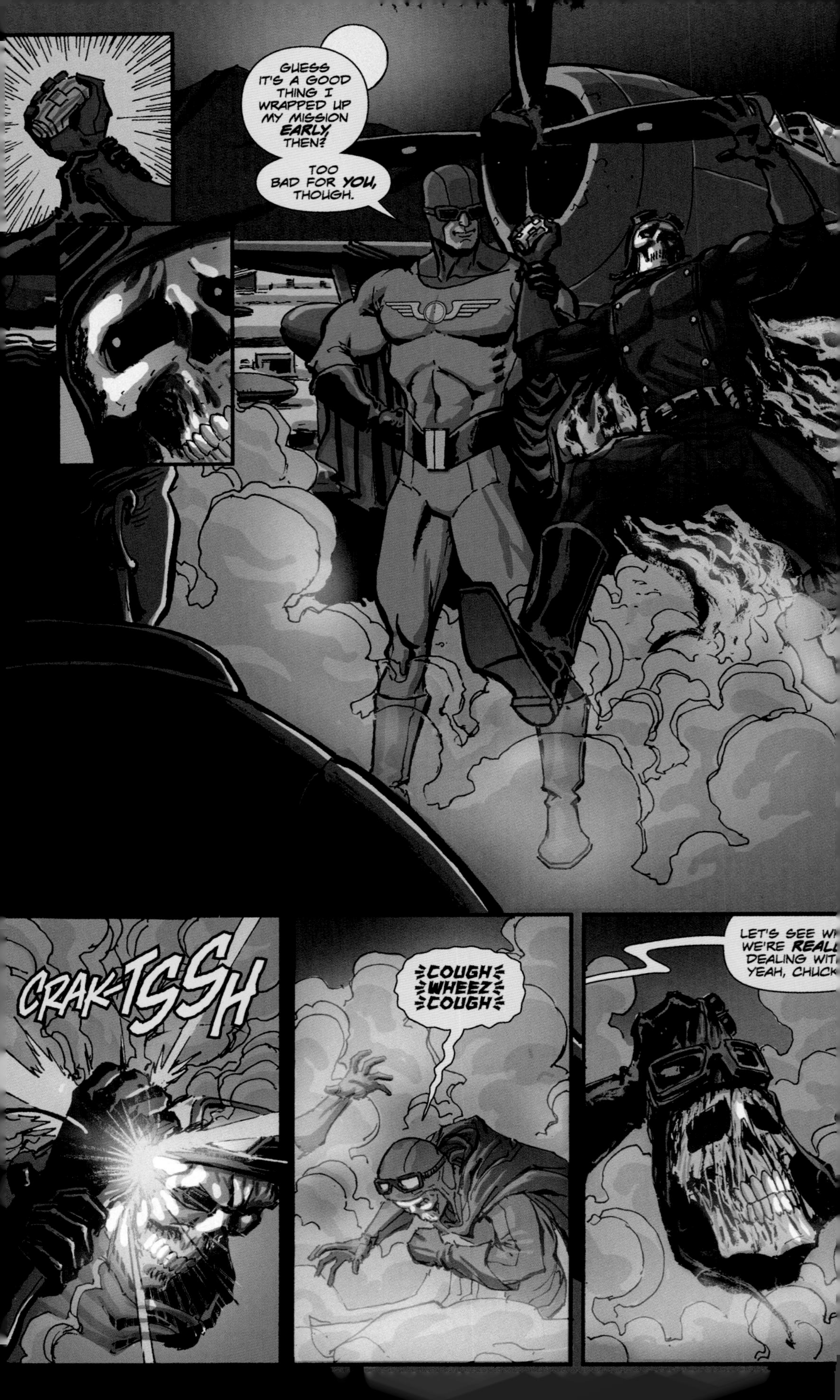
GUESS IT'S A GOOD THING I WRAPPED UP MY MISSION EARLY, THEN?
TOO BAD FOR YOU, THOUGH.
CRAK-TSSH
COUGH WHEEZ COUGH

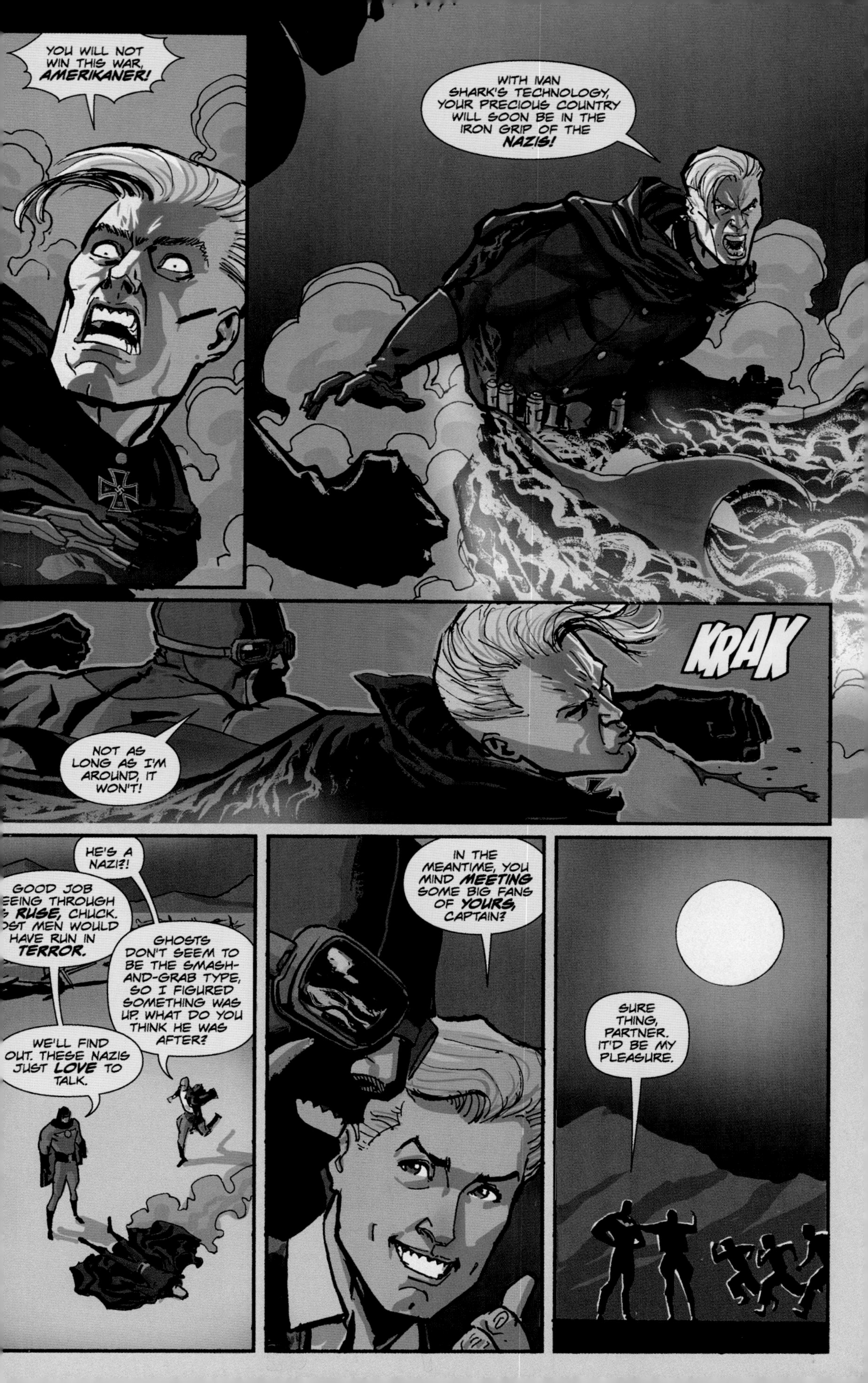

YOU WILL NOT WIN THIS WAR, AMERIKANER!
WITH IVAN SHARK'S TECHNOLOGY, YOUR PRECIOUS COUNTRY WILL SOON BE IN THE IRON GRIP OF THE NAZIS!
KRAK
NOT AS LONG AS I'M AROUND, IT WON'T!
HE'S A NAZI?!
GOOD JOB EEING THROUGH RUSE, CHUCK. OST MEN WOULD HAVE RUN IN TERROR.
GHOSTS DON'T SEEM TO BE THE SMASH-AND-GRAB TYPE, SO I FIGURED SOMETHING WAS UP. WHAT DO YOU THINK HE WAS AFTER?
WE'LL FIND OUT. THESE NAZIS JUST LOVE TO TALK.
IN THE MEANTIME, YOU MIND MEETING SOME BIG FANS OF YOURS, CAPTAIN?
SURE THING, PARTNER. IT'D BE MY PLEASURE.

WELL...?

WELL, *WHAT?*

OH, DON'T DO *THAT.* WHAT WAS THE NAZI AFTER?

THIS.

THE PICTURE?

WHEN ARE YOU GOING TO GET IT, JONES? JUST LIKE IN THE STORY...

CLICK

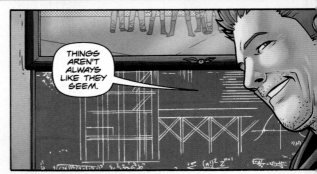

THINGS AREN'T ALWAYS LIKE THEY SEEM.

THAT'S YOUR TREASURE MAP?

JOYCE ALWAYS CALLED IT THAT IN THE STORY, BUT...I GUESS IT'S A BLUEPRINT OF CAPTAIN MIDNIGHT'S SECRET BASE.

IT MIGHT BE HARD FOR YOU TO BELIEVE, SIR, BUT THE CAPTAIN WAS MORE THAN JUST A HERO TO *ME.* HE INSPIRED EVERYONE HE CAME INTO CONTACT WITH TO BE *BETTER.*

DOESN'T CHANGE THE FACT THAT HE'S A SECURITY RISK *NOW,* MARSHALL.

BUT WITH THIS HE'S AS GOOD AS *CAUGHT.*

CHAPTER 1

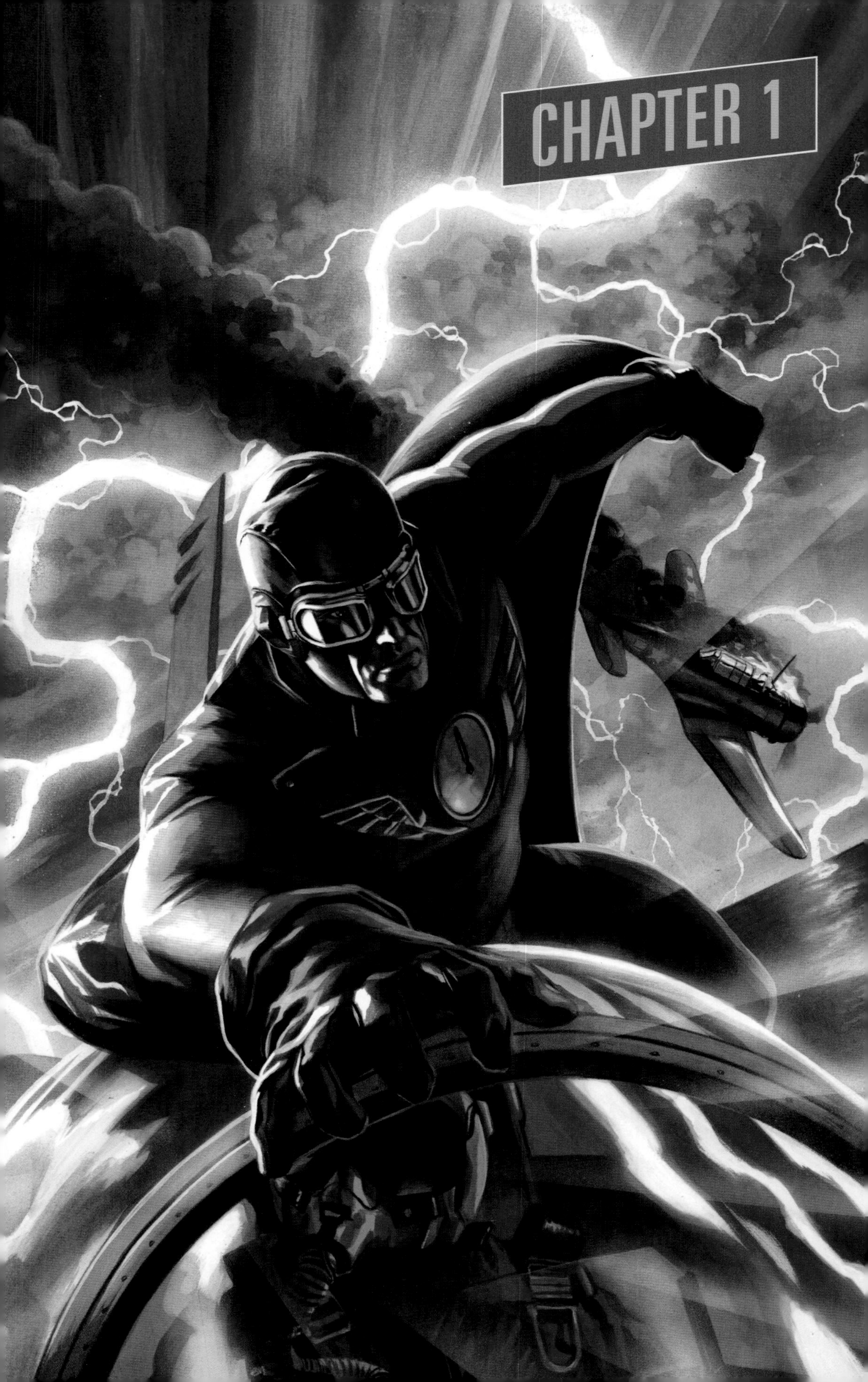

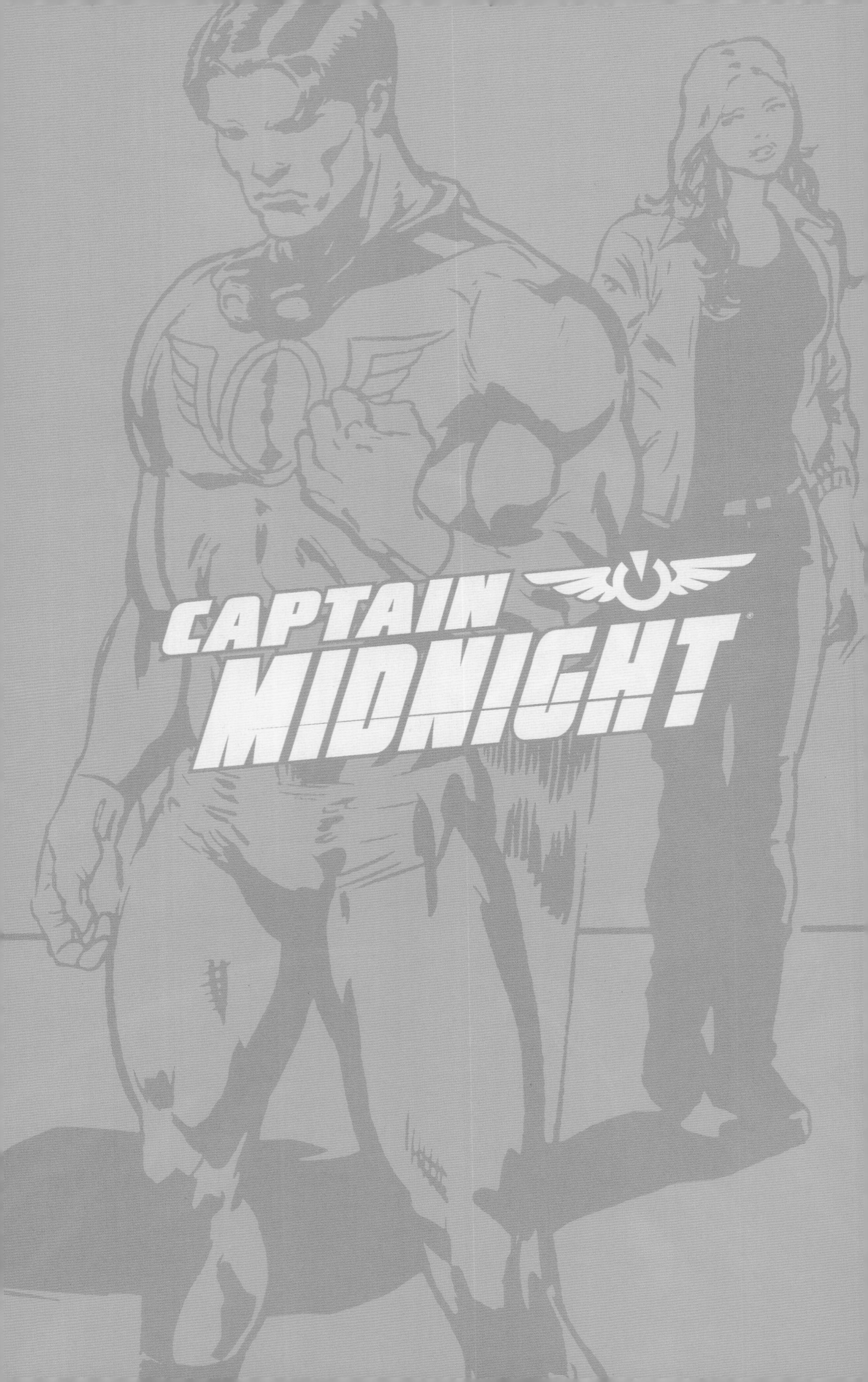
CAPTAIN
MIDNIGHT®

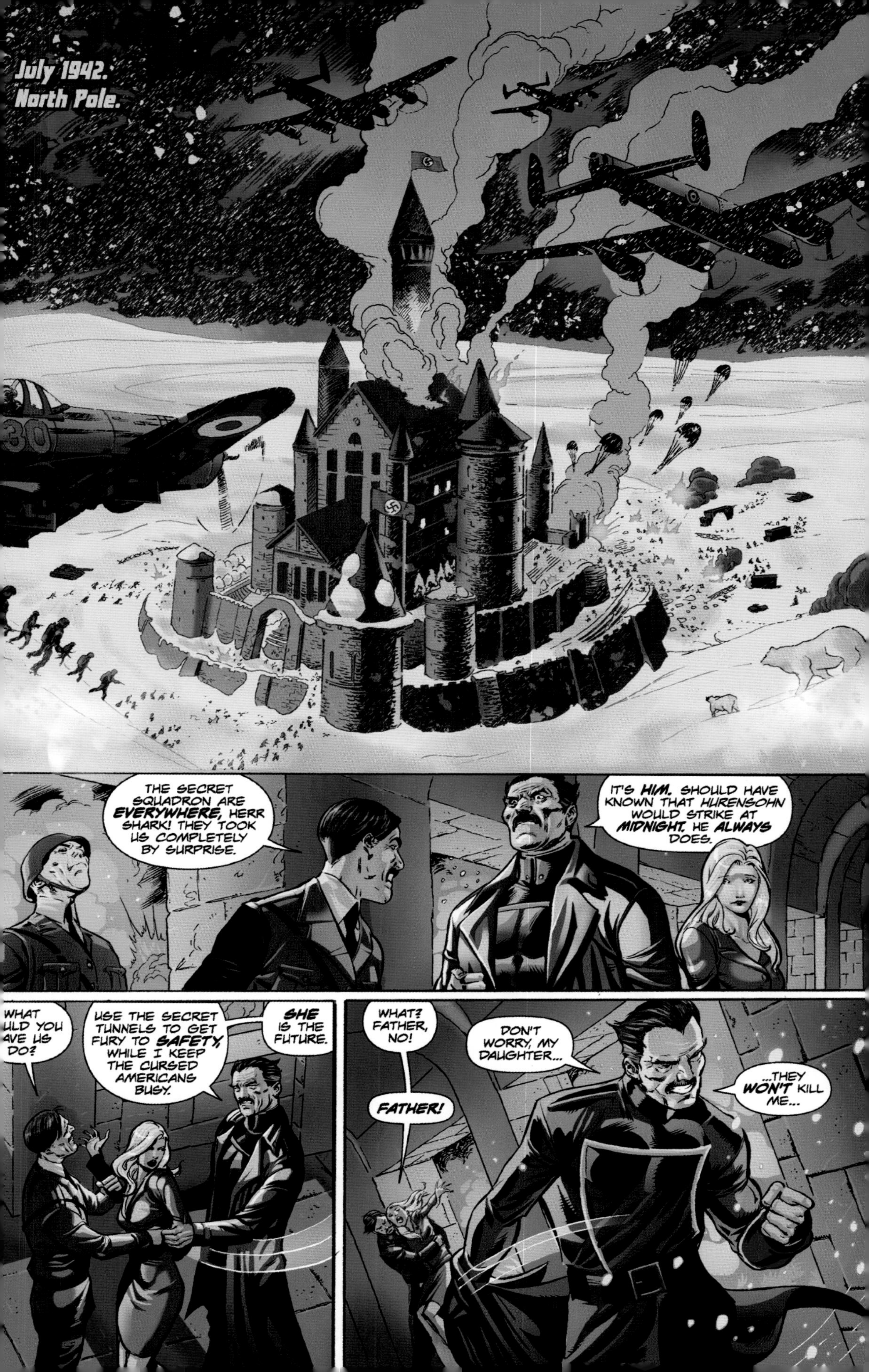

July 1942.
North Pole.
THE SECRET SQUADRON ARE EVERYWHERE, HERR SHARK! THEY TOOK US COMPLETELY BY SURPRISE.
IT'S HIM. SHOULD HAVE KNOWN THAT HURENSOHN WOULD STRIKE AT MIDNIGHT. HE ALWAYS DOES.
WHAT ULD YOU AVE US DO?
USE THE SECRET TUNNELS TO GET FURY TO SAFETY, WHILE I KEEP THE CURSED AMERICANS BUSY.
SHE IS THE FUTURE.
WHAT? FATHER, NO!
FATHER!
DON'T WORRY, MY DAUGHTER...
...THEY WON'T KILL ME...

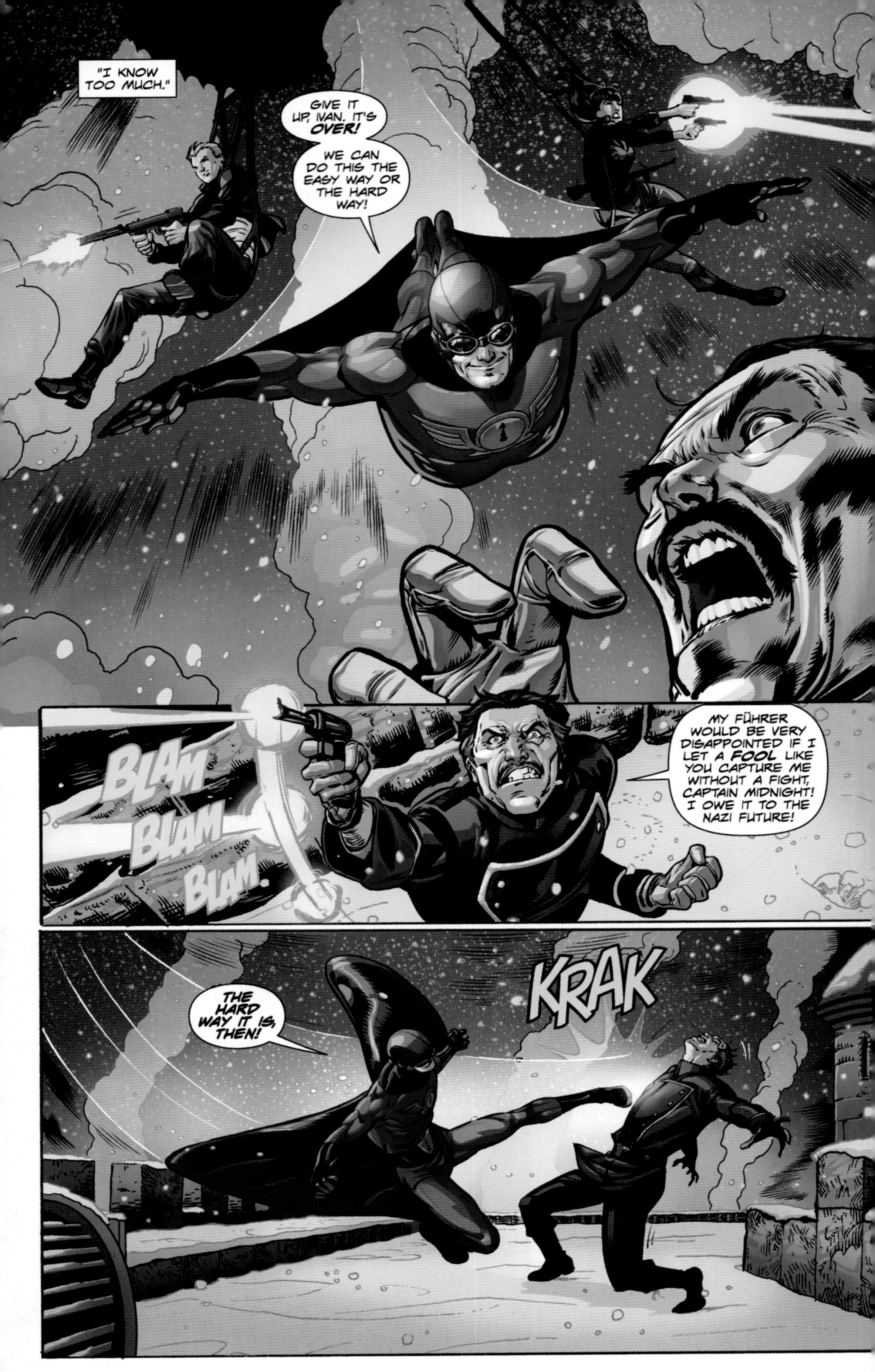
"I KNOW TOO MUCH."
GIVE IT UP, IVAN. IT'S OVER!
WE CAN DO THIS THE EASY WAY OR THE HARD WAY!
BLAM BLAM BLAM
MY FÜHRER WOULD BE VERY DISAPPOINTED IF I LET A FOOL LIKE YOU CAPTURE ME WITHOUT A FIGHT, CAPTAIN MIDNIGHT! I OWE IT TO THE NAZI FUTURE!
THE HARD WAY IT IS, THEN!
KRAK

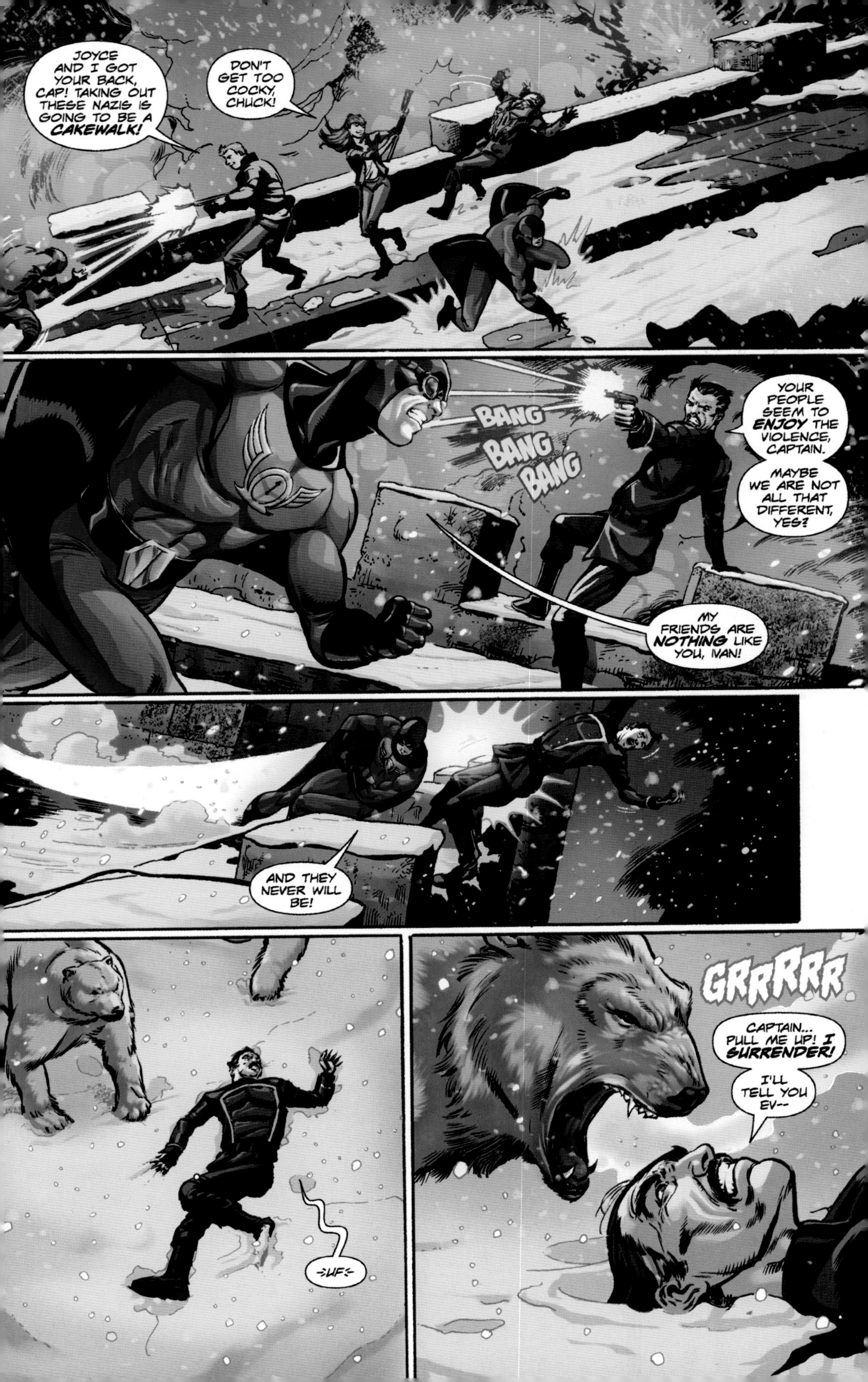
JOYCE AND I GOT YOUR BACK, CAP! TAKING OUT THESE NAZIS IS GOING TO BE A CAKEWALK!
DON'T GET TOO COCKY, CHUCK!
BANG
BANG
BANG
YOUR PEOPLE SEEM TO ENJOY THE VIOLENCE, CAPTAIN.
MAYBE WE ARE NOT ALL THAT DIFFERENT, YES?
MY FRIENDS ARE NOTHING LIKE YOU, IVAN!
AND THEY NEVER WILL BE!
-UF-
GRRRRR
CAPTAIN... PULL ME UP! I SURRENDER!
I'LL TELL YOU EV--

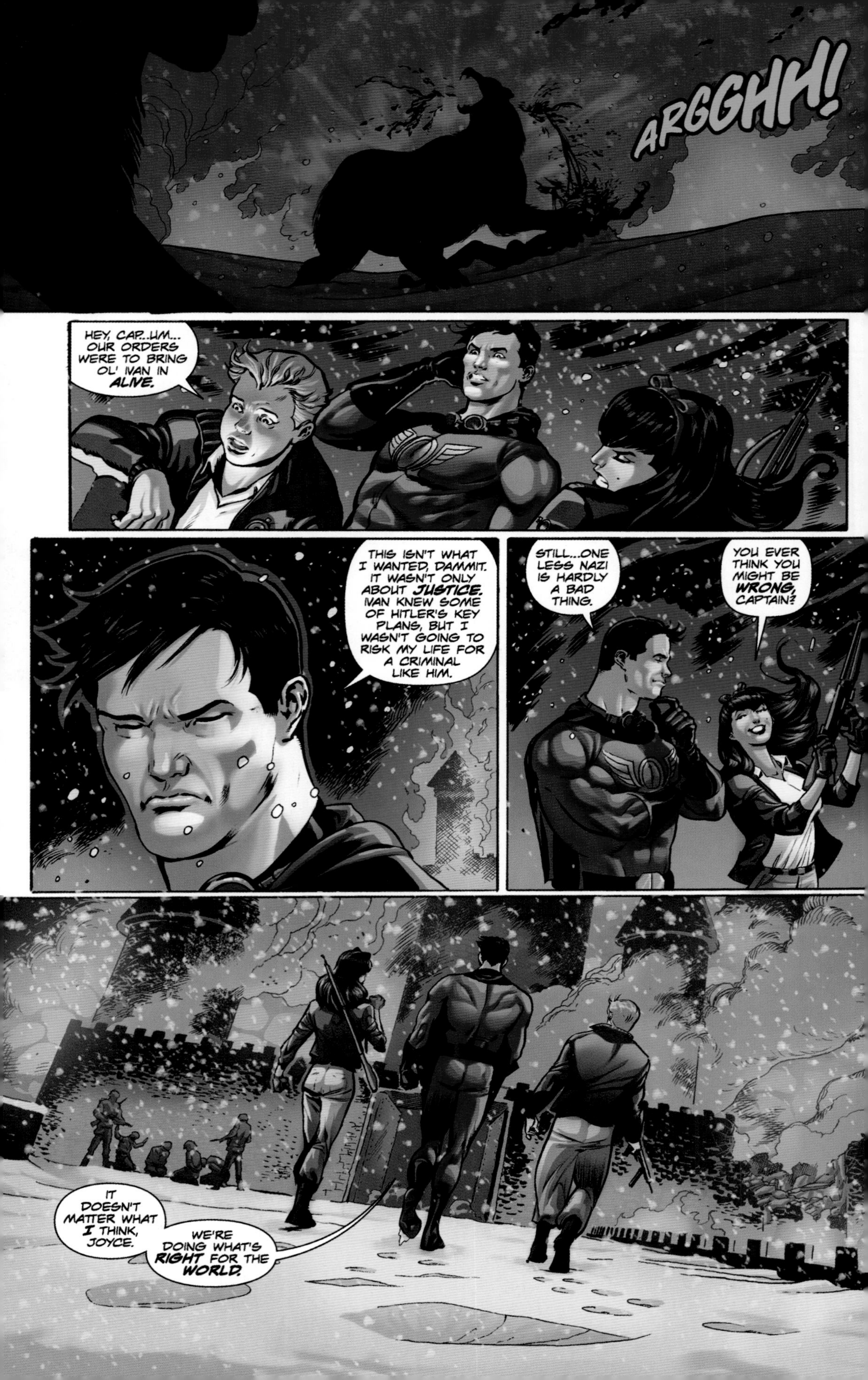
ARGGHH!
HEY, CAP...UM... OUR ORDERS WERE TO BRING OL' IVAN IN ALIVE.
THIS ISN'T WHAT I WANTED, DAMMIT. IT WASN'T ONLY ABOUT JUSTICE. IVAN KNEW SOME OF HITLER'S KEY PLANS, BUT I WASN'T GOING TO RISK MY LIFE FOR A CRIMINAL LIKE HIM.
STILL...ONE LESS NAZI IS HARDLY A BAD THING.
YOU EVER THINK YOU MIGHT BE WRONG, CAPTAIN?
IT DOESN'T MATTER WHAT I THINK, JOYCE.
WE'RE DOING WHAT'S RIGHT FOR THE WORLD.

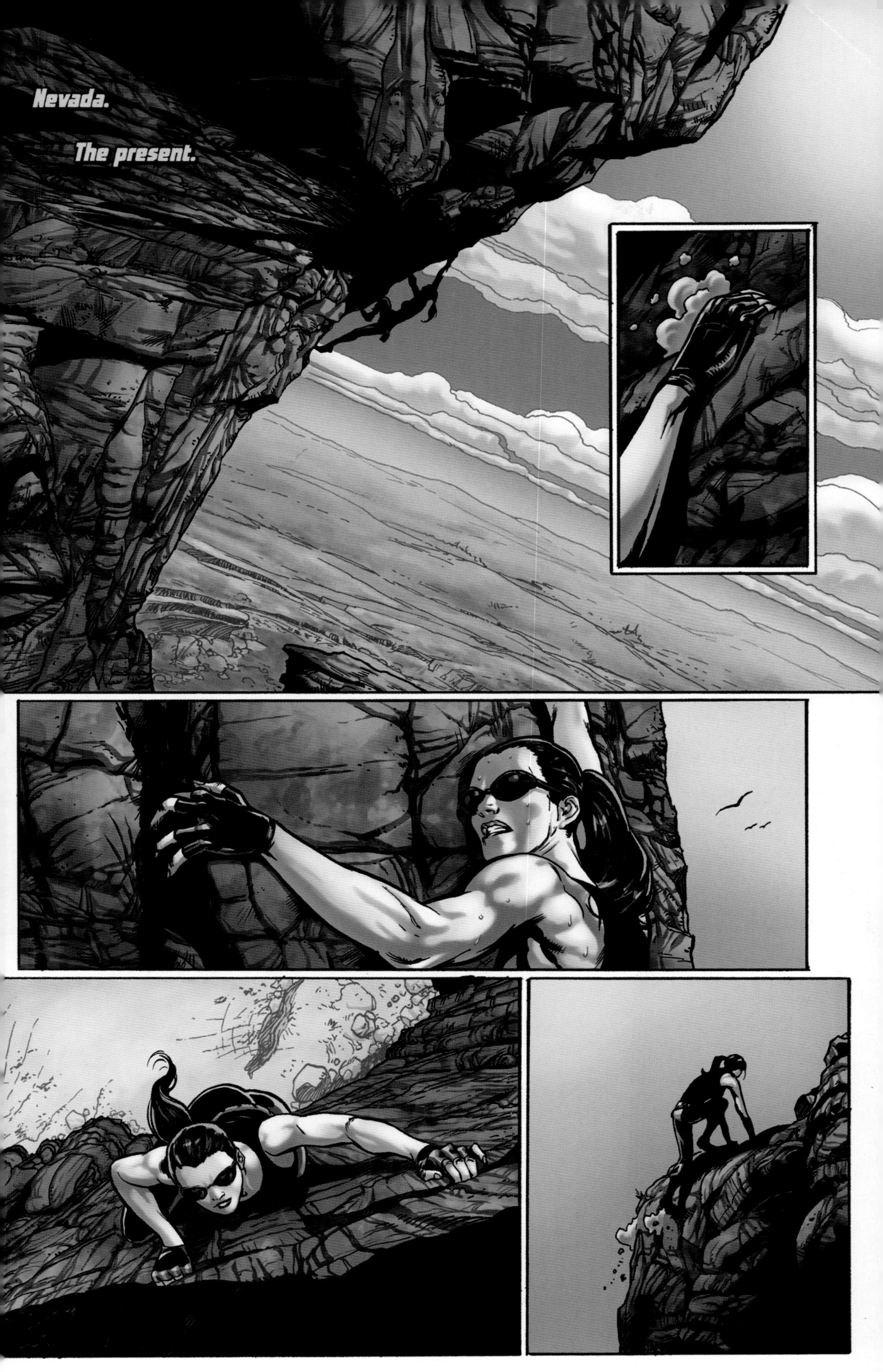
Nevada.
The present.

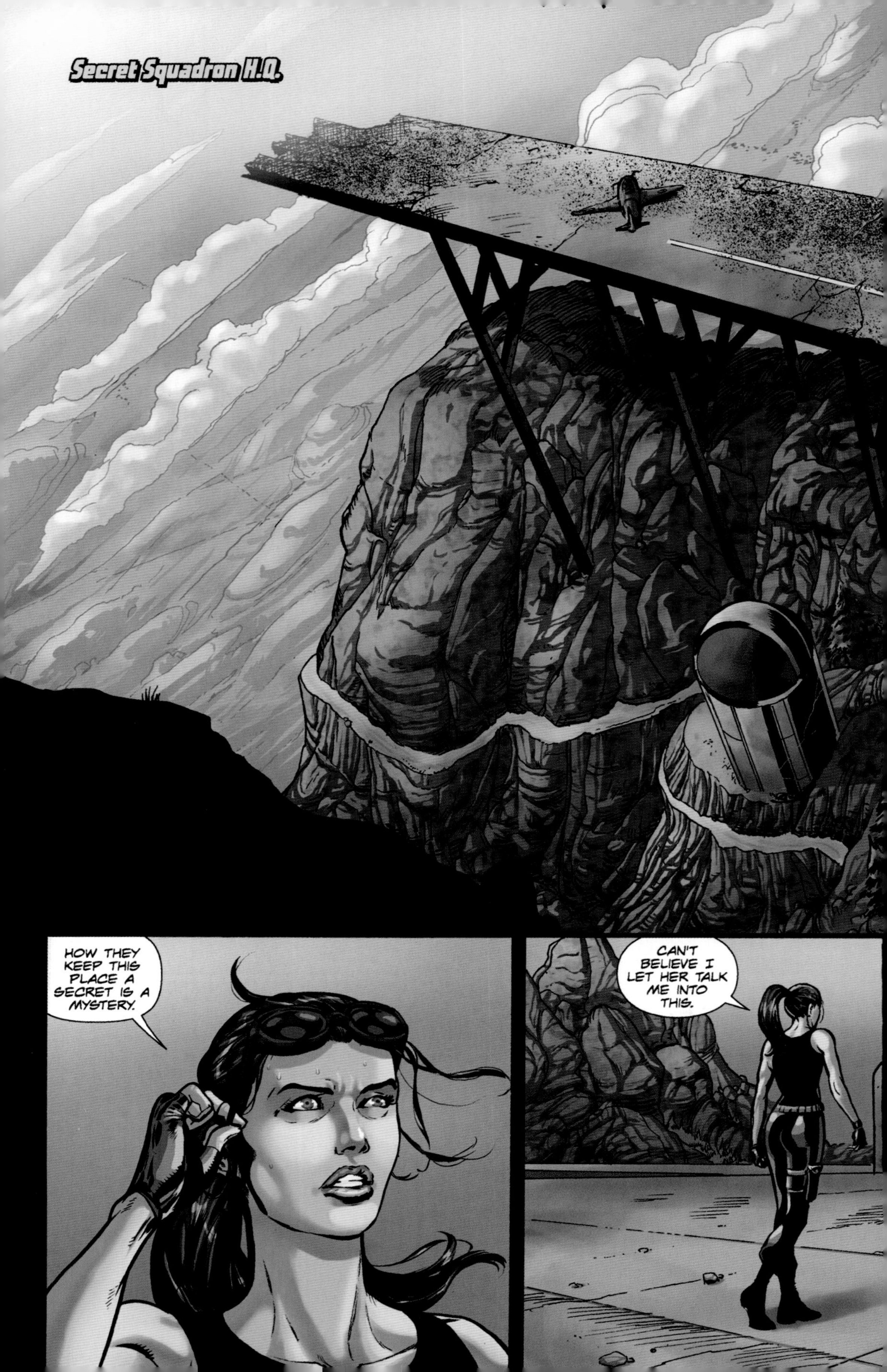
Secret Squadron H.Q.
HOW THEY KEEP THIS PLACE A SECRET IS A MYSTERY.
CAN'T BELIEVE I LET HER TALK ME INTO THIS.

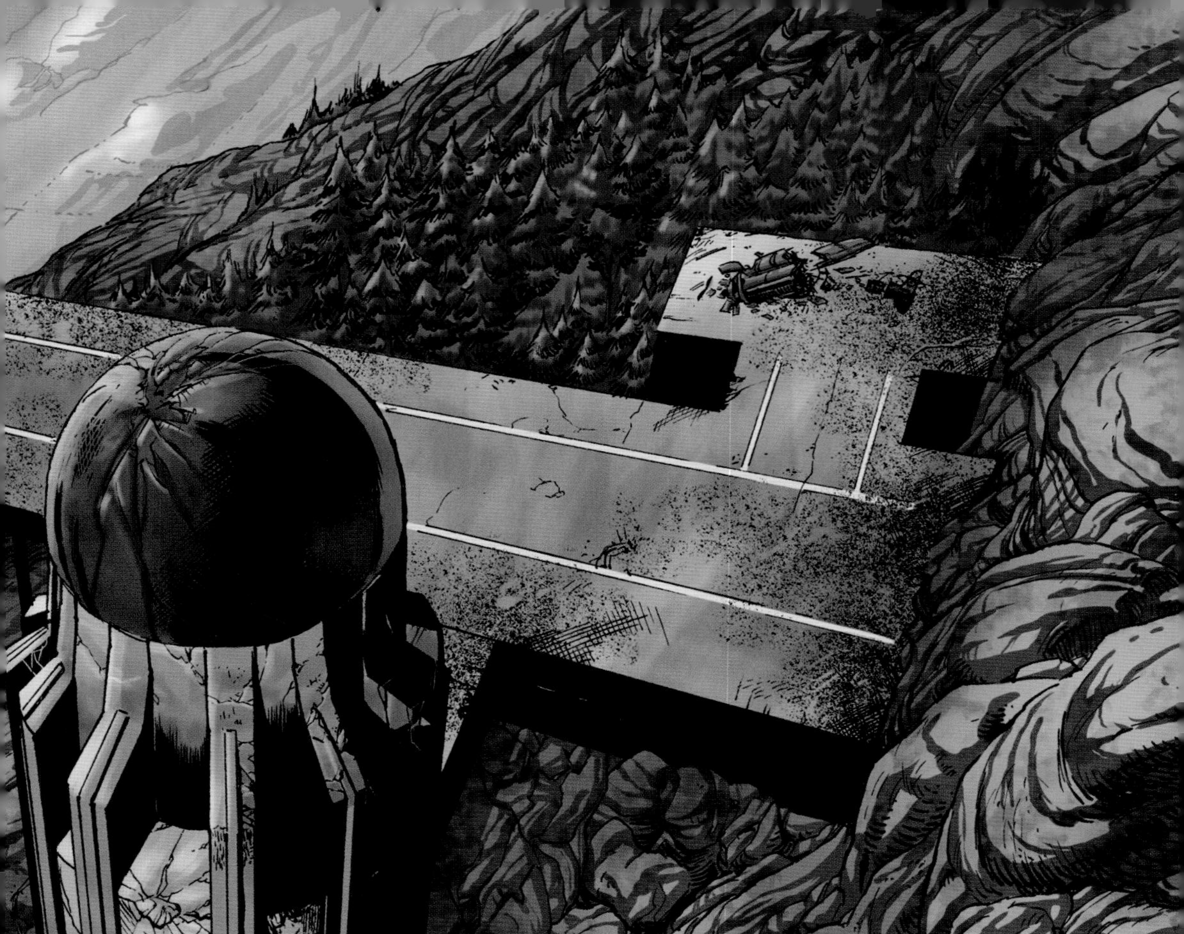

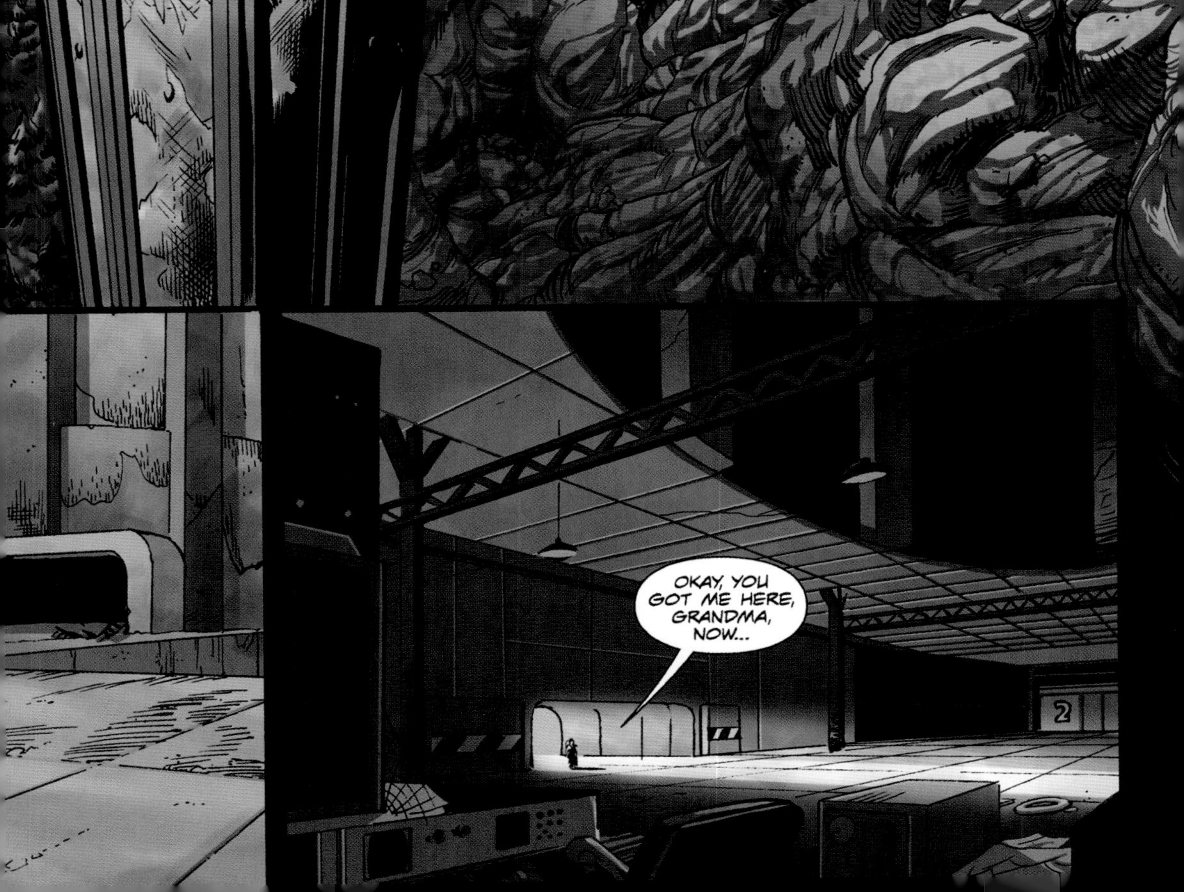
OKAY, YOU GOT ME HERE, GRANDMA, NOW...
2

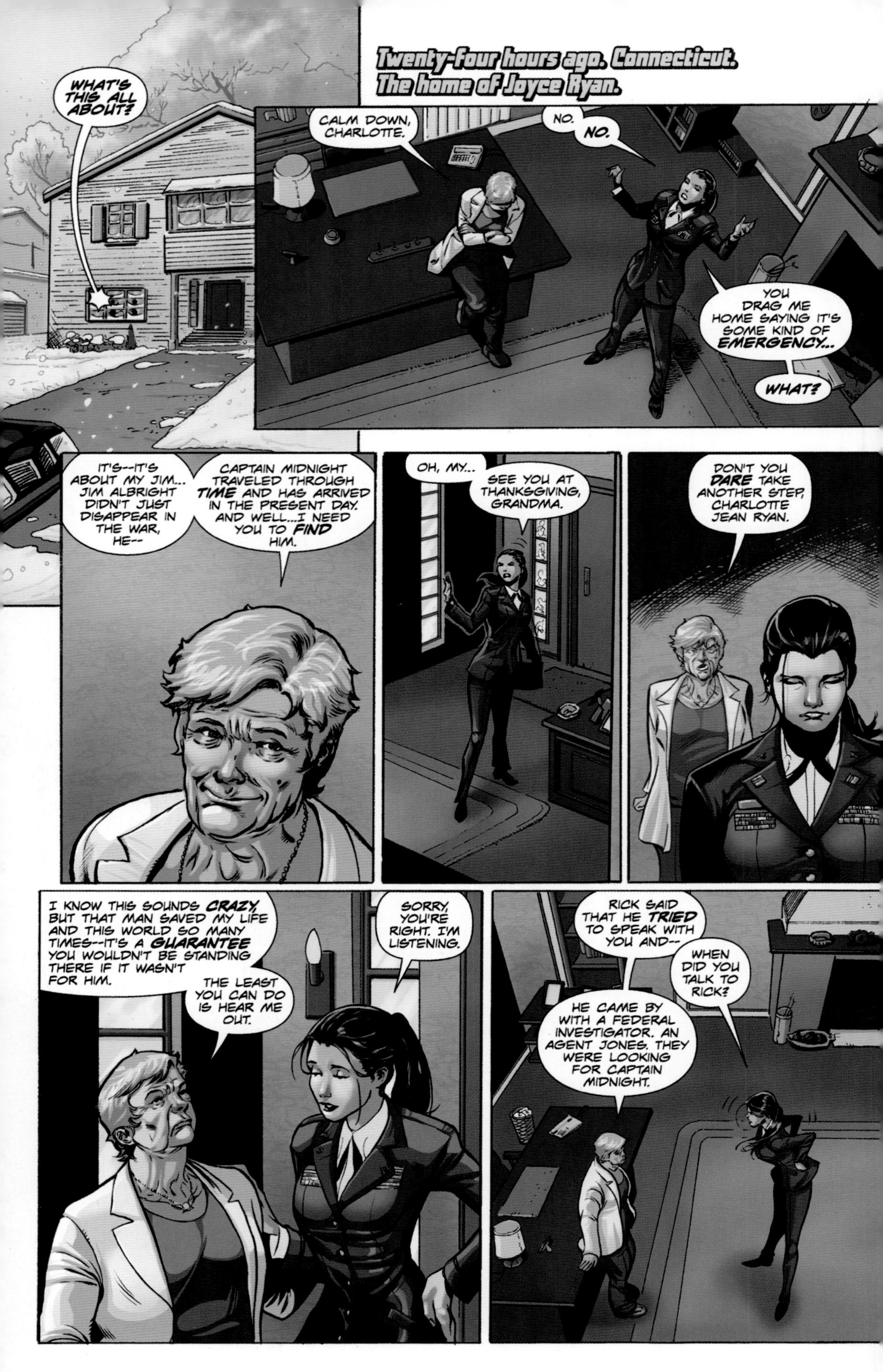
Twenty-four hours ago. Connecticut.
The home of Joyce Ryan.
WHAT'S THIS ALL ABOUT?
CALM DOWN, CHARLOTTE.
NO.
NO.
YOU DRAG ME HOME SAYING IT'S SOME KIND OF EMERGENCY...
WHAT?
IT'S--IT'S ABOUT MY JIM... JIM ALBRIGHT DIDN'T JUST DISAPPEAR IN THE WAR, HE--
CAPTAIN MIDNIGHT TRAVELED THROUGH TIME AND HAS ARRIVED IN THE PRESENT DAY. AND WELL...I NEED YOU TO FIND HIM.
OH, MY...
SEE YOU AT THANKSGIVING, GRANDMA.
DON'T YOU DARE TAKE ANOTHER STEP, CHARLOTTE JEAN RYAN.
I KNOW THIS SOUNDS CRAZY, BUT THAT MAN SAVED MY LIFE AND THIS WORLD SO MANY TIMES--IT'S A GUARANTEE YOU WOULDN'T BE STANDING THERE IF IT WASN'T FOR HIM.
THE LEAST YOU CAN DO IS HEAR ME OUT.
SORRY, YOU'RE RIGHT. I'M LISTENING.
RICK SAID THAT HE TRIED TO SPEAK WITH YOU AND--
WHEN DID YOU TALK TO RICK?
HE CAME BY WITH A FEDERAL INVESTIGATOR. AN AGENT JONES. THEY WERE LOOKING FOR CAPTAIN MIDNIGHT.

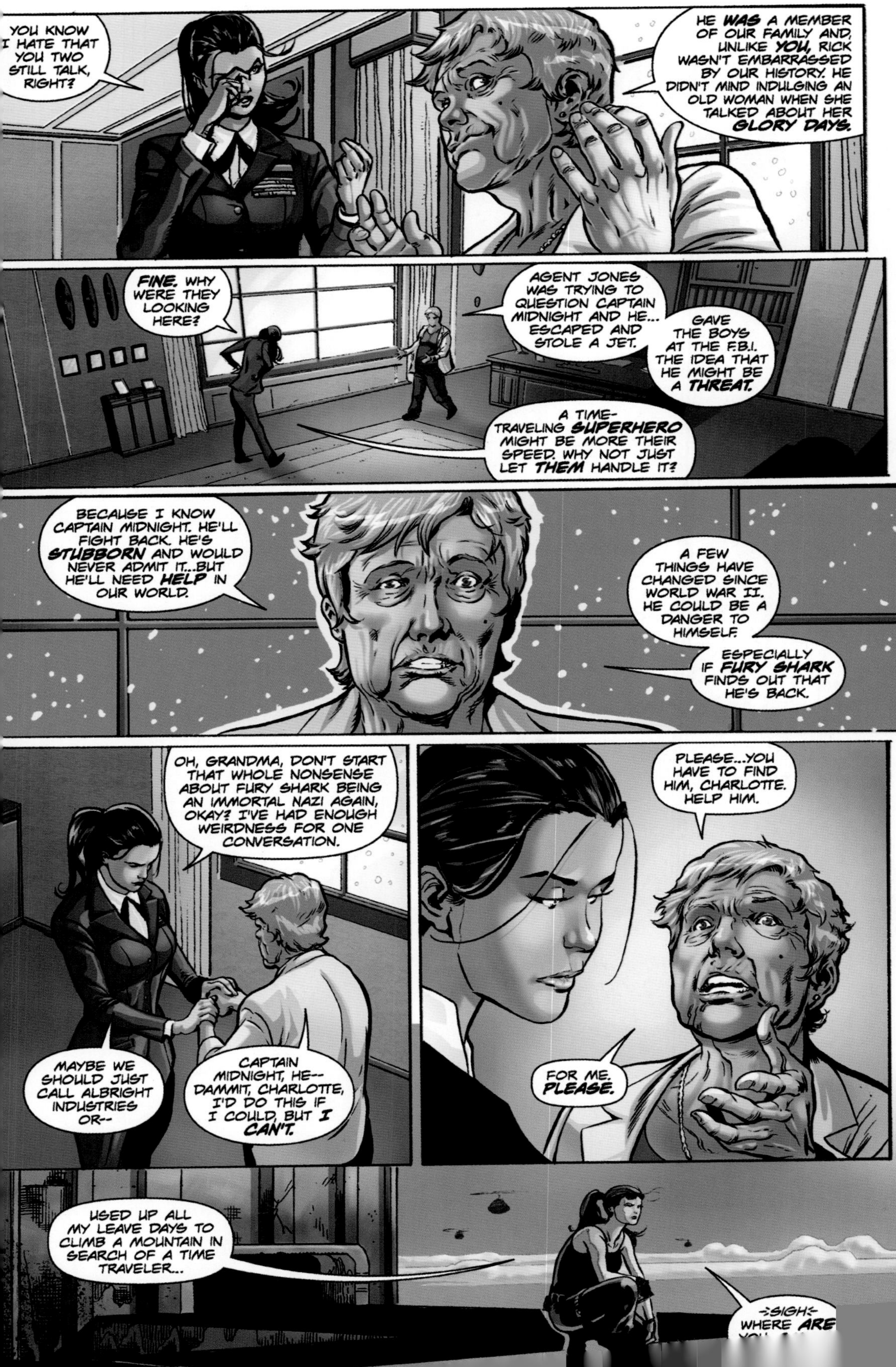

YOU KNOW I HATE THAT YOU TWO STILL TALK, RIGHT?
HE **WAS** A MEMBER OF OUR FAMILY AND, UNLIKE **YOU**, RICK WASN'T EMBARRASSED BY OUR HISTORY. HE DIDN'T MIND INDULGING AN OLD WOMAN WHEN SHE TALKED ABOUT HER **GLORY DAYS.**
FINE. WHY WERE THEY LOOKING HERE?
AGENT JONES WAS TRYING TO QUESTION CAPTAIN MIDNIGHT AND HE... ESCAPED AND STOLE A JET.
GAVE THE BOYS AT THE F.B.I. THE IDEA THAT HE MIGHT BE A **THREAT.**
A TIME-TRAVELING **SUPERHERO** MIGHT BE MORE THEIR SPEED. WHY NOT JUST LET **THEM** HANDLE IT?
BECAUSE I KNOW CAPTAIN MIDNIGHT. HE'LL FIGHT BACK. HE'S **STUBBORN** AND WOULD NEVER ADMIT IT...BUT HE'LL NEED **HELP** IN OUR WORLD.
A FEW THINGS HAVE CHANGED SINCE WORLD WAR II. HE COULD BE A DANGER TO HIMSELF.
ESPECIALLY IF **FURY SHARK** FINDS OUT THAT HE'S BACK.
OH, GRANDMA, DON'T START THAT WHOLE NONSENSE ABOUT FURY SHARK BEING AN IMMORTAL NAZI AGAIN, OKAY? I'VE HAD ENOUGH WEIRDNESS FOR ONE CONVERSATION.
MAYBE WE SHOULD JUST CALL ALBRIGHT INDUSTRIES OR--
CAPTAIN MIDNIGHT, HE-- DAMMIT, CHARLOTTE, I'D DO THIS IF I COULD, BUT **I CAN'T.**
PLEASE...YOU HAVE TO FIND HIM, CHARLOTTE. HELP HIM.
FOR ME. **PLEASE.**
USED UP ALL MY LEAVE DAYS TO CLIMB A MOUNTAIN IN SEARCH OF A TIME TRAVELER...
-SIGH- WHERE **ARE**

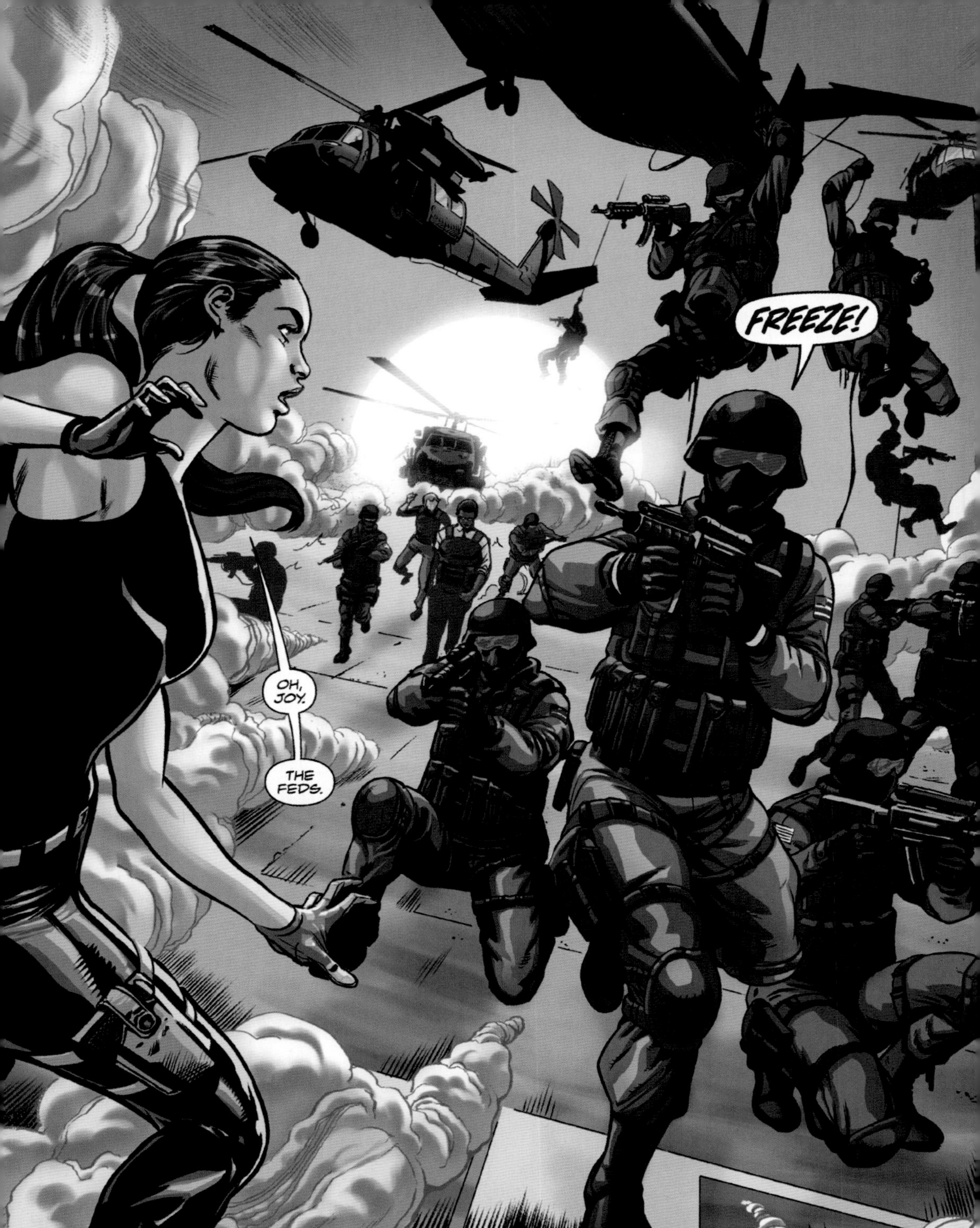
FREEZE!
OH, JOY.
THE FEDS.
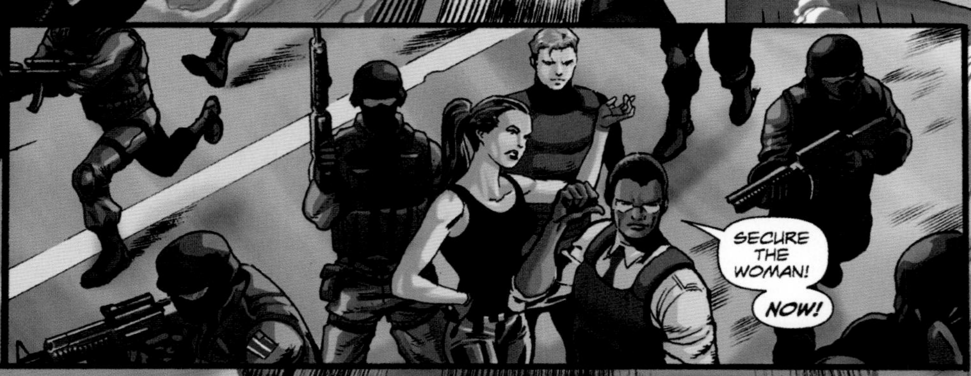
SECURE THE WOMAN!
NOW!

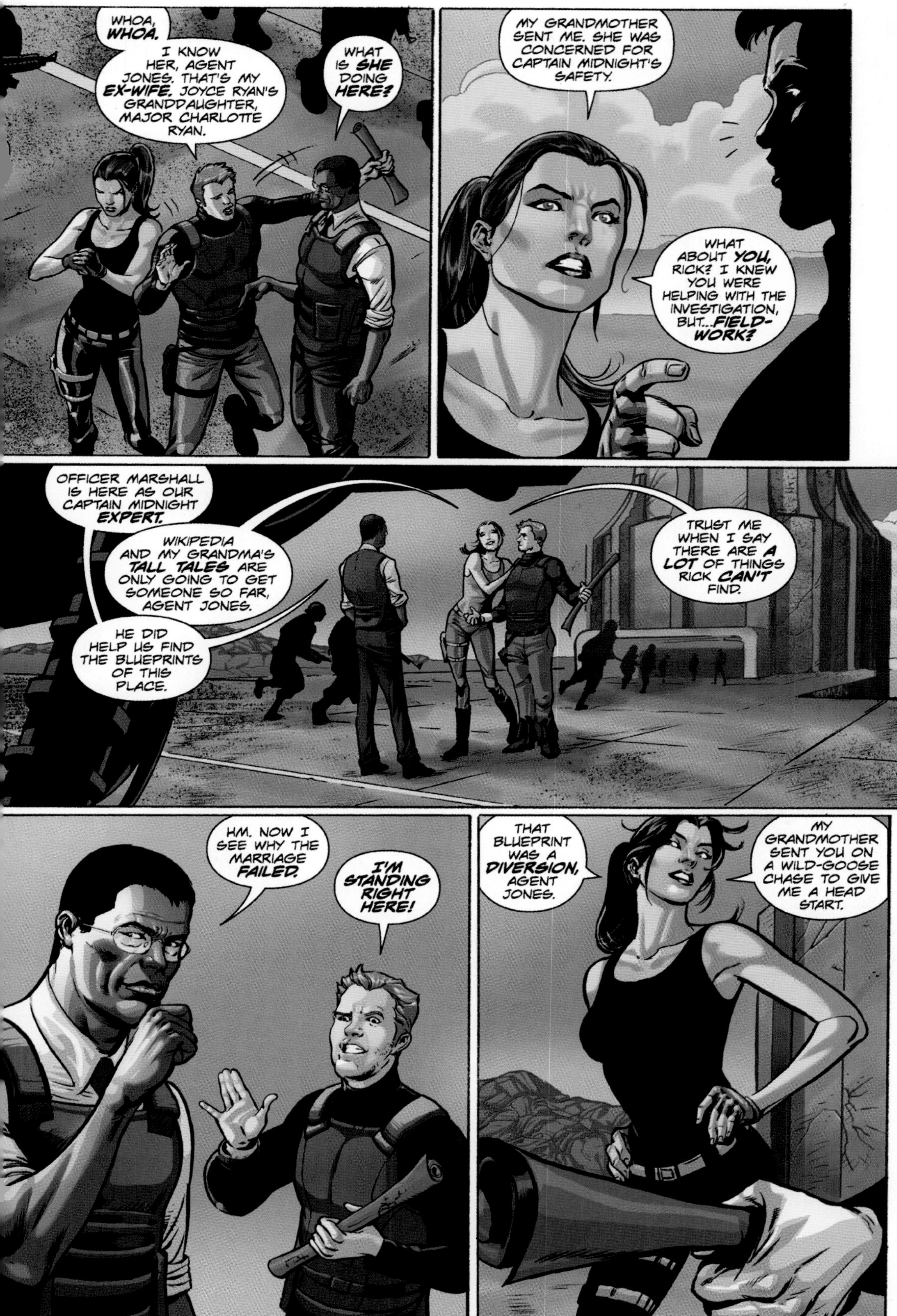
WHOA, WHOA.
I KNOW HER, AGENT JONES. THAT'S MY EX-WIFE. JOYCE RYAN'S GRANDDAUGHTER, MAJOR CHARLOTTE RYAN.
WHAT IS SHE DOING HERE?
MY GRANDMOTHER SENT ME. SHE WAS CONCERNED FOR CAPTAIN MIDNIGHT'S SAFETY.
WHAT ABOUT YOU, RICK? I KNEW YOU WERE HELPING WITH THE INVESTIGATION, BUT...FIELD-WORK?
OFFICER MARSHALL IS HERE AS OUR CAPTAIN MIDNIGHT EXPERT.
WIKIPEDIA AND MY GRANDMA'S TALL TALES ARE ONLY GOING TO GET SOMEONE SO FAR, AGENT JONES.
HE DID HELP US FIND THE BLUEPRINTS OF THIS PLACE.
TRUST ME WHEN I SAY THERE ARE A LOT OF THINGS RICK CAN'T FIND.
HM. NOW I SEE WHY THE MARRIAGE FAILED.
I'M STANDING RIGHT HERE!
THAT BLUEPRINT WAS A DIVERSION, AGENT JONES.
MY GRANDMOTHER SENT YOU ON A WILD-GOOSE CHASE TO GIVE ME A HEAD START.

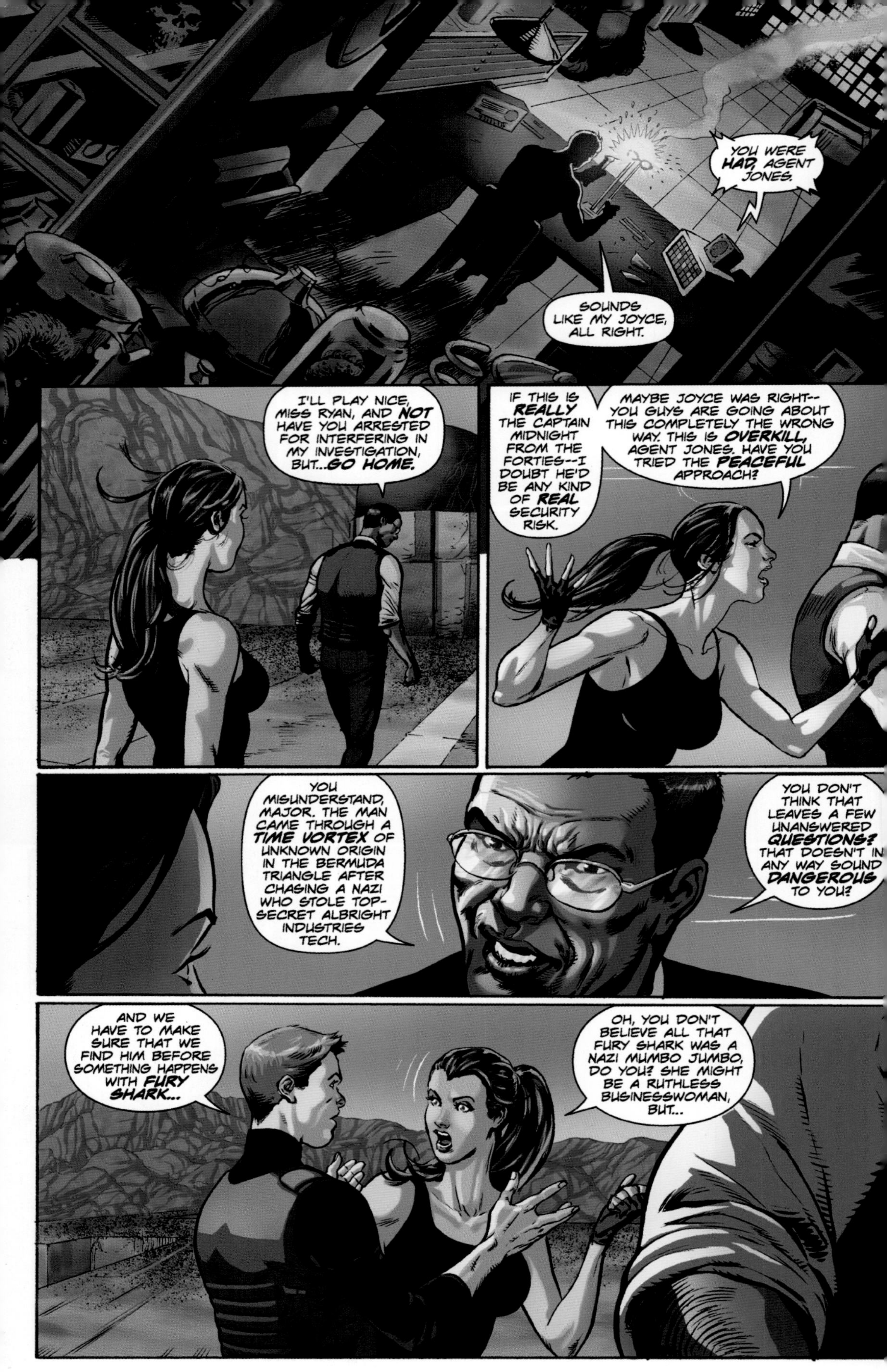

YOU WERE HAD, AGENT JONES.
SOUNDS LIKE MY JOYCE, ALL RIGHT.
I'LL PLAY NICE, MISS RYAN, AND NOT HAVE YOU ARRESTED FOR INTERFERING IN MY INVESTIGATION, BUT...GO HOME.
MAYBE JOYCE WAS RIGHT-- YOU GUYS ARE GOING ABOUT THIS COMPLETELY THE WRONG WAY. THIS IS OVERKILL, AGENT JONES. HAVE YOU TRIED THE PEACEFUL APPROACH?
IF THIS IS REALLY THE CAPTAIN MIDNIGHT FROM THE FORTIES--I DOUBT HE'D BE ANY KIND OF REAL SECURITY RISK.
YOU MISUNDERSTAND, MAJOR. THE MAN CAME THROUGH A TIME VORTEX OF UNKNOWN ORIGIN IN THE BERMUDA TRIANGLE AFTER CHASING A NAZI WHO STOLE TOP-SECRET ALBRIGHT INDUSTRIES TECH.
YOU DON'T THINK THAT LEAVES A FEW UNANSWERED QUESTIONS? THAT DOESN'T IN ANY WAY SOUND DANGEROUS TO YOU?
AND WE HAVE TO MAKE SURE THAT WE FIND HIM BEFORE SOMETHING HAPPENS WITH FURY SHARK...
OH, YOU DON'T BELIEVE ALL THAT FURY SHARK WAS A NAZI MUMBO JUMBO, DO YOU? SHE MIGHT BE A RUTHLESS BUSINESSWOMAN, BUT...

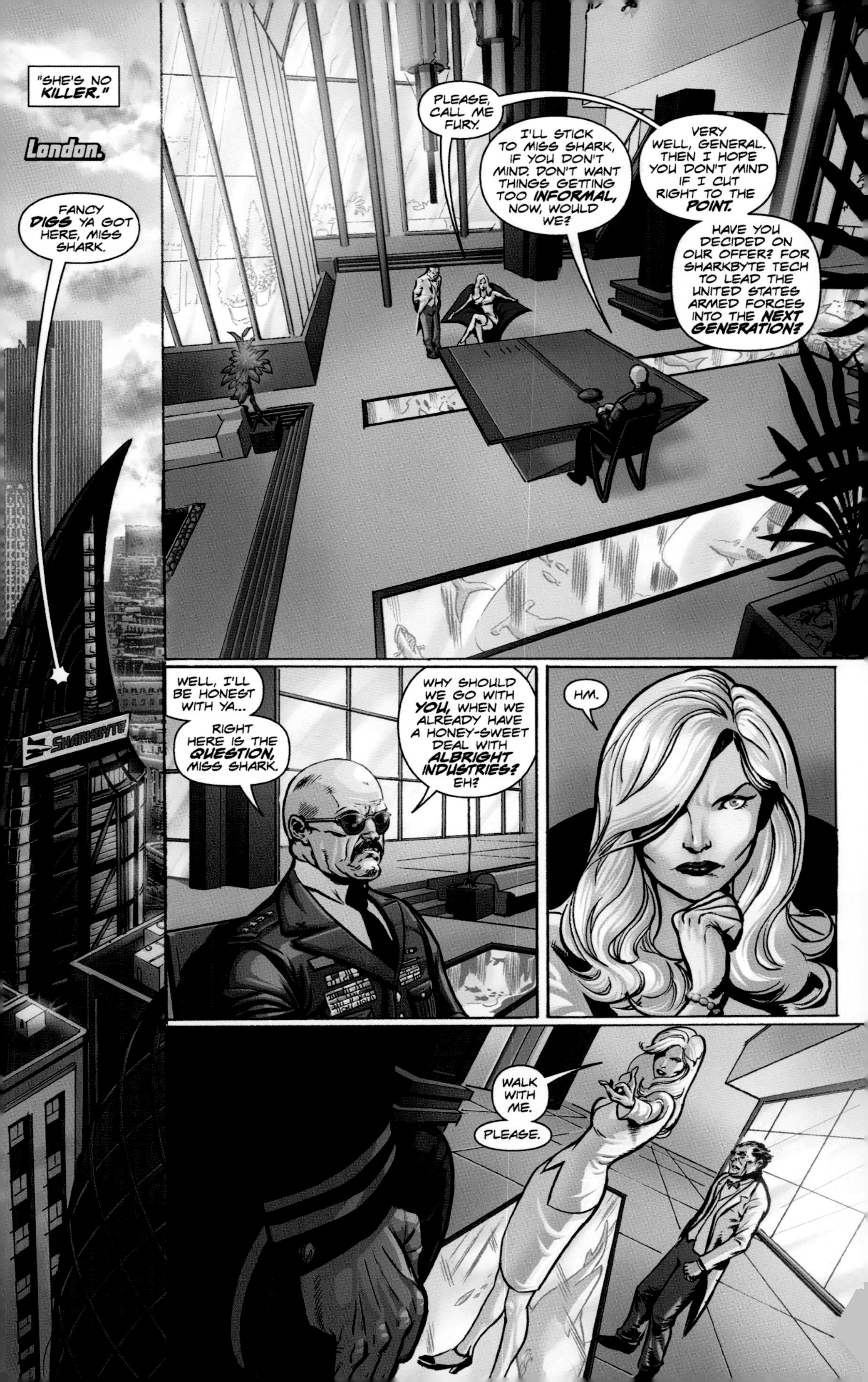
"SHE'S NO KILLER."
London.
FANCY DIGS YA GOT HERE, MISS SHARK.
PLEASE, CALL ME FURY.
I'LL STICK TO MISS SHARK, IF YOU DON'T MIND. DON'T WANT THINGS GETTING TOO INFORMAL, NOW, WOULD WE?
VERY WELL, GENERAL. THEN I HOPE YOU DON'T MIND IF I CUT RIGHT TO THE POINT.
HAVE YOU DECIDED ON OUR OFFER? FOR SHARKBYTE TECH TO LEAD THE UNITED STATES ARMED FORCES INTO THE NEXT GENERATION?
SHARKBYTE
WELL, I'LL BE HONEST WITH YA...
RIGHT HERE IS THE QUESTION, MISS SHARK.
WHY SHOULD WE GO WITH YOU, WHEN WE ALREADY HAVE A HONEY-SWEET DEAL WITH ALBRIGHT INDUSTRIES? EH?
HM.
WALK WITH ME.
PLEASE.

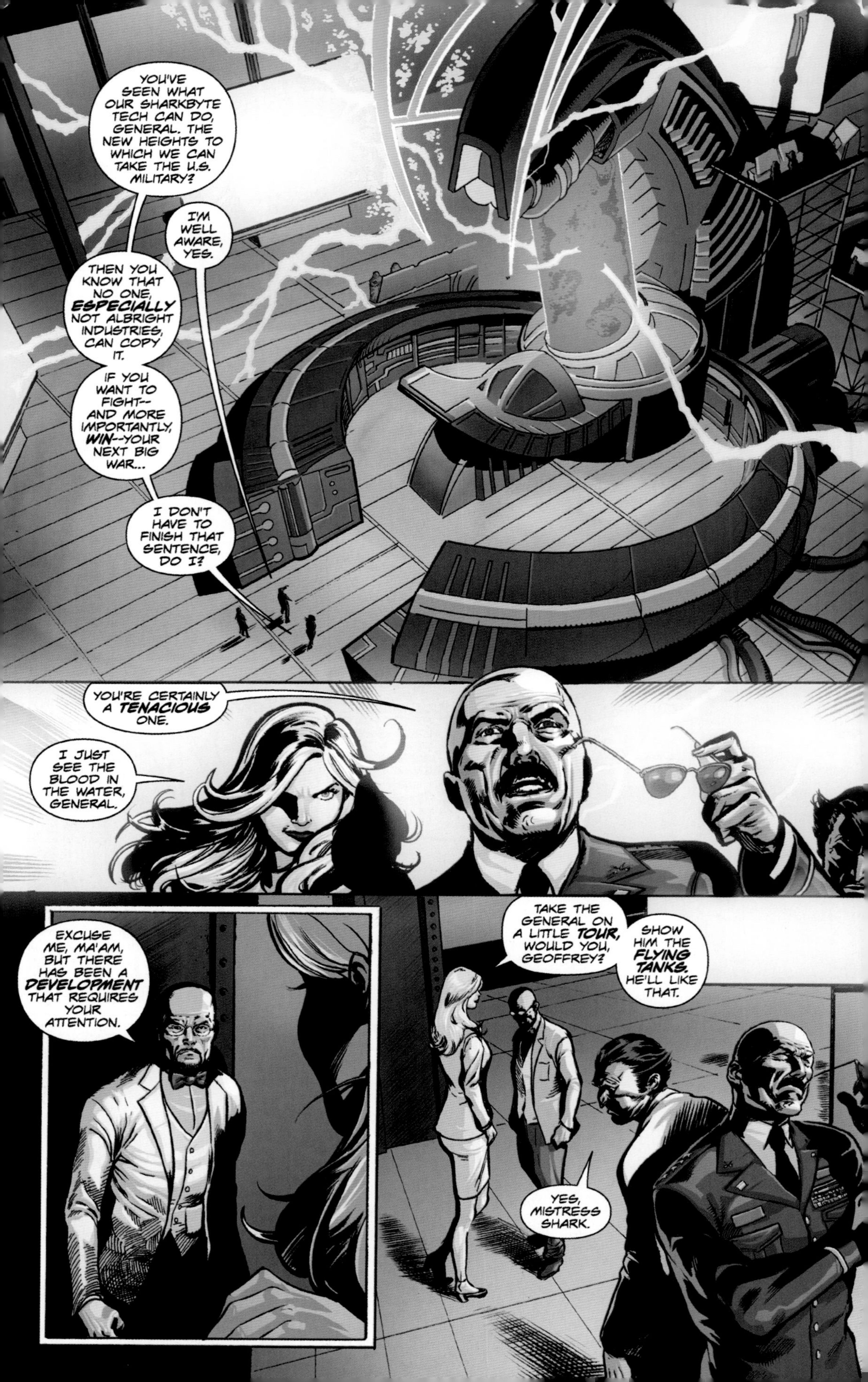
YOU'VE SEEN WHAT OUR SHARKBYTE TECH CAN DO, GENERAL. THE NEW HEIGHTS TO WHICH WE CAN TAKE THE U.S. MILITARY?
I'M WELL AWARE, YES.
THEN YOU KNOW THAT NO ONE, ESPECIALLY NOT ALBRIGHT INDUSTRIES, CAN COPY IT.
IF YOU WANT TO FIGHT-- AND MORE IMPORTANTLY, WIN--YOUR NEXT BIG WAR...
I DON'T HAVE TO FINISH THAT SENTENCE, DO I?
YOU'RE CERTAINLY A TENACIOUS ONE.
I JUST SEE THE BLOOD IN THE WATER, GENERAL.
EXCUSE ME, MA'AM, BUT THERE HAS BEEN A DEVELOPMENT THAT REQUIRES YOUR ATTENTION.
TAKE THE GENERAL ON A LITTLE TOUR, WOULD YOU, GEOFFREY?
SHOW HIM THE FLYING TANKS. HE'LL LIKE THAT.
YES, MISTRESS SHARK.

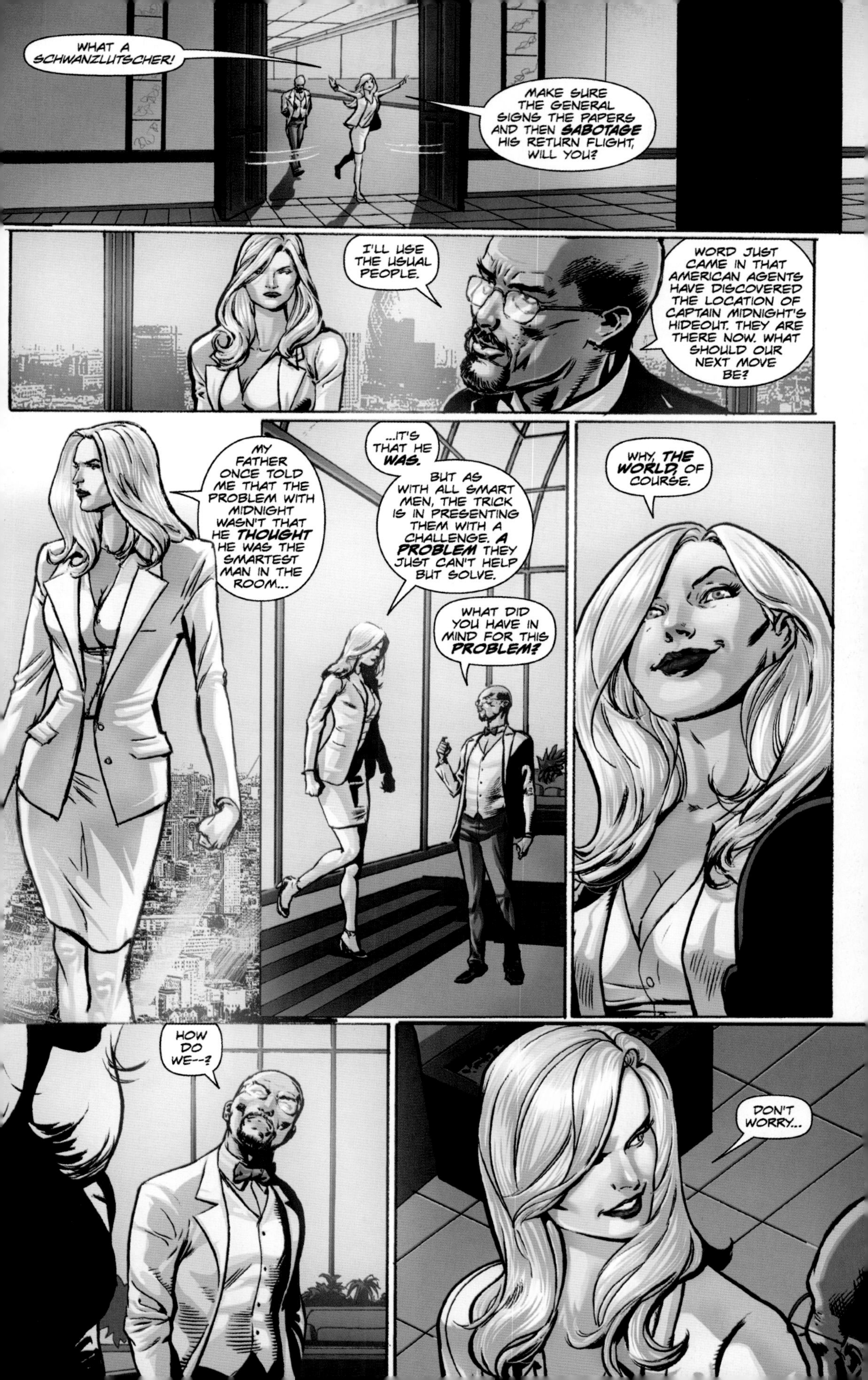
WHAT A SCHWANZLUTSCHER!
MAKE SURE THE GENERAL SIGNS THE PAPERS AND THEN SABOTAGE HIS RETURN FLIGHT, WILL YOU?
I'LL USE THE USUAL PEOPLE.
WORD JUST CAME IN THAT AMERICAN AGENTS HAVE DISCOVERED THE LOCATION OF CAPTAIN MIDNIGHT'S HIDEOUT. THEY ARE THERE NOW. WHAT SHOULD OUR NEXT MOVE BE?
MY FATHER ONCE TOLD ME THAT THE PROBLEM WITH MIDNIGHT WASN'T THAT HE THOUGHT HE WAS THE SMARTEST MAN IN THE ROOM...
...IT'S THAT HE WAS.
BUT AS WITH ALL SMART MEN, THE TRICK IS IN PRESENTING THEM WITH A CHALLENGE. A PROBLEM THEY JUST CAN'T HELP BUT SOLVE.
WHAT DID YOU HAVE IN MIND FOR THIS PROBLEM?
WHY, THE WORLD, OF COURSE.
HOW DO WE--?
DON'T WORRY...

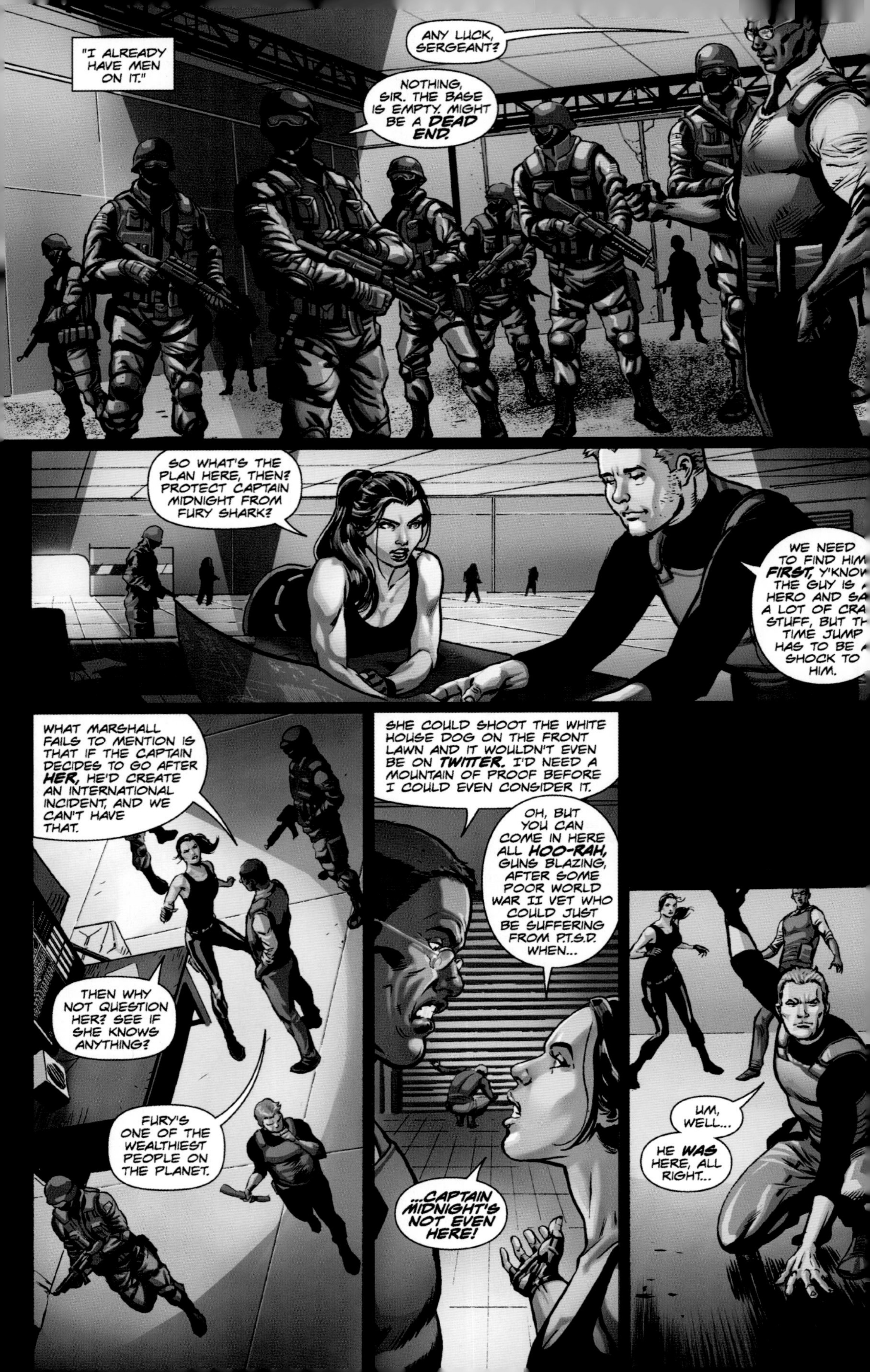
"I ALREADY HAVE MEN ON IT."
ANY LUCK, SERGEANT?
NOTHING, SIR. THE BASE IS EMPTY. MIGHT BE A DEAD END.
SO WHAT'S THE PLAN HERE, THEN? PROTECT CAPTAIN MIDNIGHT FROM FURY SHARK?
WE NEED TO FIND HIM FIRST, Y'KNOW THE GUY IS HERO AND SA A LOT OF CRA STUFF, BUT TH TIME JUMP HAS TO BE SHOCK TO HIM.
WHAT MARSHALL FAILS TO MENTION IS THAT IF THE CAPTAIN DECIDES TO GO AFTER HER, HE'D CREATE AN INTERNATIONAL INCIDENT, AND WE CAN'T HAVE THAT.
THEN WHY NOT QUESTION HER? SEE IF SHE KNOWS ANYTHING?
FURY'S ONE OF THE WEALTHIEST PEOPLE ON THE PLANET.
SHE COULD SHOOT THE WHITE HOUSE DOG ON THE FRONT LAWN AND IT WOULDN'T EVEN BE ON TWITTER. I'D NEED A MOUNTAIN OF PROOF BEFORE I COULD EVEN CONSIDER IT.
OH, BUT YOU CAN COME IN HERE ALL HOO-RAH, GUNS BLAZING, AFTER SOME POOR WORLD WAR II VET WHO COULD JUST BE SUFFERING FROM P.T.S.D. WHEN...
...CAPTAIN MIDNIGHT'S NOT EVEN HERE!
UM, WELL...
HE WAS HERE, ALL RIGHT...

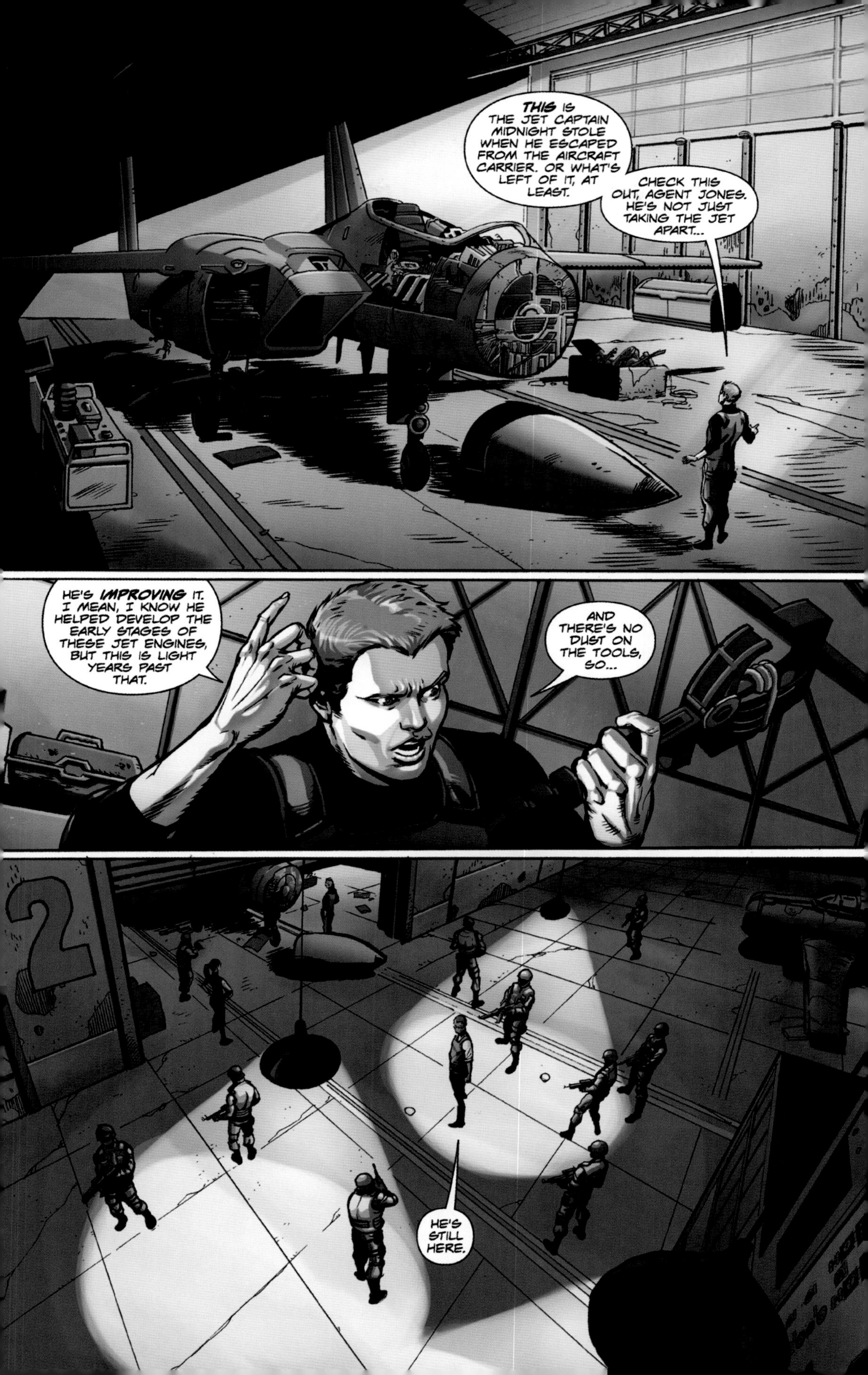
THIS IS THE JET CAPTAIN MIDNIGHT STOLE WHEN HE ESCAPED FROM THE AIRCRAFT CARRIER. OR WHAT'S LEFT OF IT, AT LEAST.
CHECK THIS OUT, AGENT JONES. HE'S NOT JUST TAKING THE JET APART...
HE'S IMPROVING IT. I MEAN, I KNOW HE HELPED DEVELOP THE EARLY STAGES OF THESE JET ENGINES, BUT THIS IS LIGHT YEARS PAST THAT.
AND THERE'S NO DUST ON THE TOOLS, SO...
2
HE'S STILL HERE.

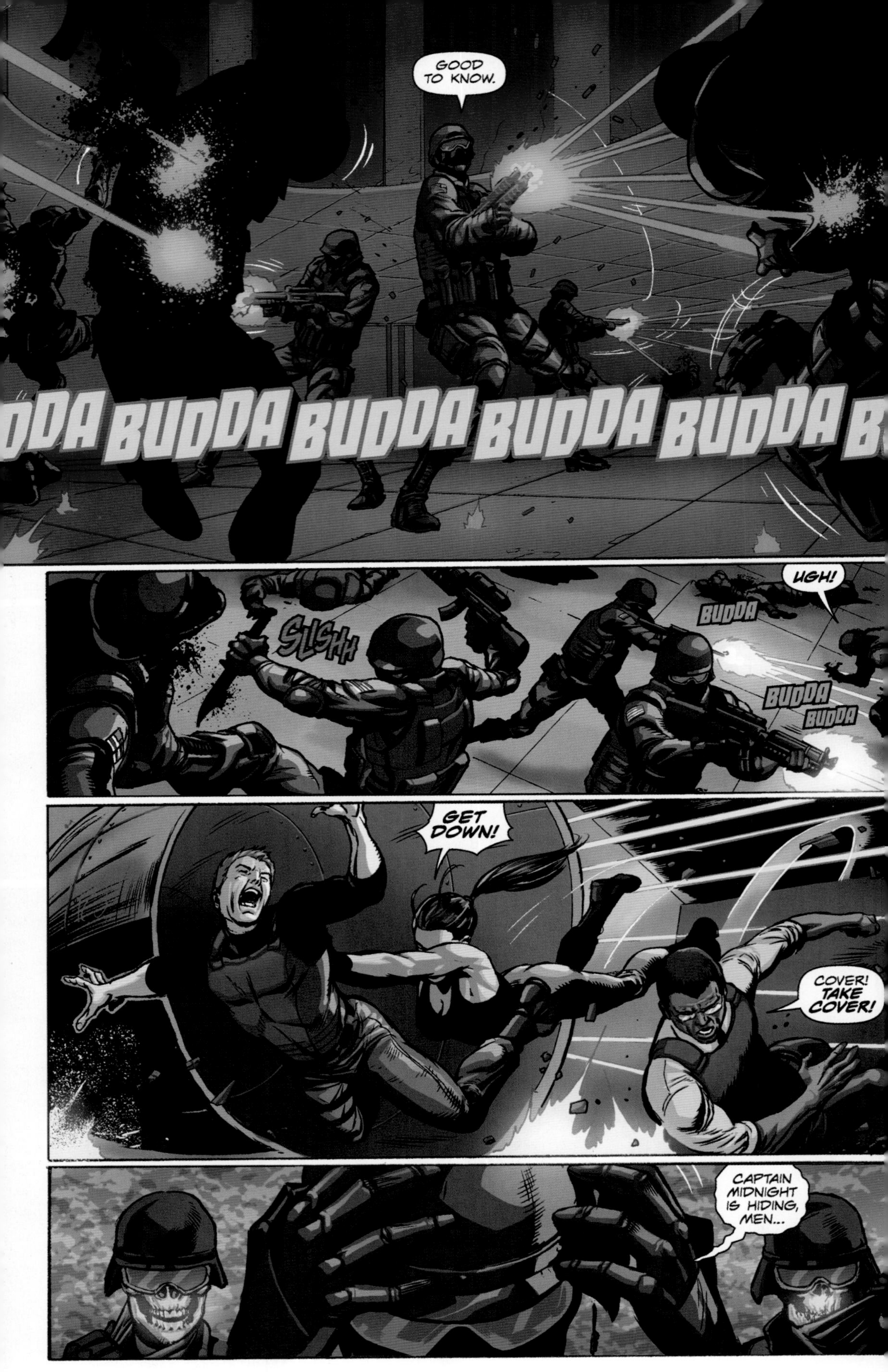
GOOD TO KNOW.
DDA BUDDA BUDDA BUDDA BUDDA B
SLISHH
UGH!
BUDDA
BUDDA
BUDDA
GET DOWN!
COVER! TAKE COVER!
CAPTAIN MIDNIGHT IS HIDING, MEN...

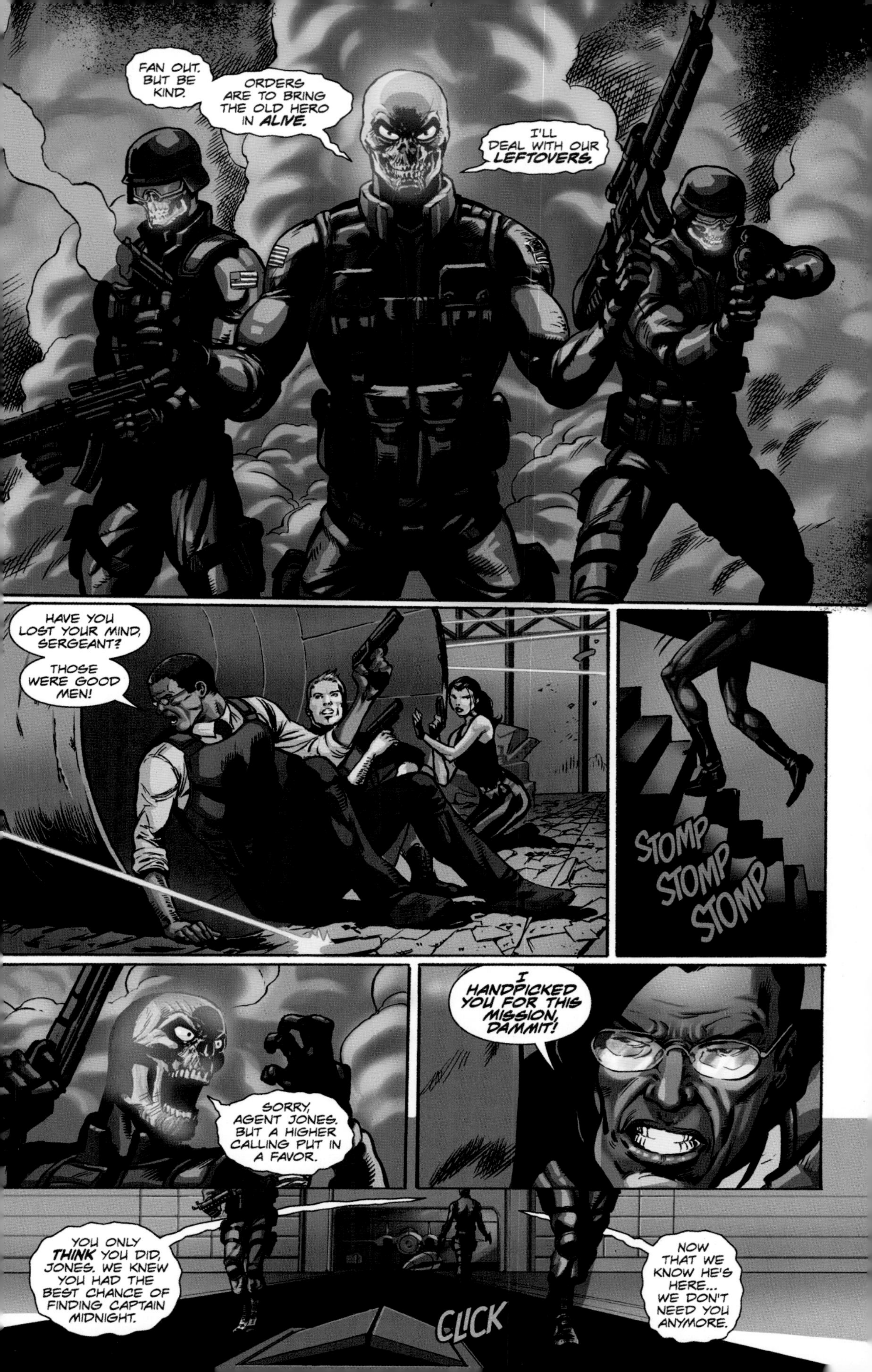
FAN OUT. BUT BE KIND.
ORDERS ARE TO BRING THE OLD HERO IN ALIVE.
I'LL DEAL WITH OUR LEFTOVERS.
HAVE YOU LOST YOUR MIND, SERGEANT?
THOSE WERE GOOD MEN!
STOMP STOMP STOMP
SORRY, AGENT JONES. BUT A HIGHER CALLING PUT IN A FAVOR.
I HANDPICKED YOU FOR THIS MISSION, DAMMIT!
YOU ONLY THINK YOU DID, JONES. WE KNEW YOU HAD THE BEST CHANCE OF FINDING CAPTAIN MIDNIGHT.
CLICK
NOW THAT WE KNOW HE'S HERE... WE DON'T NEED YOU ANYMORE.

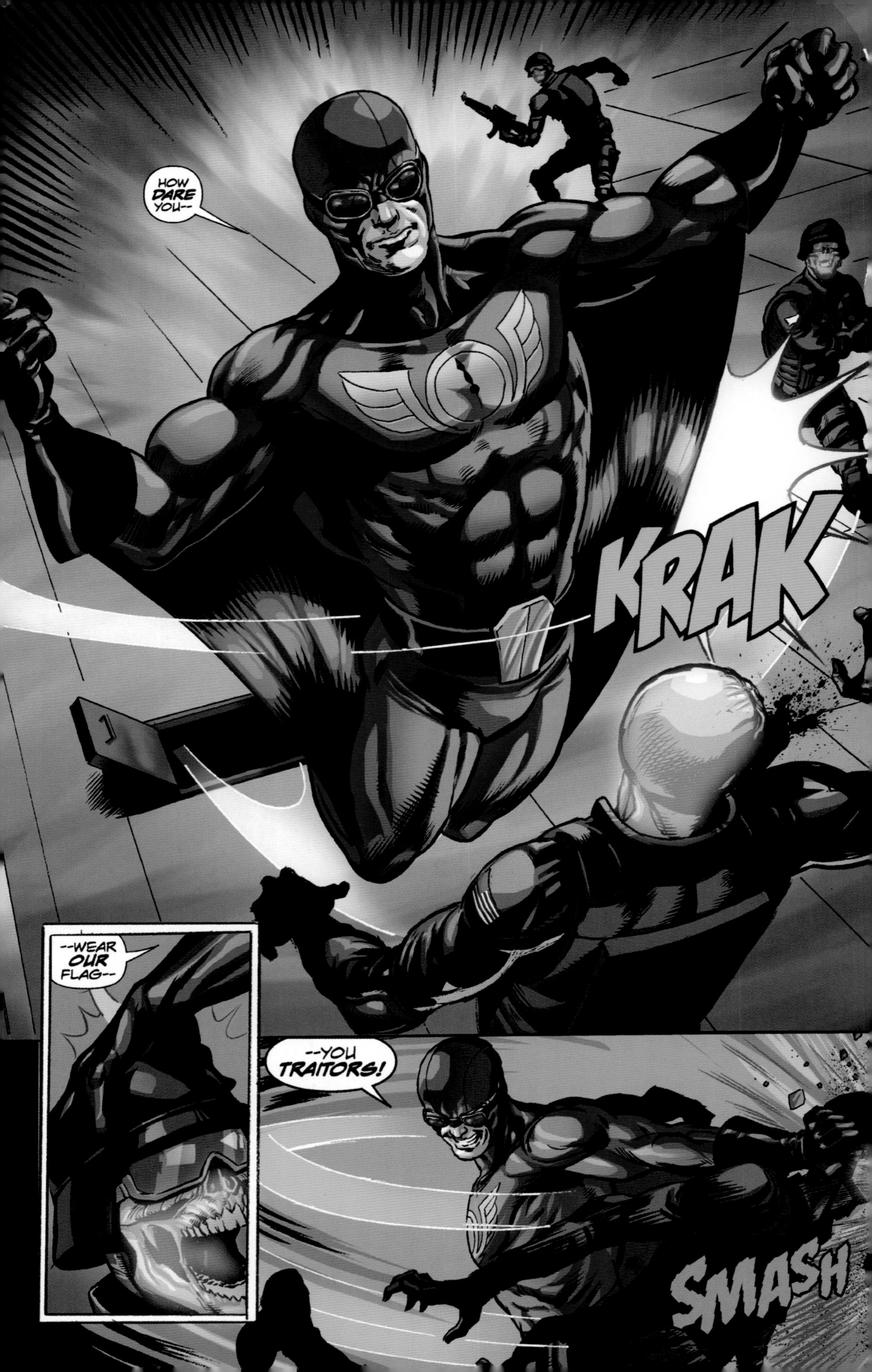
HOW DARE YOU--
KRAK
--WEAR OUR FLAG--
--YOU TRAITORS!
SMASH

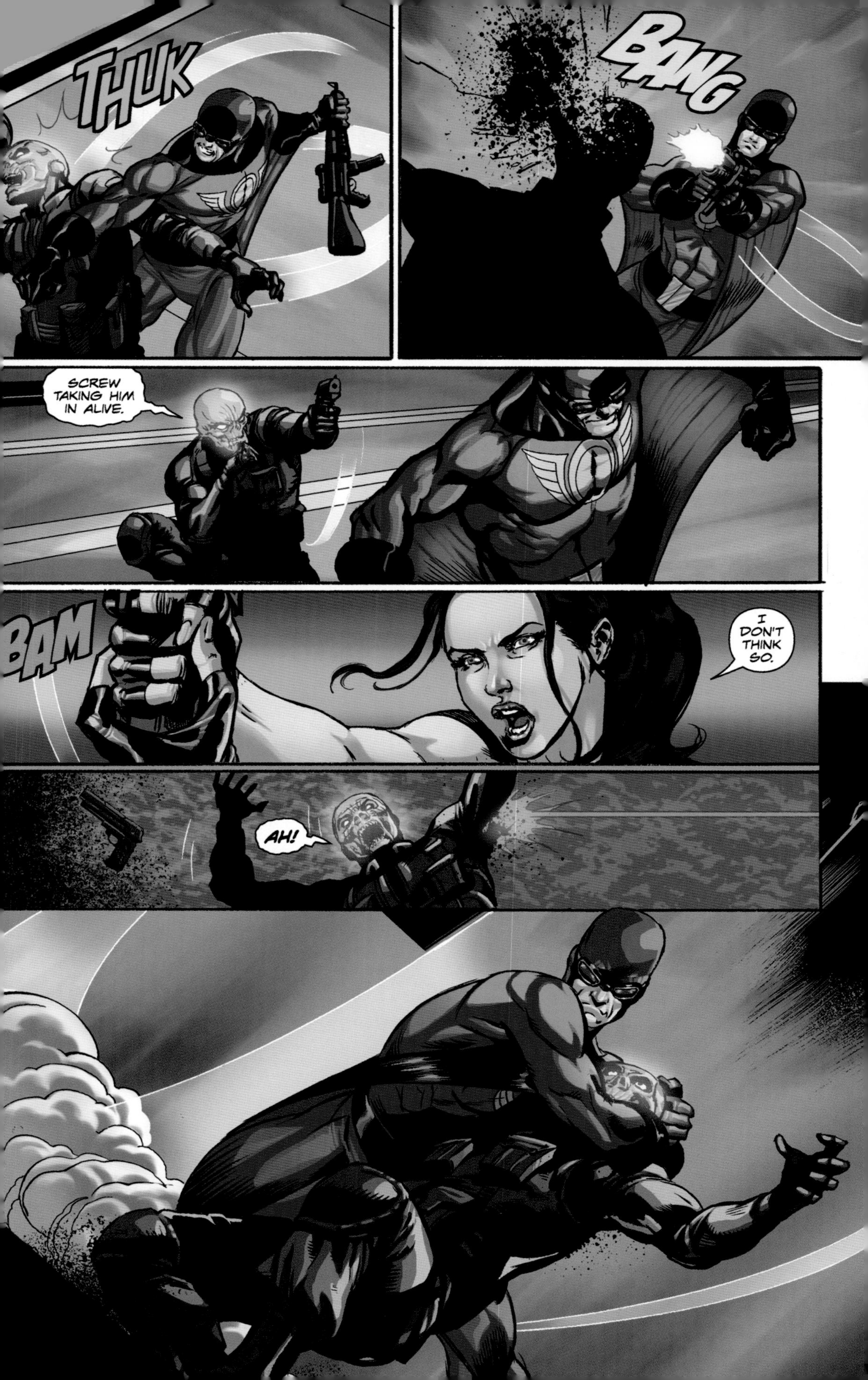
THUK
BANG
SCREW TAKING HIM IN ALIVE.
BAM
I DON'T THINK SO.
AH!

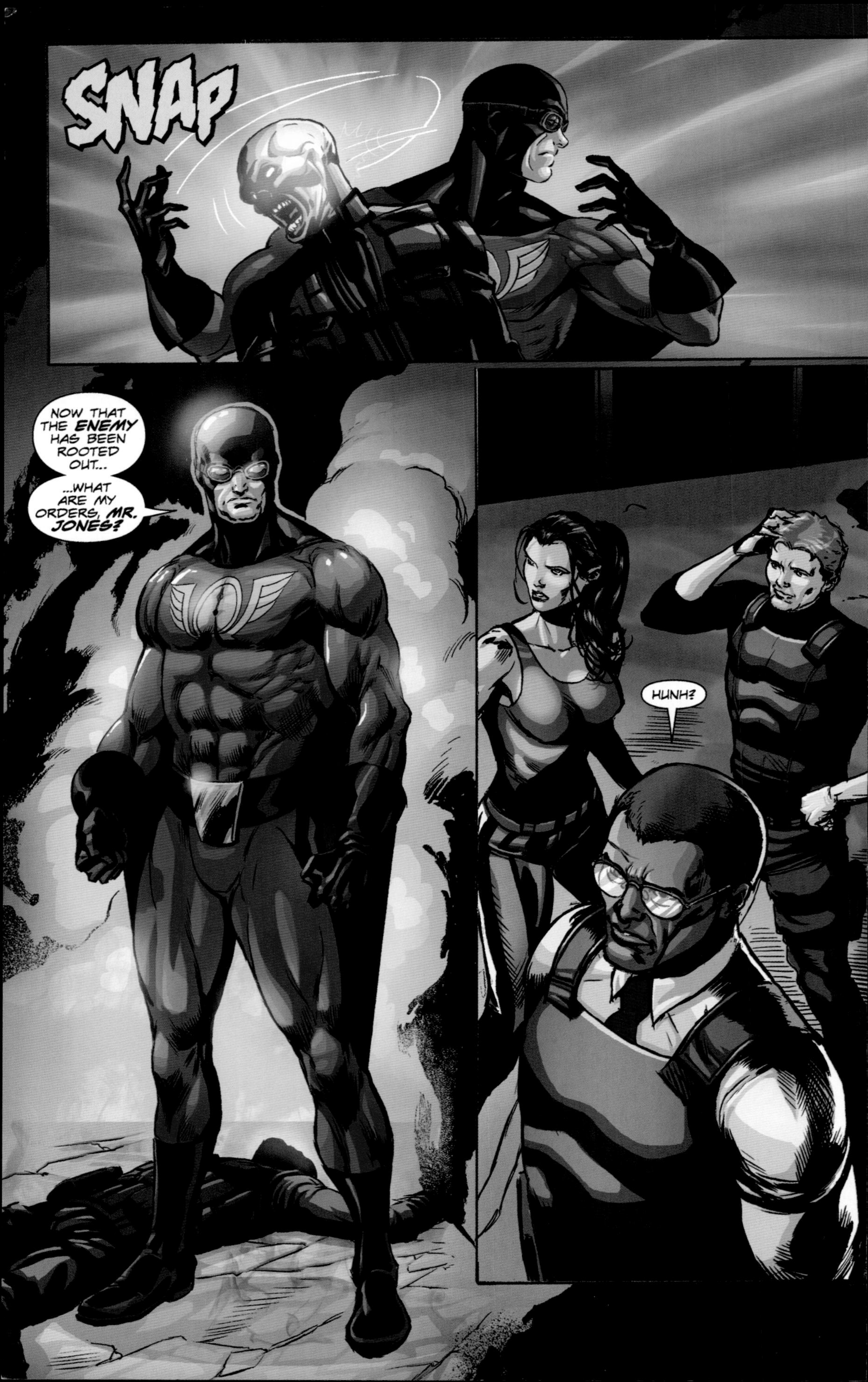
SNAP
NOW THAT THE ENEMY HAS BEEN ROOTED OUT...
...WHAT ARE MY ORDERS, MR. JONES?
HUNH?

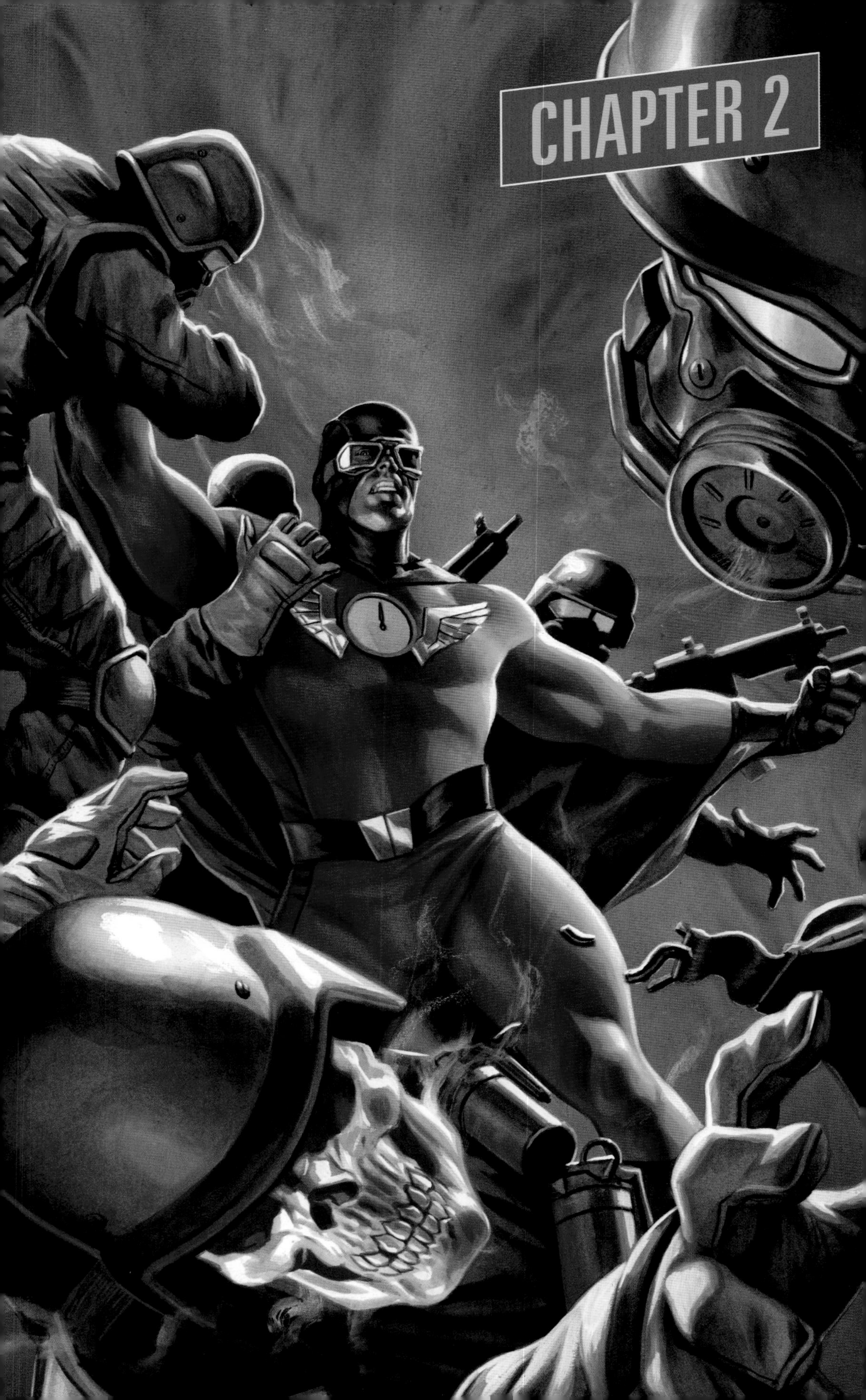
CHAPTER 2

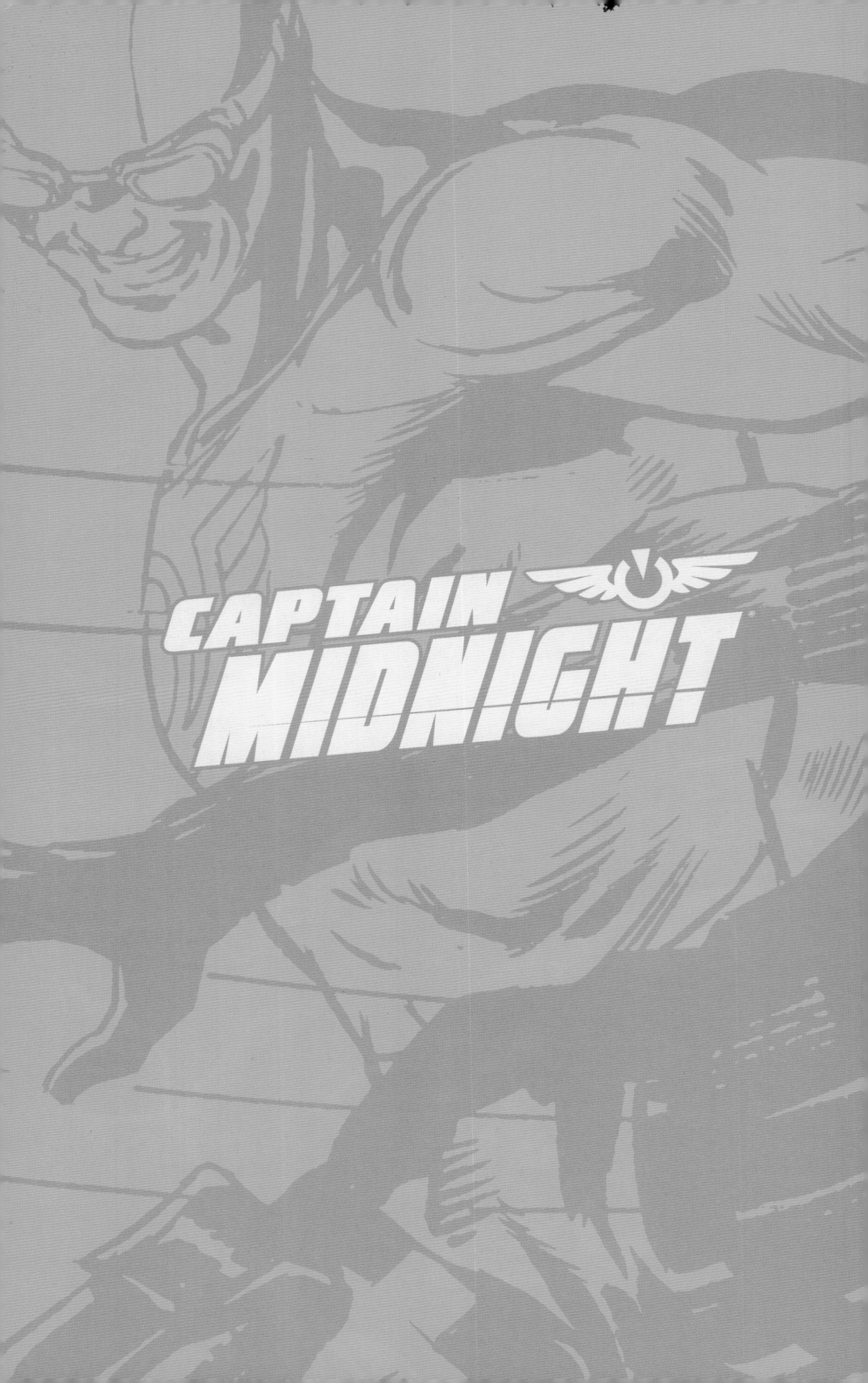
CAPTAIN
MIDNIGHT

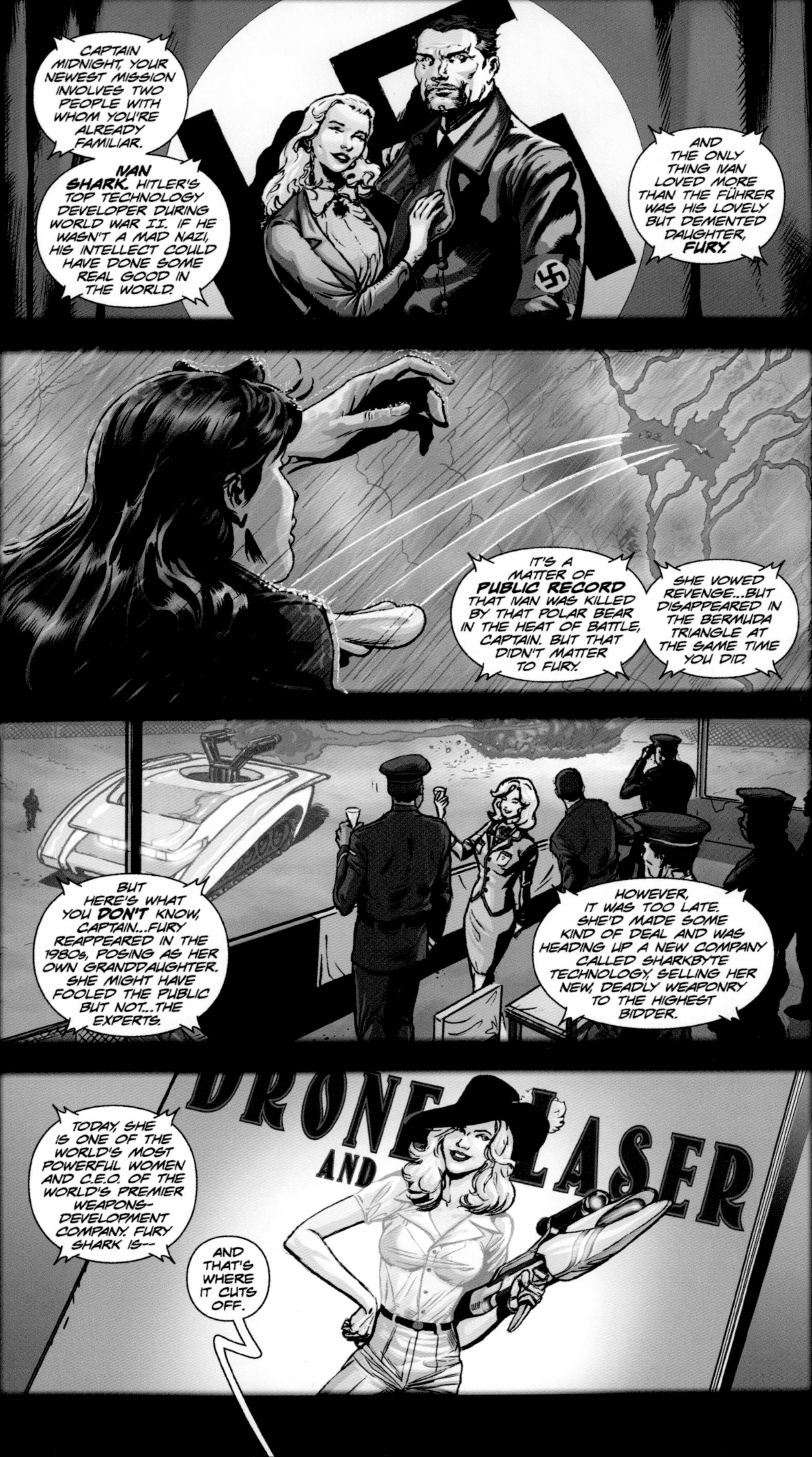
CAPTAIN MIDNIGHT, YOUR NEWEST MISSION INVOLVES TWO PEOPLE WITH WHOM YOU'RE ALREADY FAMILIAR.
IVAN SHARK. HITLER'S TOP TECHNOLOGY DEVELOPER DURING WORLD WAR II. IF HE WASN'T A MAD NAZI, HIS INTELLECT COULD HAVE DONE SOME REAL GOOD IN THE WORLD.
AND THE ONLY THING IVAN LOVED MORE THAN THE FÜHRER WAS HIS LOVELY BUT DEMENTED DAUGHTER, FURY.
IT'S A MATTER OF PUBLIC RECORD THAT IVAN WAS KILLED BY THAT POLAR BEAR IN THE HEAT OF BATTLE, CAPTAIN. BUT THAT DIDN'T MATTER TO FURY.
SHE VOWED REVENGE...BUT DISAPPEARED IN THE BERMUDA TRIANGLE AT THE SAME TIME YOU DID.
BUT HERE'S WHAT YOU DON'T KNOW, CAPTAIN...FURY REAPPEARED IN THE 1980s, POSING AS HER OWN GRANDDAUGHTER. SHE MIGHT HAVE FOOLED THE PUBLIC BUT NOT...THE EXPERTS.
HOWEVER, IT WAS TOO LATE. SHE'D MADE SOME KIND OF DEAL AND WAS HEADING UP A NEW COMPANY CALLED SHARKBYTE TECHNOLOGY, SELLING HER NEW, DEADLY WEAPONRY TO THE HIGHEST BIDDER.
DRONE LASER
AND
TODAY, SHE IS ONE OF THE WORLD'S MOST POWERFUL WOMEN AND C.E.O. OF THE WORLD'S PREMIER WEAPONS-DEVELOPMENT COMPANY. FURY SHARK IS--
AND THAT'S WHERE IT CUTS OFF.

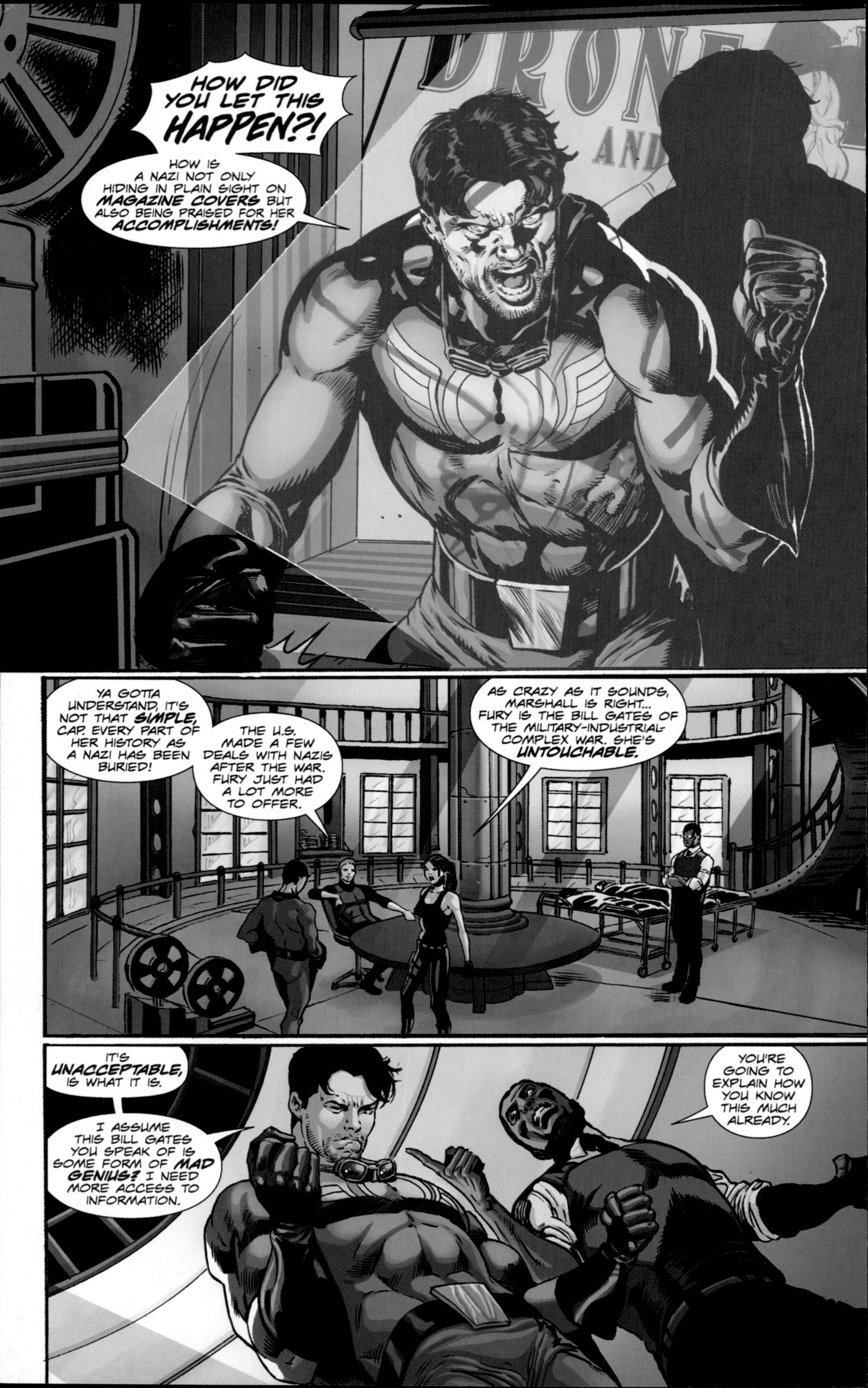
DRONE
AND
HOW DID YOU LET THIS HAPPEN?!
HOW IS A NAZI NOT ONLY HIDING IN PLAIN SIGHT ON MAGAZINE COVERS BUT ALSO BEING PRAISED FOR HER ACCOMPLISHMENTS!
YA GOTTA UNDERSTAND, IT'S NOT THAT SIMPLE, CAP. EVERY PART OF HER HISTORY AS A NAZI HAS BEEN BURIED!
THE U.S. MADE A FEW DEALS WITH NAZIS AFTER THE WAR. FURY JUST HAD A LOT MORE TO OFFER.
AS CRAZY AS IT SOUNDS, MARSHALL IS RIGHT... FURY IS THE BILL GATES OF THE MILITARY-INDUSTRIAL-COMPLEX WAR. SHE'S UNTOUCHABLE.
IT'S UNACCEPTABLE, IS WHAT IT IS.
I ASSUME THIS BILL GATES YOU SPEAK OF IS SOME FORM OF MAD GENIUS? I NEED MORE ACCESS TO INFORMATION.
YOU'RE GOING TO EXPLAIN HOW YOU KNOW THIS MUCH ALREADY.

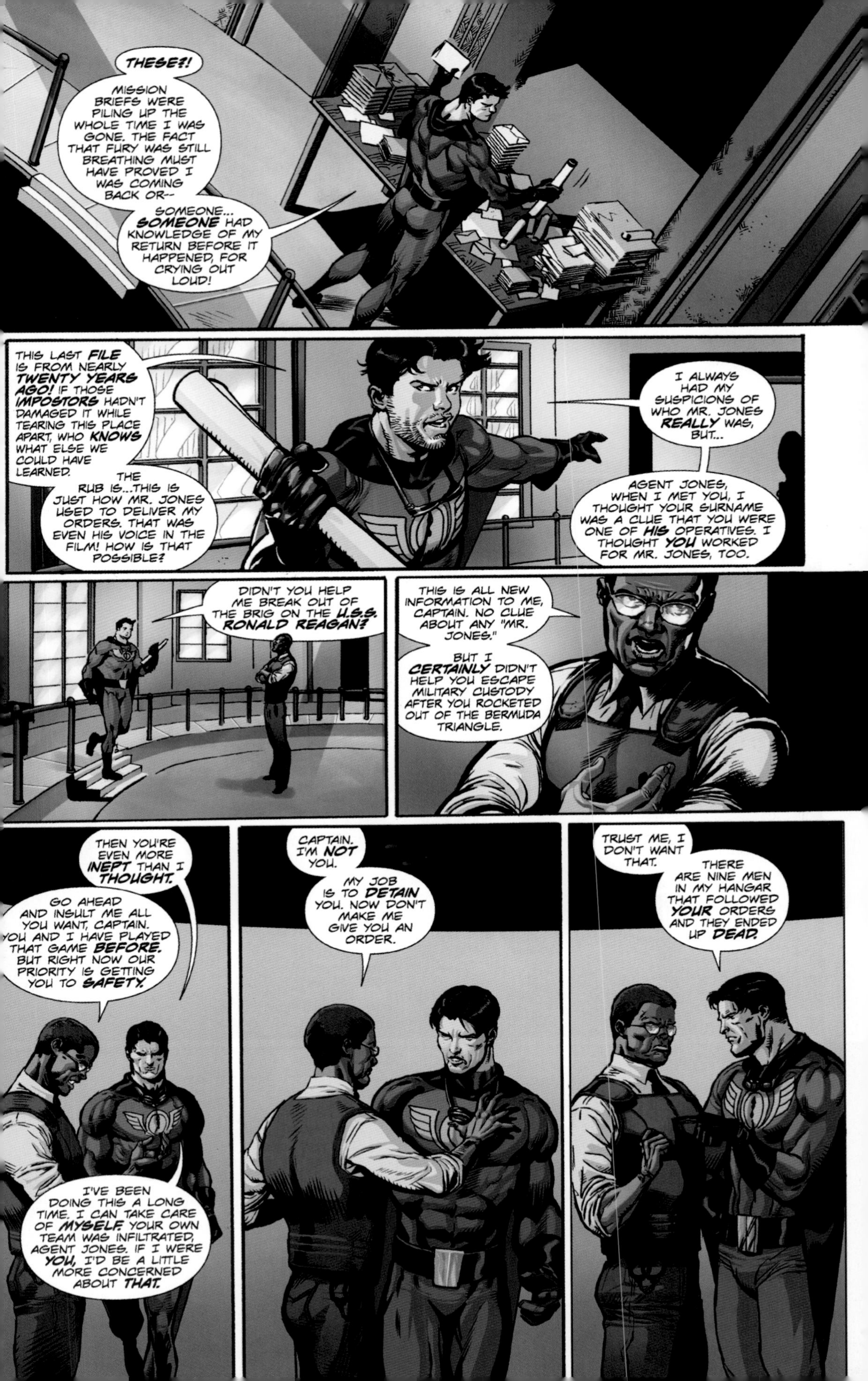
THESE?!
MISSION BRIEFS WERE PILING UP THE WHOLE TIME I WAS GONE. THE FACT THAT FURY WAS STILL BREATHING MUST HAVE PROVED I WAS COMING BACK OR--
SOMEONE... SOMEONE HAD KNOWLEDGE OF MY RETURN BEFORE IT HAPPENED, FOR CRYING OUT LOUD!
THIS LAST FILE IS FROM NEARLY TWENTY YEARS AGO! IF THOSE IMPOSTORS HADN'T DAMAGED IT WHILE TEARING THIS PLACE APART, WHO KNOWS WHAT ELSE WE COULD HAVE LEARNED.
THE RUB IS...THIS IS JUST HOW MR. JONES USED TO DELIVER MY ORDERS. THAT WAS EVEN HIS VOICE IN THE FILM! HOW IS THAT POSSIBLE?
I ALWAYS HAD MY SUSPICIONS OF WHO MR. JONES REALLY WAS, BUT...
AGENT JONES, WHEN I MET YOU, I THOUGHT YOUR SURNAME WAS A CLUE THAT YOU WERE ONE OF HIS OPERATIVES. I THOUGHT YOU WORKED FOR MR. JONES, TOO.
DIDN'T YOU HELP ME BREAK OUT OF THE BRIG ON THE U.S.S. RONALD REAGAN?
THIS IS ALL NEW INFORMATION TO ME, CAPTAIN. NO CLUE ABOUT ANY "MR. JONES."
BUT I CERTAINLY DIDN'T HELP YOU ESCAPE MILITARY CUSTODY AFTER YOU ROCKETED OUT OF THE BERMUDA TRIANGLE.
THEN YOU'RE EVEN MORE INEPT THAN I THOUGHT.
GO AHEAD AND INSULT ME ALL YOU WANT, CAPTAIN. YOU AND I HAVE PLAYED THAT GAME BEFORE. BUT RIGHT NOW OUR PRIORITY IS GETTING YOU TO SAFETY.
I'VE BEEN DOING THIS A LONG TIME. I CAN TAKE CARE OF MYSELF. YOUR OWN TEAM WAS INFILTRATED, AGENT JONES. IF I WERE YOU, I'D BE A LITTLE MORE CONCERNED ABOUT THAT.
CAPTAIN. I'M NOT YOU.
MY JOB IS TO DETAIN YOU. NOW DON'T MAKE ME GIVE YOU AN ORDER.
TRUST ME, I DON'T WANT THAT.
THERE ARE NINE MEN IN MY HANGAR THAT FOLLOWED YOUR ORDERS AND THEY ENDED UP DEAD.

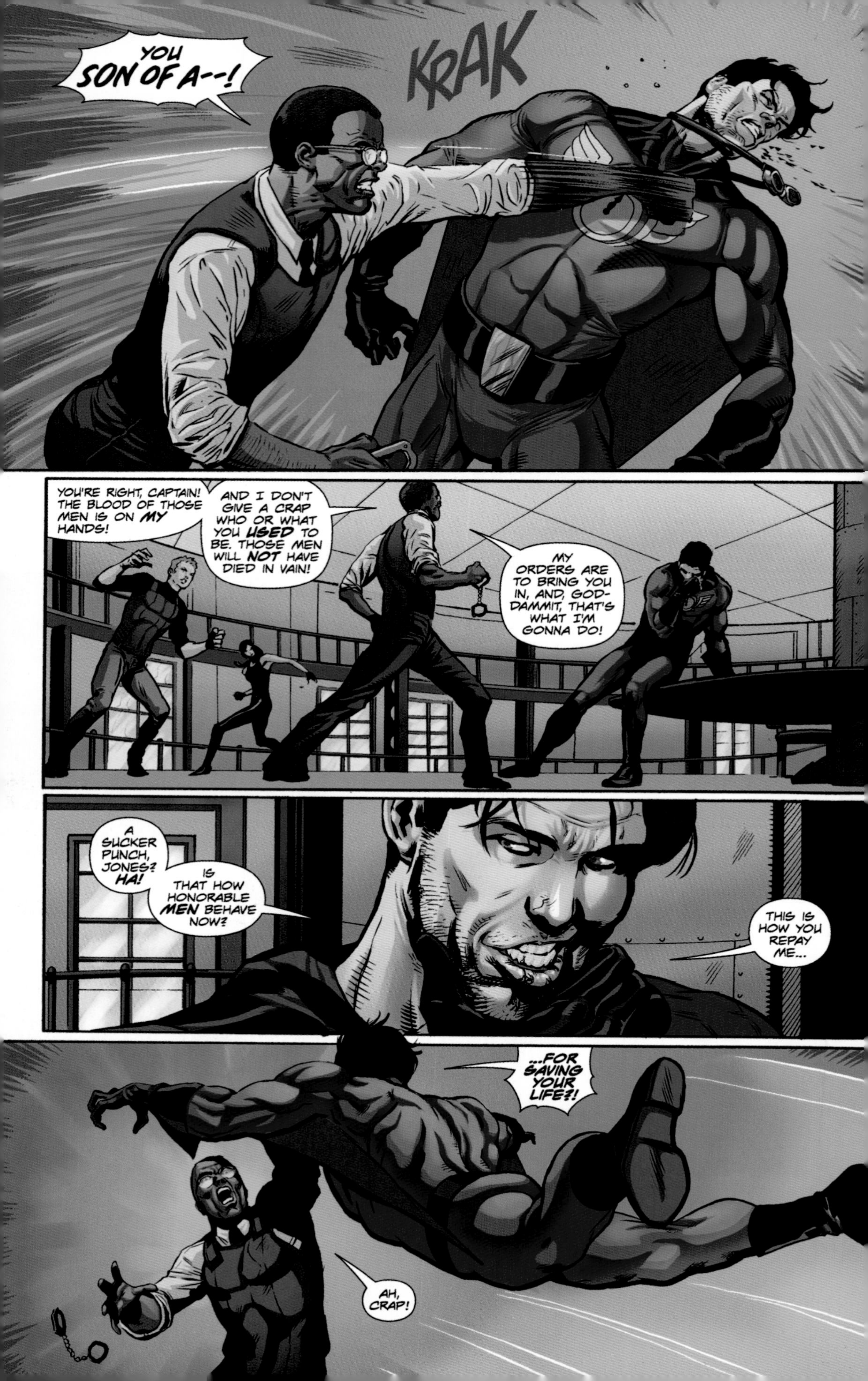

YOU SON OF A--!
KRAK
YOU'RE RIGHT, CAPTAIN! THE BLOOD OF THOSE MEN IS ON MY HANDS!
AND I DON'T GIVE A CRAP WHO OR WHAT YOU USED TO BE. THOSE MEN WILL NOT HAVE DIED IN VAIN!
MY ORDERS ARE TO BRING YOU IN, AND, GOD-DAMMIT, THAT'S WHAT I'M GONNA DO!
A SUCKER PUNCH, JONES? HA!
IS THAT HOW HONORABLE MEN BEHAVE NOW?
THIS IS HOW YOU REPAY ME...
...FOR SAVING YOUR LIFE?!
AH, CRAP!

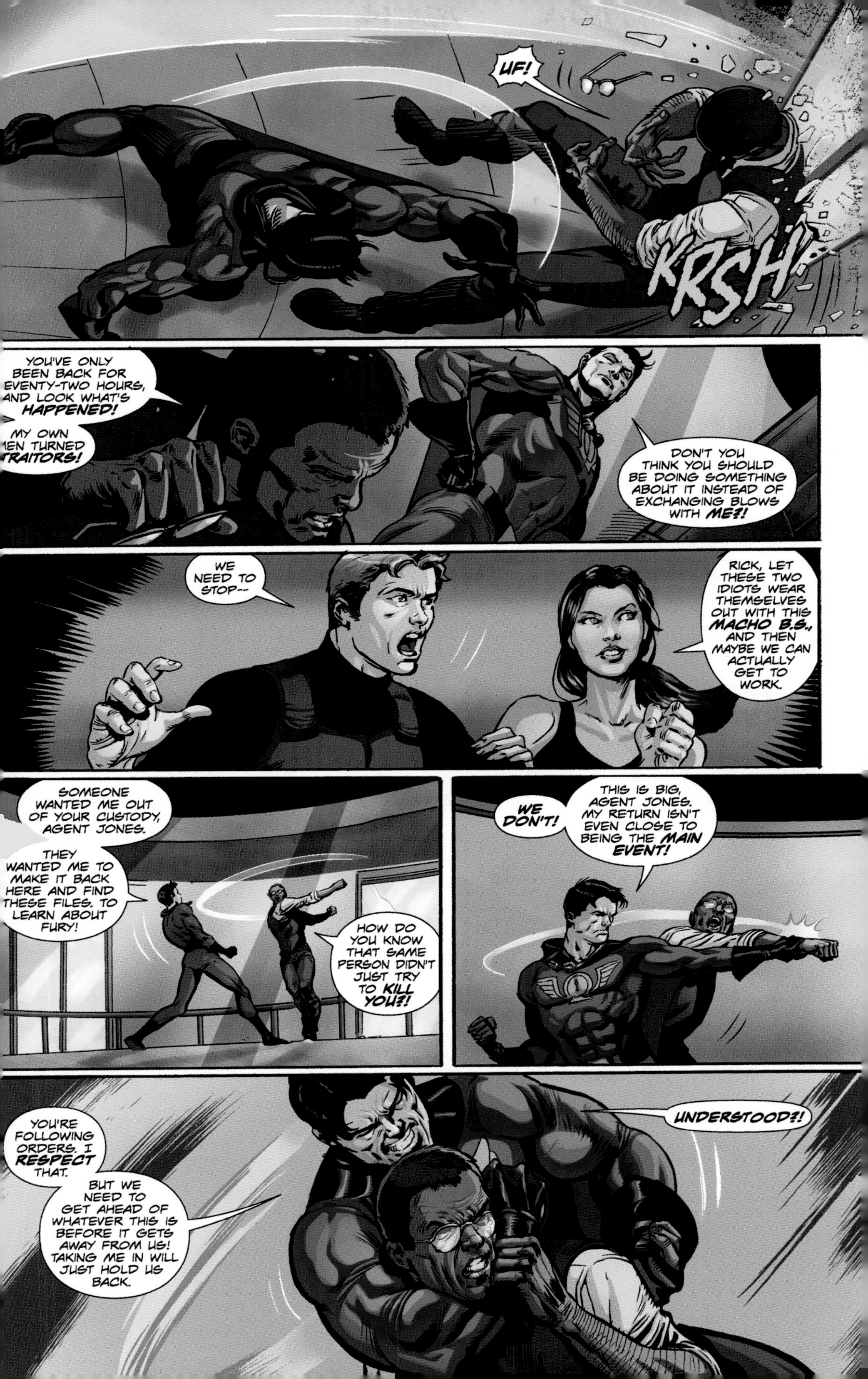
UF!
KRSH!
YOU'VE ONLY BEEN BACK FOR EVENTY-TWO HOURS, AND LOOK WHAT'S HAPPENED!
MY OWN MEN TURNED TRAITORS!
DON'T YOU THINK YOU SHOULD BE DOING SOMETHING ABOUT IT INSTEAD OF EXCHANGING BLOWS WITH ME?!
WE NEED TO STOP--
RICK, LET THESE TWO IDIOTS WEAR THEMSELVES OUT WITH THIS MACHO B.S., AND THEN MAYBE WE CAN ACTUALLY GET TO WORK.
SOMEONE WANTED ME OUT OF YOUR CUSTODY, AGENT JONES.
THEY WANTED ME TO MAKE IT BACK HERE AND FIND THESE FILES. TO LEARN ABOUT FURY!
HOW DO YOU KNOW THAT SAME PERSON DIDN'T JUST TRY TO KILL YOU?!
WE DON'T!
THIS IS BIG, AGENT JONES. MY RETURN ISN'T EVEN CLOSE TO BEING THE MAIN EVENT!
YOU'RE FOLLOWING ORDERS. I RESPECT THAT.
BUT WE NEED TO GET AHEAD OF WHATEVER THIS IS BEFORE IT GETS AWAY FROM US! TAKING ME IN WILL JUST HOLD US BACK.
UNDERSTOOD?!

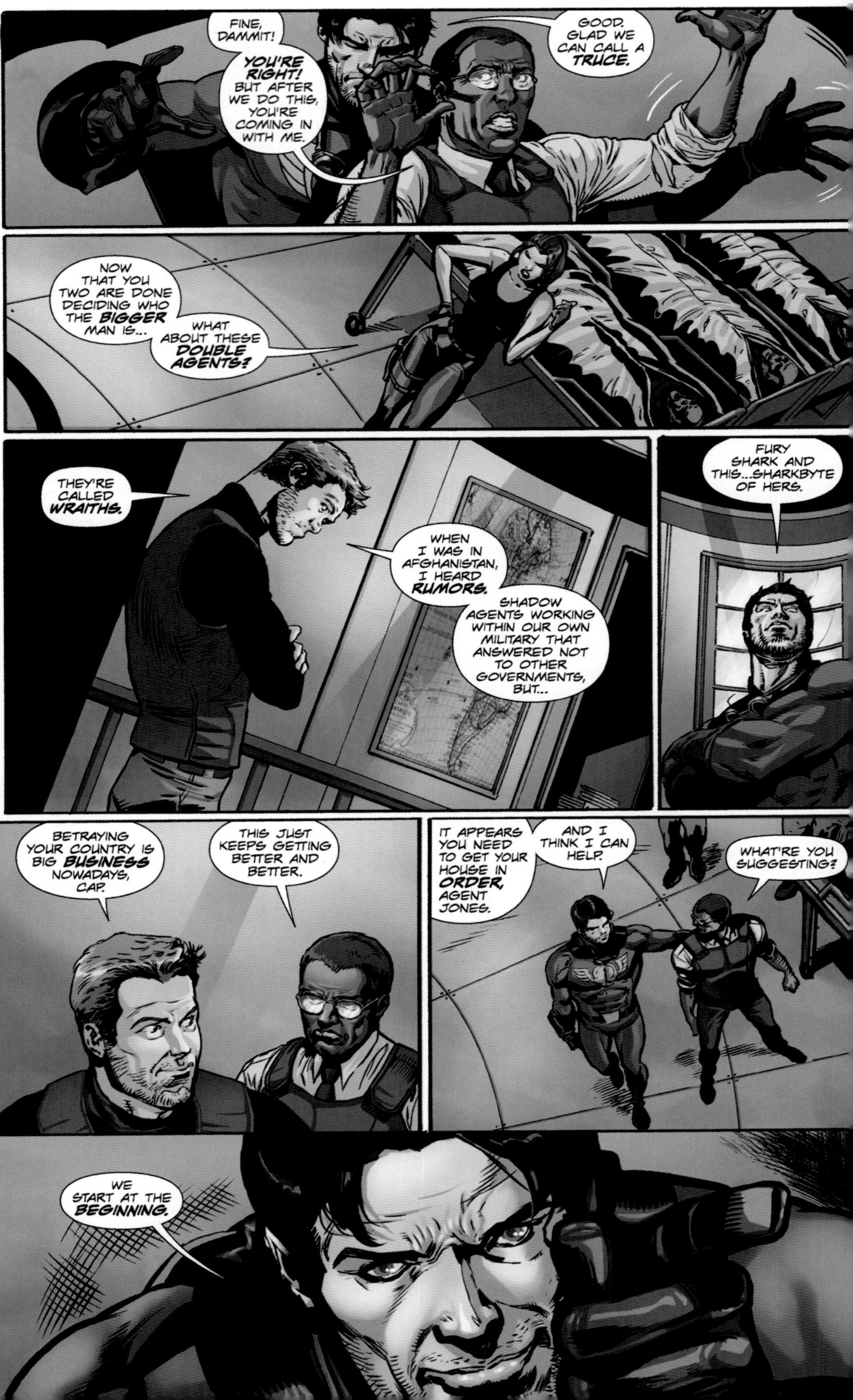
FINE, DAMMIT!
YOU'RE RIGHT! BUT AFTER WE DO THIS, YOU'RE COMING IN WITH ME.
GOOD. GLAD WE CAN CALL A TRUCE.
NOW THAT YOU TWO ARE DONE DECIDING WHO THE BIGGER MAN IS...
WHAT ABOUT THESE DOUBLE AGENTS?
THEY'RE CALLED WRAITHS.
WHEN I WAS IN AFGHANISTAN, I HEARD RUMORS.
SHADOW AGENTS WORKING WITHIN OUR OWN MILITARY THAT ANSWERED NOT TO OTHER GOVERNMENTS, BUT...
FURY SHARK AND THIS...SHARKBYTE OF HERS.
BETRAYING YOUR COUNTRY IS BIG BUSINESS NOWADAYS, CAP.
THIS JUST KEEPS GETTING BETTER AND BETTER.
IT APPEARS YOU NEED TO GET YOUR HOUSE IN ORDER, AGENT JONES.
AND I THINK I CAN HELP.
WHAT'RE YOU SUGGESTING?
WE START AT THE BEGINNING.

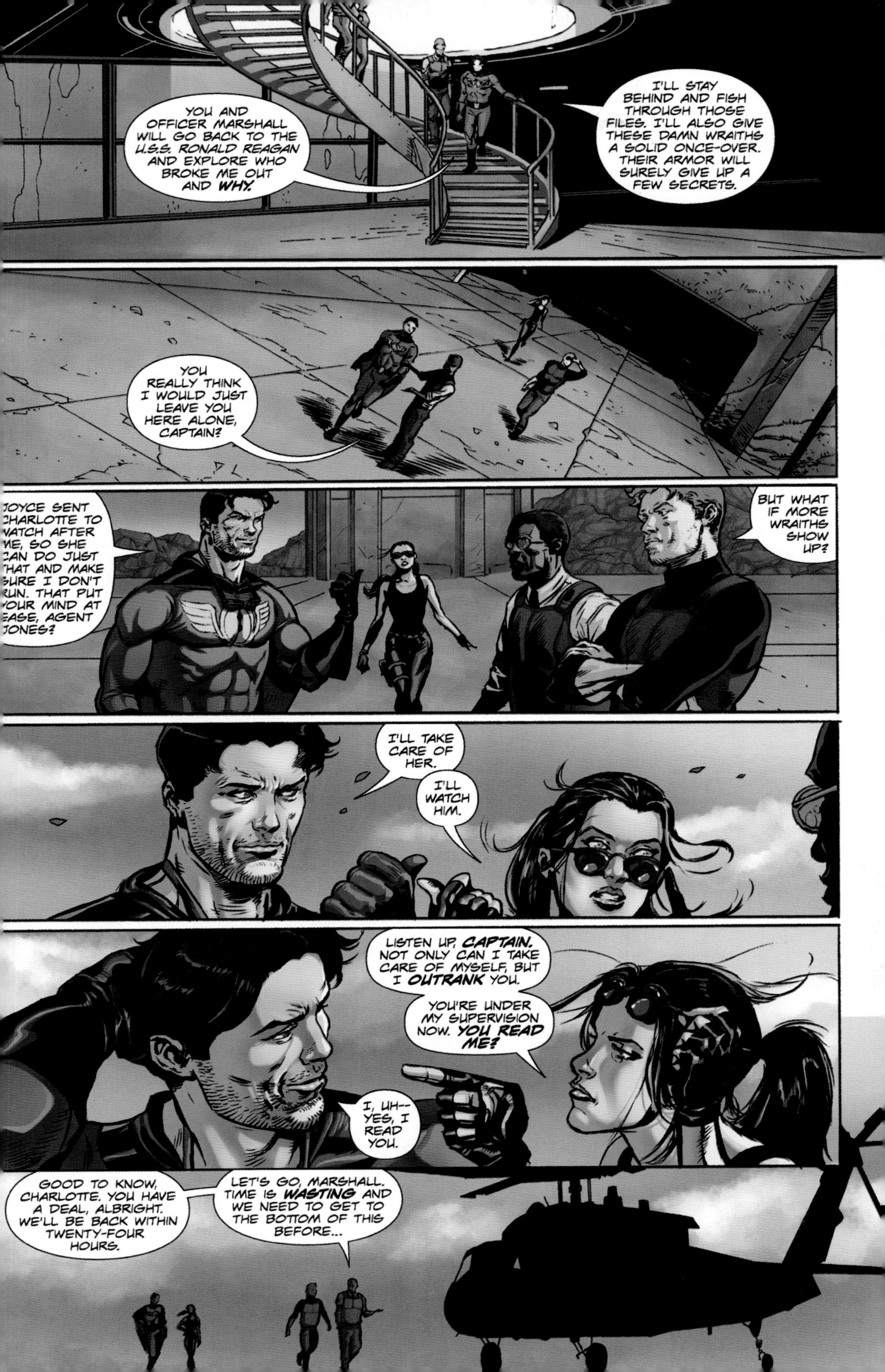
YOU AND OFFICER MARSHALL WILL GO BACK TO THE U.S.S. RONALD REAGAN AND EXPLORE WHO BROKE ME OUT AND WHY.
I'LL STAY BEHIND AND FISH THROUGH THOSE FILES. I'LL ALSO GIVE THESE DAMN WRAITHS A SOLID ONCE-OVER. THEIR ARMOR WILL SURELY GIVE UP A FEW SECRETS.
YOU REALLY THINK I WOULD JUST LEAVE YOU HERE ALONE, CAPTAIN?
JOYCE SENT CHARLOTTE TO WATCH AFTER ME, SO SHE CAN DO JUST THAT AND MAKE SURE I DON'T RUN. THAT PUT YOUR MIND AT EASE, AGENT JONES?
BUT WHAT IF MORE WRAITHS SHOW UP?
I'LL TAKE CARE OF HER.
I'LL WATCH HIM.
LISTEN UP, CAPTAIN. NOT ONLY CAN I TAKE CARE OF MYSELF, BUT I OUTRANK YOU.
YOU'RE UNDER MY SUPERVISION NOW. YOU READ ME?
I, UH-- YES, I READ YOU.
GOOD TO KNOW, CHARLOTTE. YOU HAVE A DEAL, ALBRIGHT. WE'LL BE BACK WITHIN TWENTY-FOUR HOURS.
LET'S GO, MARSHALL. TIME IS WASTING AND WE NEED TO GET TO THE BOTTOM OF THIS BEFORE...

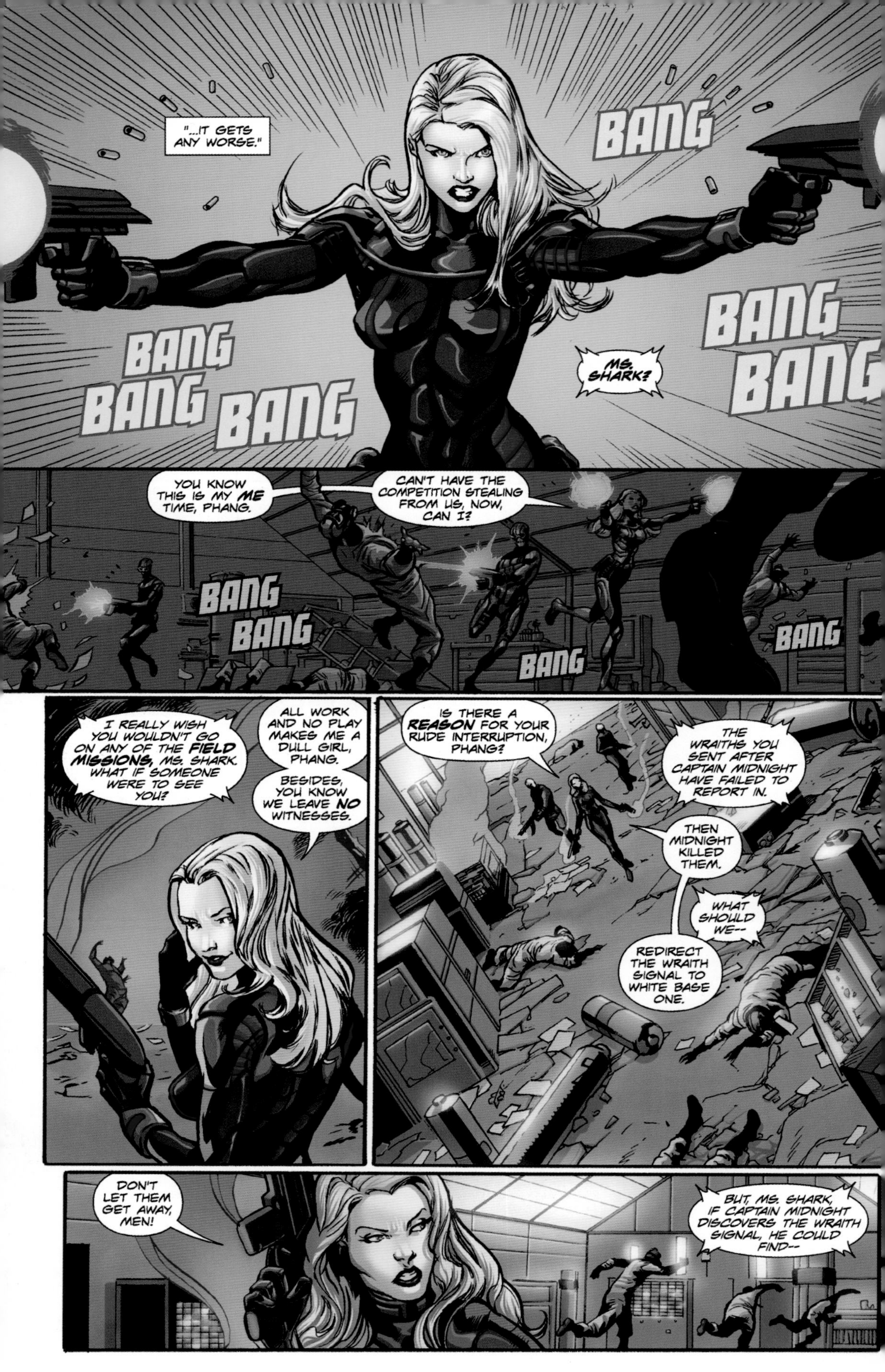
"...IT GETS ANY WORSE."
BANG
BANG BANG BANG
MS. SHARK?
BANG BANG
YOU KNOW THIS IS MY ME TIME, PHANG.
CAN'T HAVE THE COMPETITION STEALING FROM US, NOW, CAN I?
BANG BANG
BANG
BANG
I REALLY WISH YOU WOULDN'T GO ON ANY OF THE FIELD MISSIONS, MS. SHARK. WHAT IF SOMEONE WERE TO SEE YOU?
ALL WORK AND NO PLAY MAKES ME A DULL GIRL, PHANG.
BESIDES, YOU KNOW WE LEAVE NO WITNESSES.
IS THERE A REASON FOR YOUR RUDE INTERRUPTION, PHANG?
THE WRAITHS YOU SENT AFTER CAPTAIN MIDNIGHT HAVE FAILED TO REPORT IN.
THEN MIDNIGHT KILLED THEM.
WHAT SHOULD WE--
REDIRECT THE WRAITH SIGNAL TO WHITE BASE ONE.
DON'T LET THEM GET AWAY, MEN!
BUT, MS. SHARK, IF CAPTAIN MIDNIGHT DISCOVERS THE WRAITH SIGNAL, HE COULD FIND--

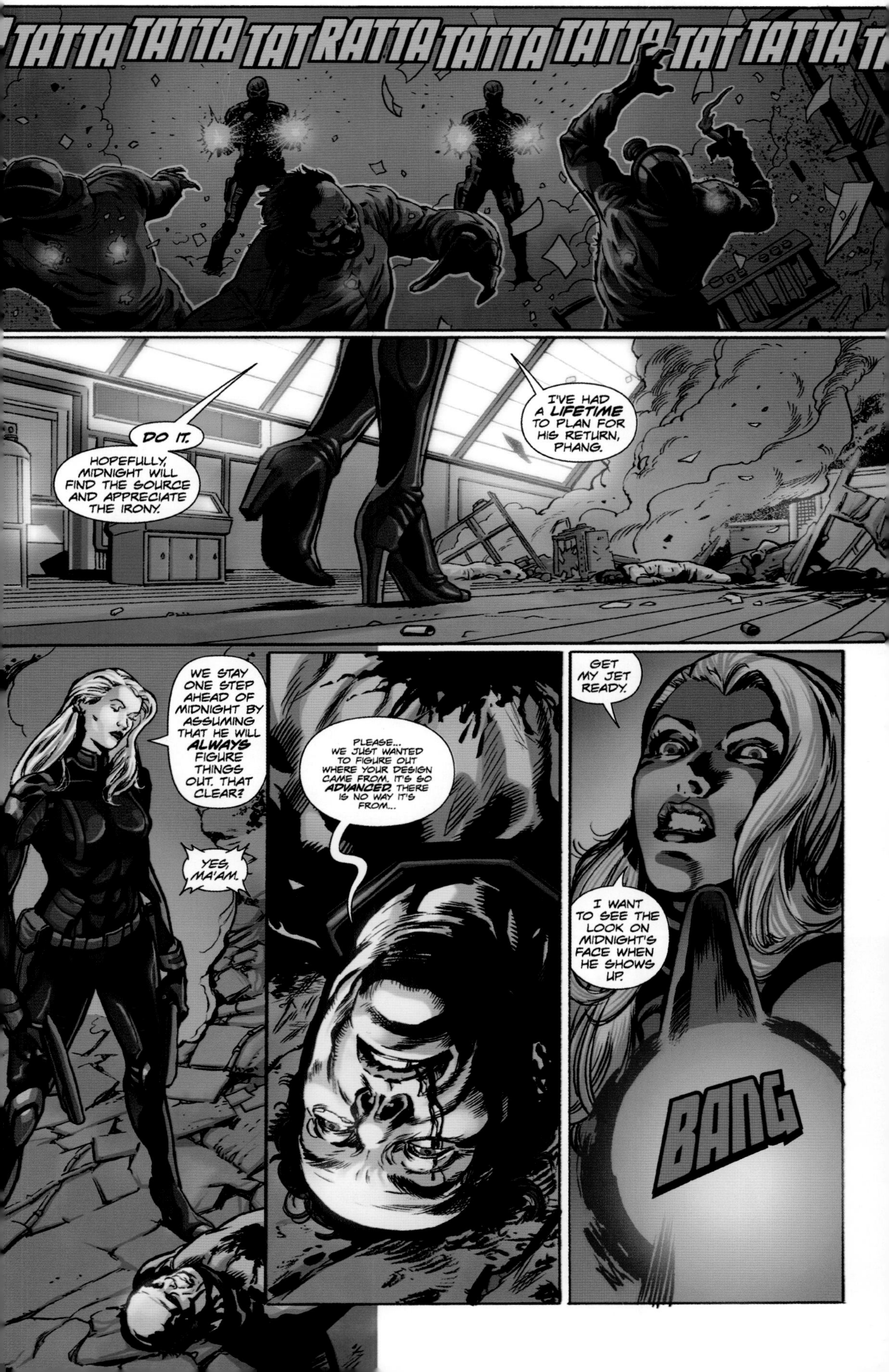
TATTA TATTA TAT RATTA TATTA TATTA TAT TATTA
DO IT.
HOPEFULLY, MIDNIGHT WILL FIND THE SOURCE AND APPRECIATE THE IRONY.
I'VE HAD A LIFETIME TO PLAN FOR HIS RETURN, PHANG.
WE STAY ONE STEP AHEAD OF MIDNIGHT BY ASSUMING THAT HE WILL ALWAYS FIGURE THINGS OUT. THAT CLEAR?
YES, MA'AM.
PLEASE... WE JUST WANTED TO FIGURE OUT WHERE YOUR DESIGN CAME FROM. IT'S SO ADVANCED, THERE IS NO WAY IT'S FROM...
GET MY JET READY.
I WANT TO SEE THE LOOK ON MIDNIGHT'S FACE WHEN HE SHOWS UP.
BANG

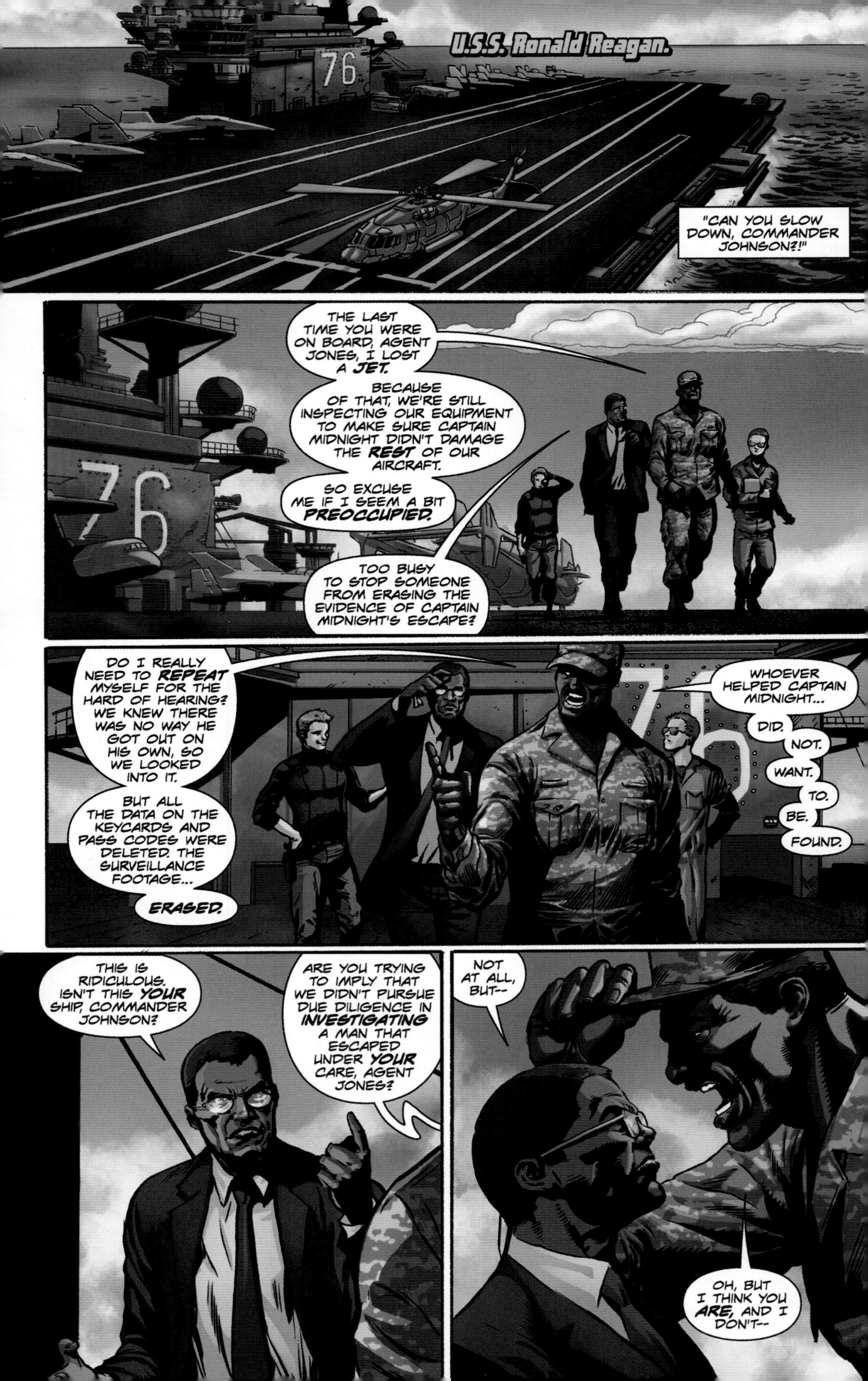
U.S.S. Ronald Reagan.
"CAN YOU SLOW DOWN, COMMANDER JOHNSON?!"
THE LAST TIME YOU WERE ON BOARD, AGENT JONES, I LOST A JET.
BECAUSE OF THAT, WE'RE STILL INSPECTING OUR EQUIPMENT TO MAKE SURE CAPTAIN MIDNIGHT DIDN'T DAMAGE THE REST OF OUR AIRCRAFT.
SO EXCUSE ME IF I SEEM A BIT PREOCCUPIED.
TOO BUSY TO STOP SOMEONE FROM ERASING THE EVIDENCE OF CAPTAIN MIDNIGHT'S ESCAPE?
DO I REALLY NEED TO REPEAT MYSELF FOR THE HARD OF HEARING? WE KNEW THERE WAS NO WAY HE GOT OUT ON HIS OWN, SO WE LOOKED INTO IT.
BUT ALL THE DATA ON THE KEYCARDS AND PASS CODES WERE DELETED. THE SURVEILLANCE FOOTAGE...
ERASED.
WHOEVER HELPED CAPTAIN MIDNIGHT...
DID.
NOT.
WANT.
TO.
BE.
FOUND.
THIS IS RIDICULOUS. ISN'T THIS YOUR SHIP, COMMANDER JOHNSON?
ARE YOU TRYING TO IMPLY THAT WE DIDN'T PURSUE DUE DILIGENCE IN INVESTIGATING A MAN THAT ESCAPED UNDER YOUR CARE, AGENT JONES?
NOT AT ALL, BUT--
OH, BUT I THINK YOU ARE, AND I DON'T--

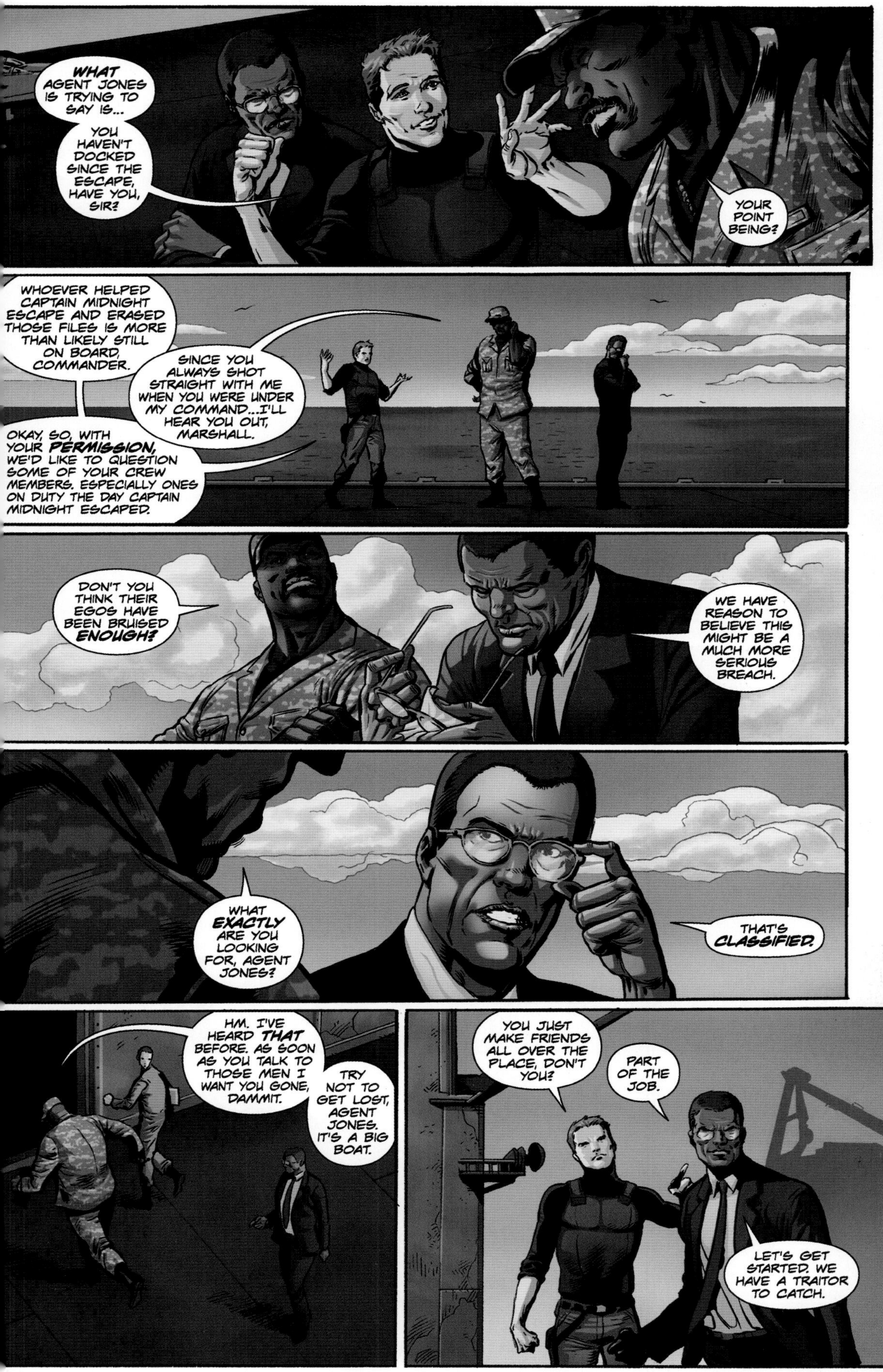
WHAT AGENT JONES IS TRYING TO SAY IS...
YOU HAVEN'T DOCKED SINCE THE ESCAPE, HAVE YOU, SIR?
YOUR POINT BEING?
WHOEVER HELPED CAPTAIN MIDNIGHT ESCAPE AND ERASED THOSE FILES IS MORE THAN LIKELY STILL ON BOARD, COMMANDER.
SINCE YOU ALWAYS SHOT STRAIGHT WITH ME WHEN YOU WERE UNDER MY COMMAND...I'LL HEAR YOU OUT, MARSHALL.
OKAY, SO, WITH YOUR PERMISSION, WE'D LIKE TO QUESTION SOME OF YOUR CREW MEMBERS. ESPECIALLY ONES ON DUTY THE DAY CAPTAIN MIDNIGHT ESCAPED.
DON'T YOU THINK THEIR EGOS HAVE BEEN BRUISED ENOUGH?
WE HAVE REASON TO BELIEVE THIS MIGHT BE A MUCH MORE SERIOUS BREACH.
WHAT EXACTLY ARE YOU LOOKING FOR, AGENT JONES?
THAT'S CLASSIFIED.
HM. I'VE HEARD THAT BEFORE. AS SOON AS YOU TALK TO THOSE MEN I WANT YOU GONE, DAMMIT.
TRY NOT TO GET LOST, AGENT JONES. IT'S A BIG BOAT.
YOU JUST MAKE FRIENDS ALL OVER THE PLACE, DON'T YOU?
PART OF THE JOB.
LET'S GET STARTED. WE HAVE A TRAITOR TO CATCH.

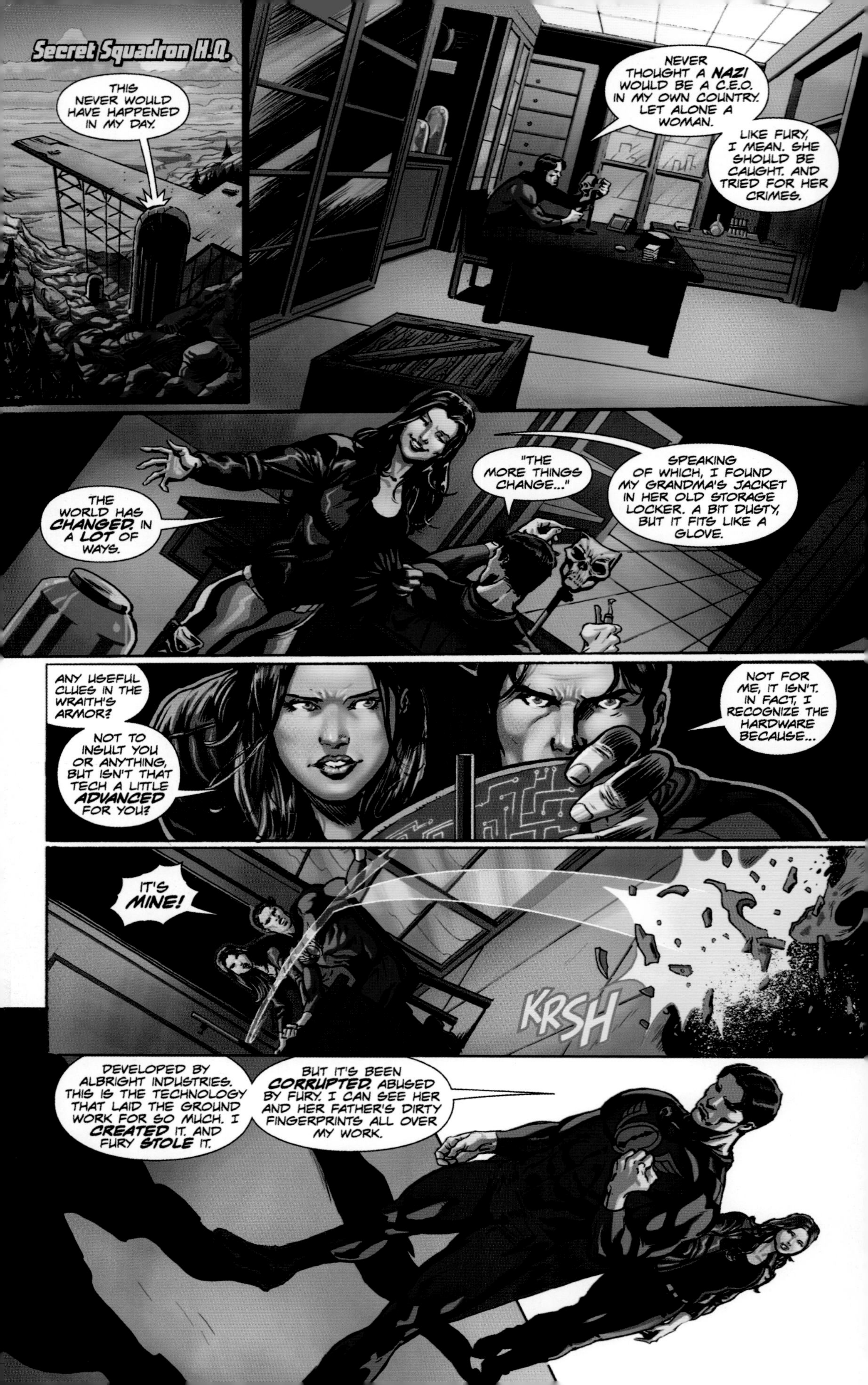
Secret Squadron H.Q.
THIS NEVER WOULD HAVE HAPPENED IN MY DAY.
NEVER THOUGHT A NAZI WOULD BE A C.E.O. IN MY OWN COUNTRY. LET ALONE A WOMAN.
LIKE FURY, I MEAN. SHE SHOULD BE CAUGHT. AND TRIED FOR HER CRIMES.
THE WORLD HAS CHANGED. IN A LOT OF WAYS.
"THE MORE THINGS CHANGE..."
SPEAKING OF WHICH, I FOUND MY GRANDMA'S JACKET IN HER OLD STORAGE LOCKER. A BIT DUSTY, BUT IT FITS LIKE A GLOVE.
ANY USEFUL CLUES IN THE WRAITH'S ARMOR?
NOT TO INSULT YOU OR ANYTHING, BUT ISN'T THAT TECH A LITTLE ADVANCED FOR YOU?
NOT FOR ME, IT ISN'T. IN FACT, I RECOGNIZE THE HARDWARE BECAUSE...
IT'S MINE!
KRSH
DEVELOPED BY ALBRIGHT INDUSTRIES. THIS IS THE TECHNOLOGY THAT LAID THE GROUND WORK FOR SO MUCH. I CREATED IT. AND FURY STOLE IT.
BUT IT'S BEEN CORRUPTED. ABUSED BY FURY. I CAN SEE HER AND HER FATHER'S DIRTY FINGERPRINTS ALL OVER MY WORK.

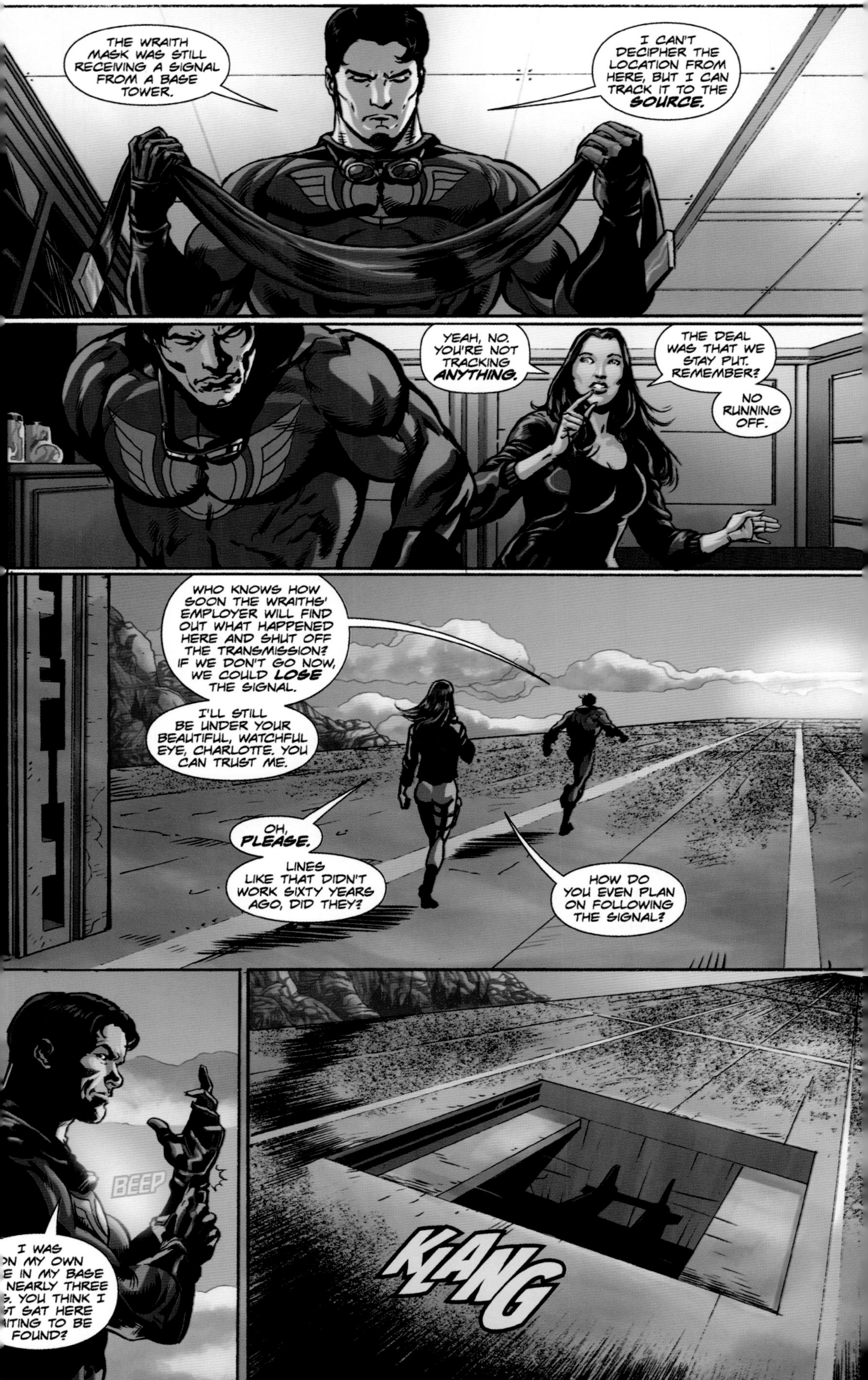
THE WRAITH MASK WAS STILL RECEIVING A SIGNAL FROM A BASE TOWER.
I CAN'T DECIPHER THE LOCATION FROM HERE, BUT I CAN TRACK IT TO THE **SOURCE.**
YEAH, NO. YOU'RE NOT TRACKING **ANYTHING.**
THE DEAL WAS THAT WE STAY PUT. REMEMBER?
NO RUNNING OFF.
WHO KNOWS HOW SOON THE WRAITHS' EMPLOYER WILL FIND OUT WHAT HAPPENED HERE AND SHUT OFF THE TRANSMISSION? IF WE DON'T GO NOW, WE COULD **LOSE** THE SIGNAL.
I'LL STILL BE UNDER YOUR BEAUTIFUL, WATCHFUL EYE, CHARLOTTE. YOU CAN TRUST ME.
OH, **PLEASE.**
LINES LIKE THAT DIDN'T WORK SIXTY YEARS AGO, DID THEY?
HOW DO YOU EVEN PLAN ON FOLLOWING THE SIGNAL?
BEEP
KLANG

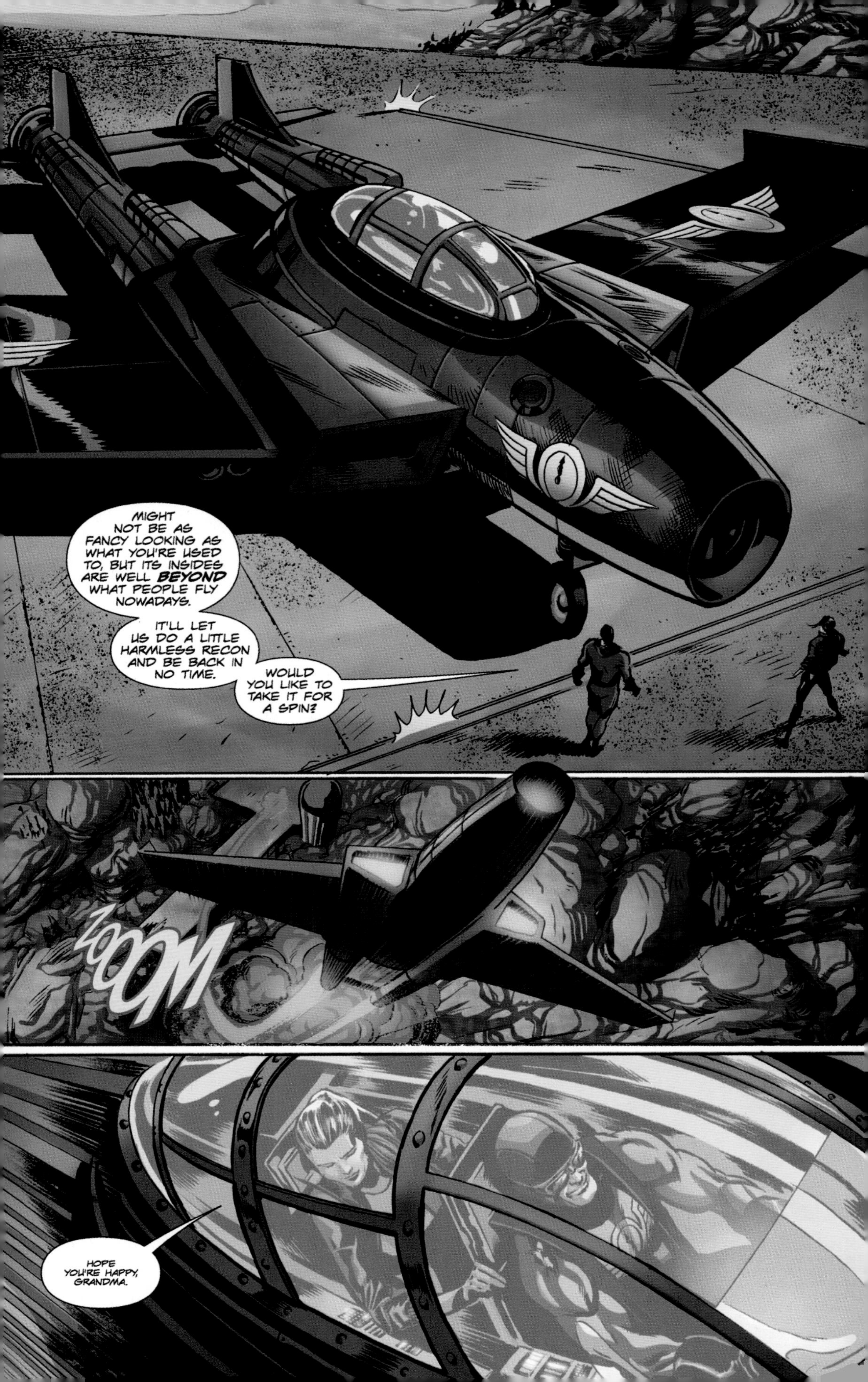
MIGHT NOT BE AS FANCY LOOKING AS WHAT YOU'RE USED TO, BUT ITS INSIDES ARE WELL BEYOND WHAT PEOPLE FLY NOWADAYS.
IT'LL LET US DO A LITTLE HARMLESS RECON AND BE BACK IN NO TIME.
WOULD YOU LIKE TO TAKE IT FOR A SPIN?
ZOOOM
HOPE YOU'RE HAPPY, GRANDMA.

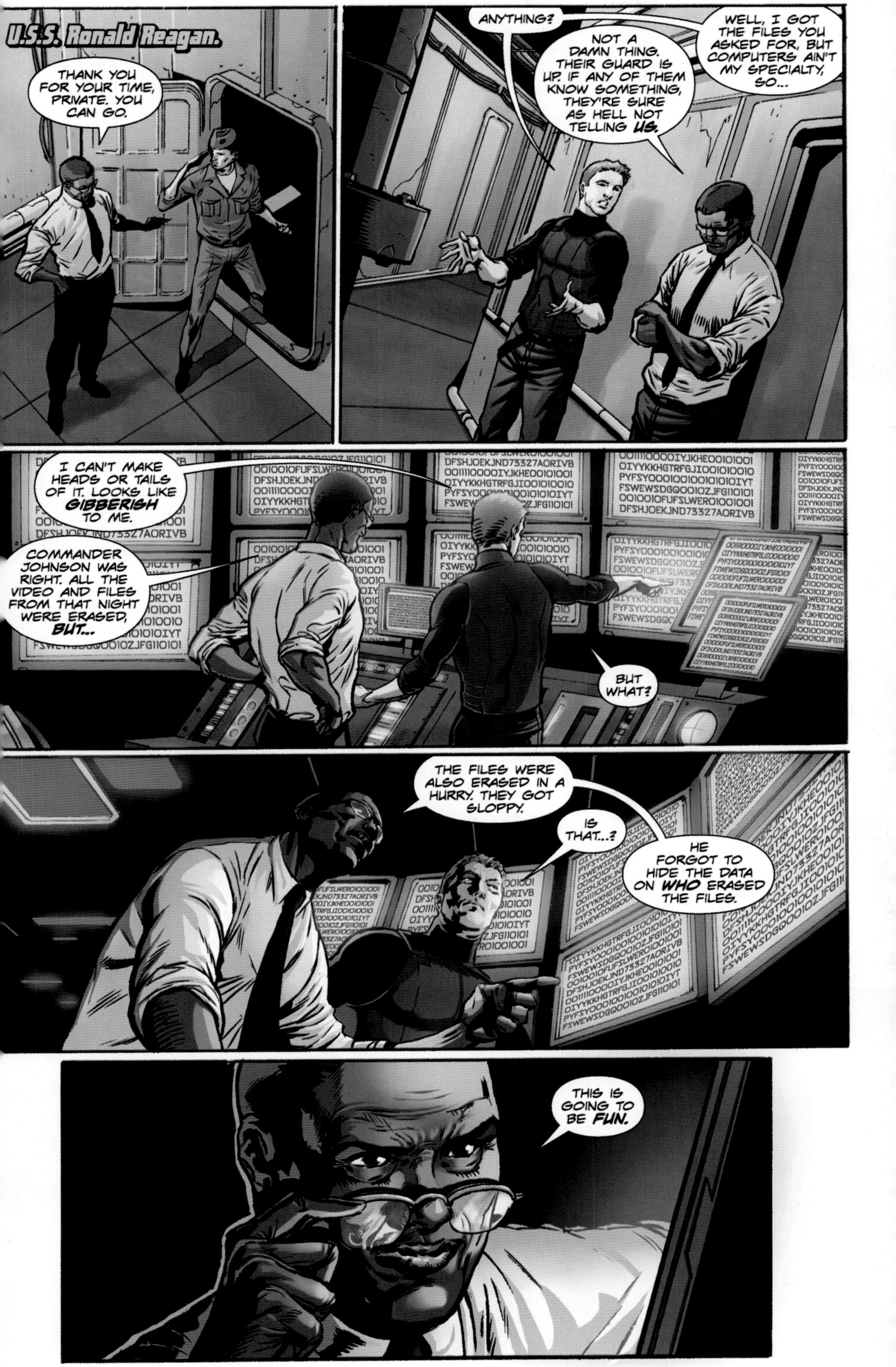
U.S.S. Ronald Reagan.
THANK YOU FOR YOUR TIME, PRIVATE. YOU CAN GO.
ANYTHING?
NOT A DAMN THING. THEIR GUARD IS UP. IF ANY OF THEM KNOW SOMETHING, THEY'RE SURE AS HELL NOT TELLING US.
WELL, I GOT THE FILES YOU ASKED FOR, BUT COMPUTERS AIN'T MY SPECIALTY, SO...
I CAN'T MAKE HEADS OR TAILS OF IT. LOOKS LIKE GIBBERISH TO ME.
COMMANDER JOHNSON WAS RIGHT. ALL THE VIDEO AND FILES FROM THAT NIGHT WERE ERASED, BUT...
BUT WHAT?
THE FILES WERE ALSO ERASED IN A HURRY. THEY GOT SLOPPY.
IS THAT...?
HE FORGOT TO HIDE THE DATA ON WHO ERASED THE FILES.
THIS IS GOING TO BE FUN.

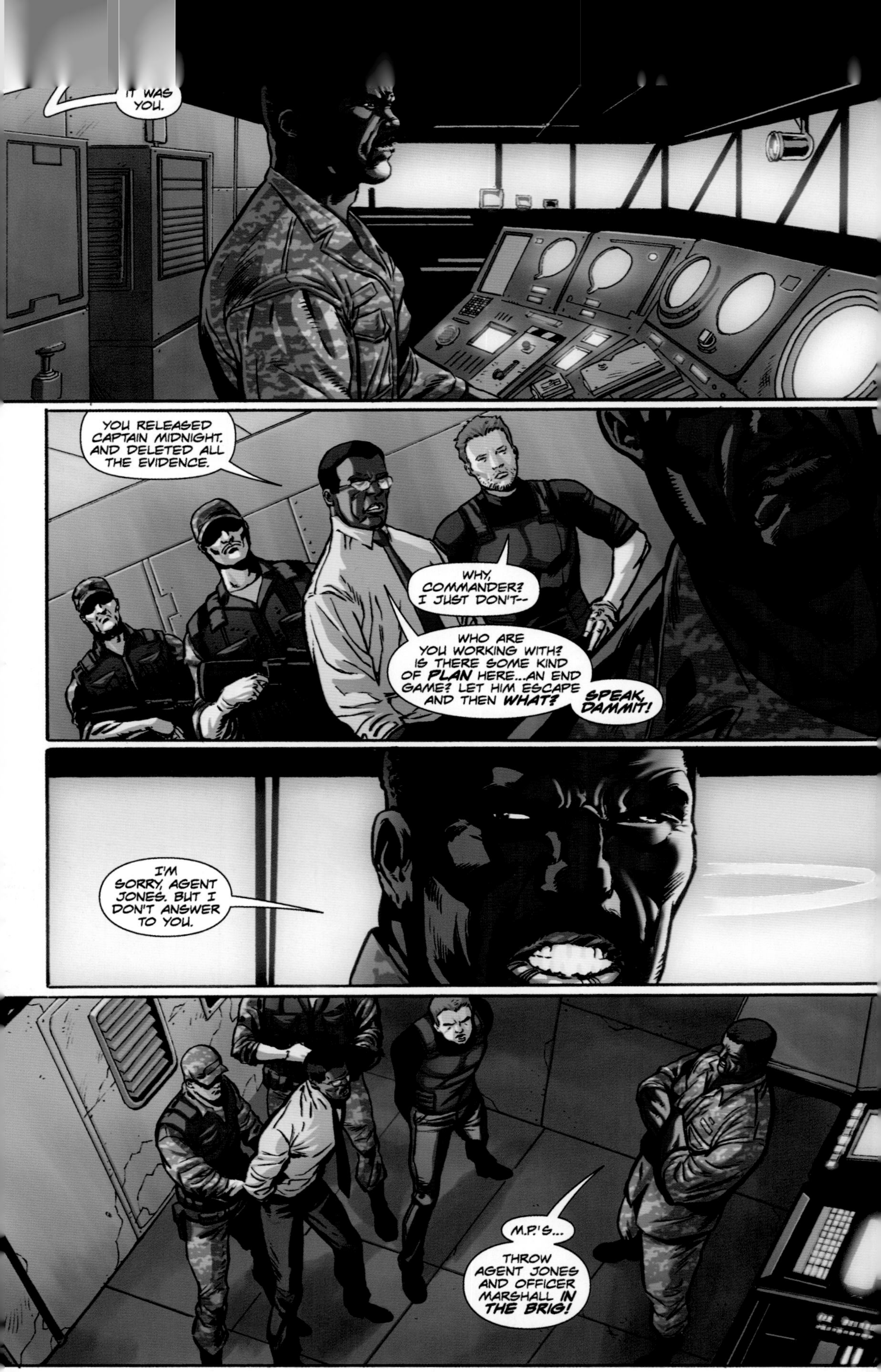
IT WAS YOU.
YOU RELEASED CAPTAIN MIDNIGHT. AND DELETED ALL THE EVIDENCE.
WHY, COMMANDER? I JUST DON'T--
WHO ARE YOU WORKING WITH? IS THERE SOME KIND OF PLAN HERE...AN END GAME? LET HIM ESCAPE AND THEN WHAT?
SPEAK, DAMMIT!
I'M SORRY, AGENT JONES. BUT I DON'T ANSWER TO YOU.
M.P.'S...
THROW AGENT JONES AND OFFICER MARSHALL IN THE BRIG!

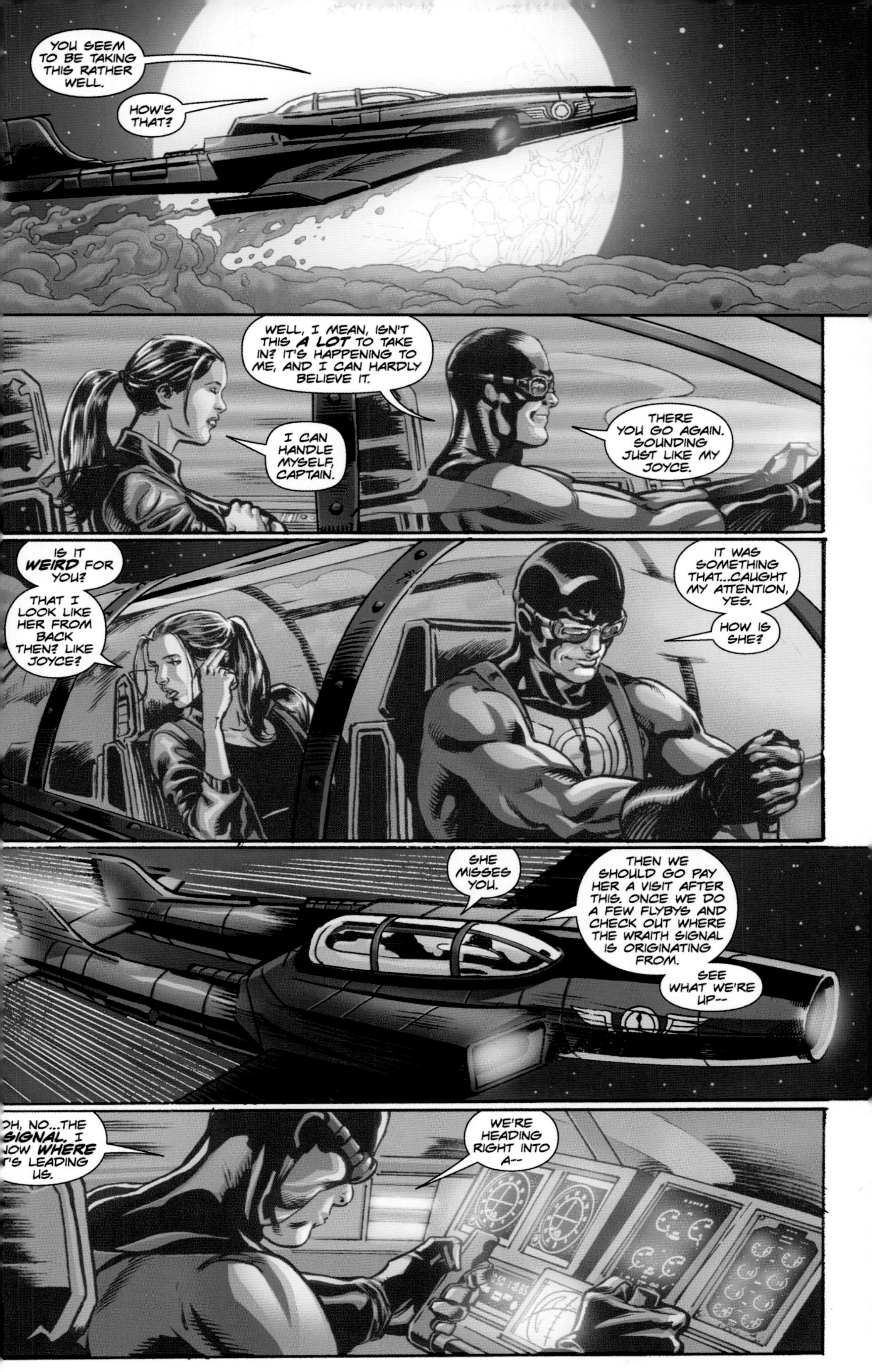

YOU SEEM TO BE TAKING THIS RATHER WELL.
HOW'S THAT?
WELL, I MEAN, ISN'T THIS A LOT TO TAKE IN? IT'S HAPPENING TO ME, AND I CAN HARDLY BELIEVE IT.
I CAN HANDLE MYSELF, CAPTAIN.
THERE YOU GO AGAIN. SOUNDING JUST LIKE MY JOYCE.
IS IT WEIRD FOR YOU?
THAT I LOOK LIKE HER FROM BACK THEN? LIKE JOYCE?
IT WAS SOMETHING THAT...CAUGHT MY ATTENTION, YES.
HOW IS SHE?
SHE MISSES YOU.
THEN WE SHOULD GO PAY HER A VISIT AFTER THIS. ONCE WE DO A FEW FLYBYS AND CHECK OUT WHERE THE WRAITH SIGNAL IS ORIGINATING FROM.
SEE WHAT WE'RE UP--
OH, NO...THE SIGNAL. I KNOW WHERE IT'S LEADING US.
WE'RE HEADING RIGHT INTO A--

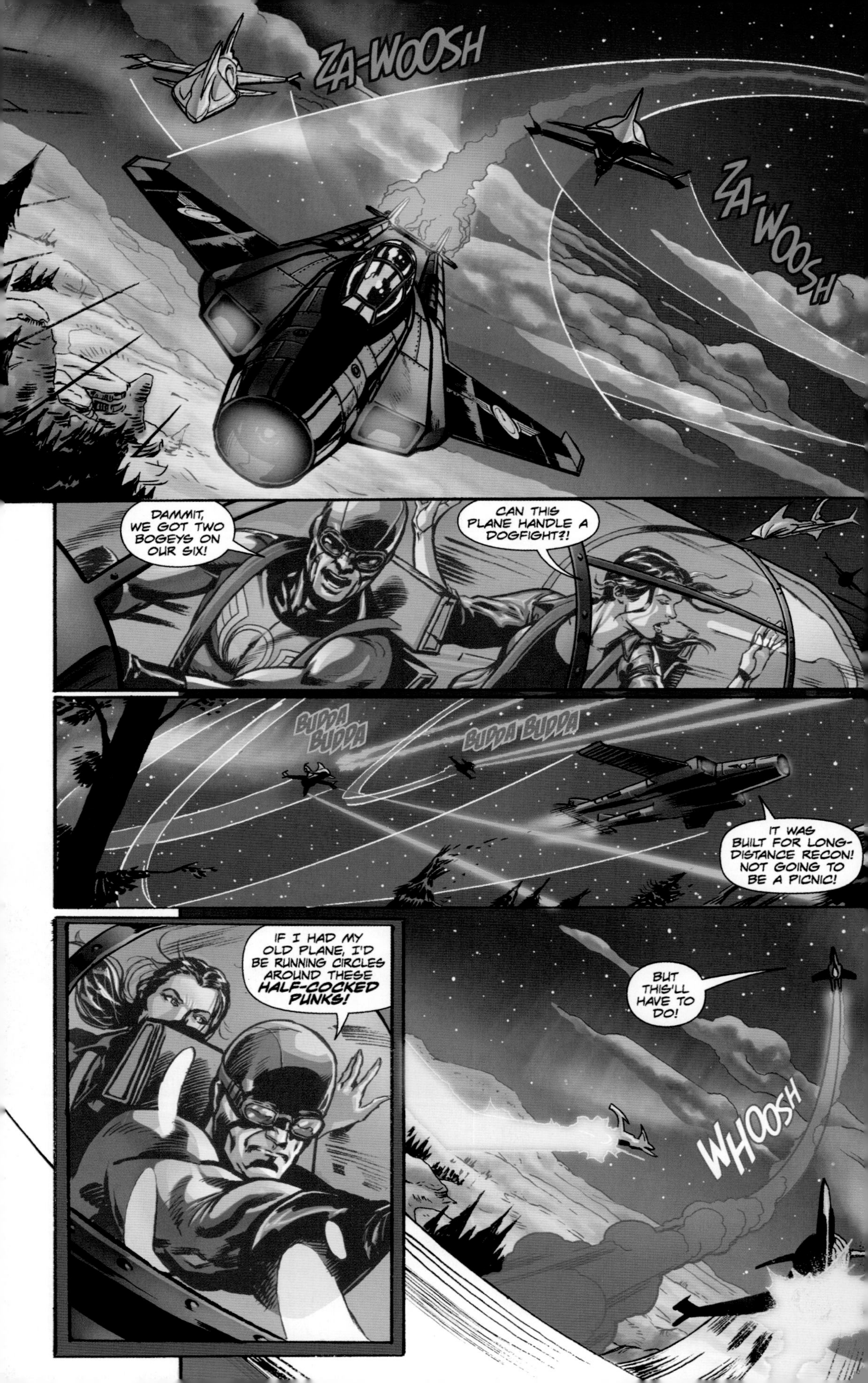
ZA-WOOSH
ZA-WOOSH
DAMMIT, WE GOT TWO BOGEYS ON OUR SIX!
CAN THIS PLANE HANDLE A DOGFIGHT?!
BUDDA BUDDA
BUDDA BUDDA
IT WAS BUILT FOR LONG-DISTANCE RECON! NOT GOING TO BE A PICNIC!
IF I HAD MY OLD PLANE, I'D BE RUNNING CIRCLES AROUND THESE HALF-COCKED PUNKS!
BUT THIS'LL HAVE TO DO!
WHOOSH

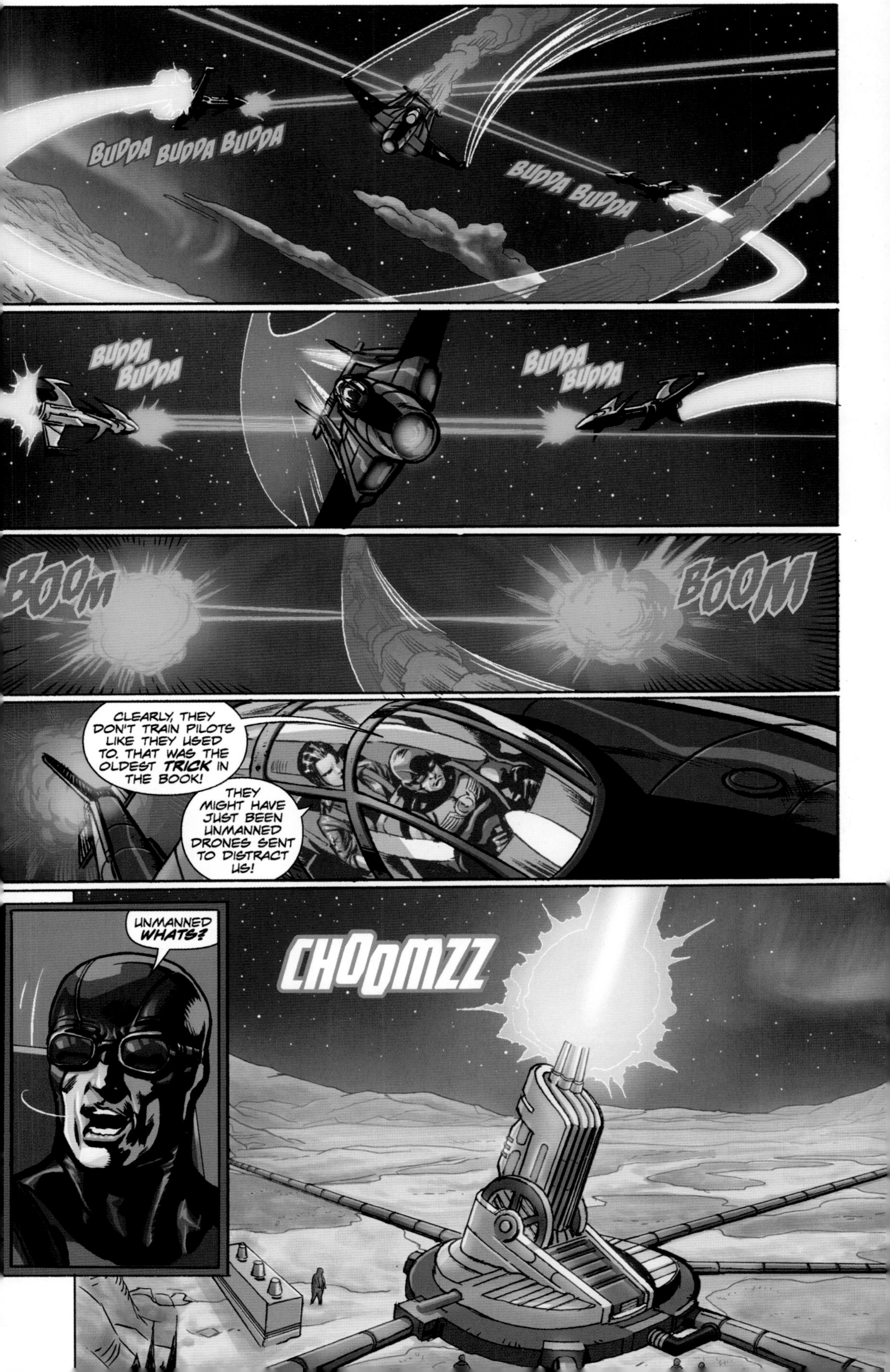
BUDDA BUDDA BUDDA
BUDDA BUDDA
BUDDA BUDDA
BUDDA BUDDA
BOOM
BOOM
CLEARLY, THEY DON'T TRAIN PILOTS LIKE THEY USED TO. THAT WAS THE OLDEST TRICK IN THE BOOK!
THEY MIGHT HAVE JUST BEEN UNMANNED DRONES SENT TO DISTRACT US!
UNMANNED WHATS?
CHOOMZZ

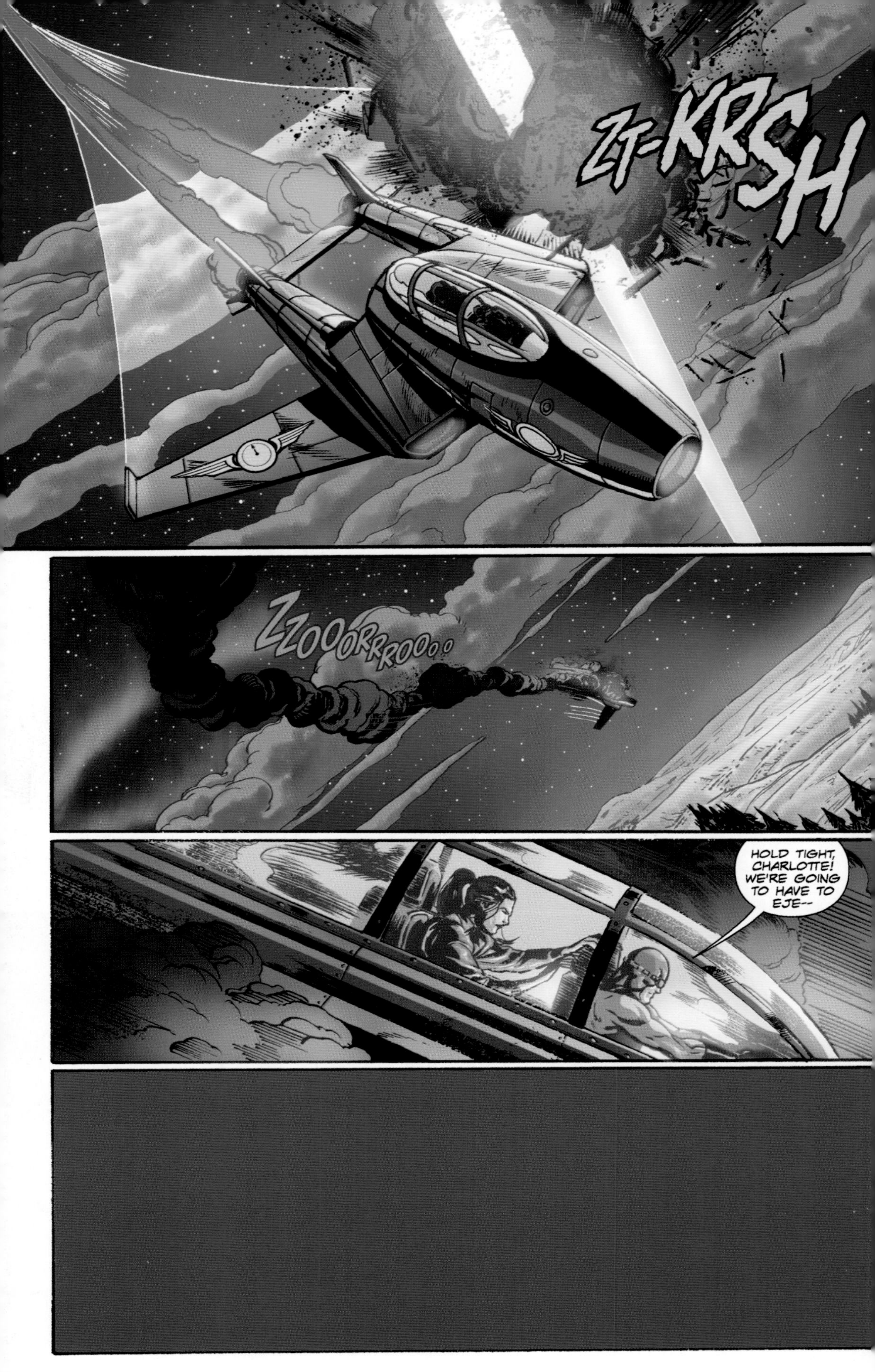
ZT-KRSH
ZZOOORRROOooo
HOLD TIGHT, CHARLOTTE! WE'RE GOING TO HAVE TO EJE--

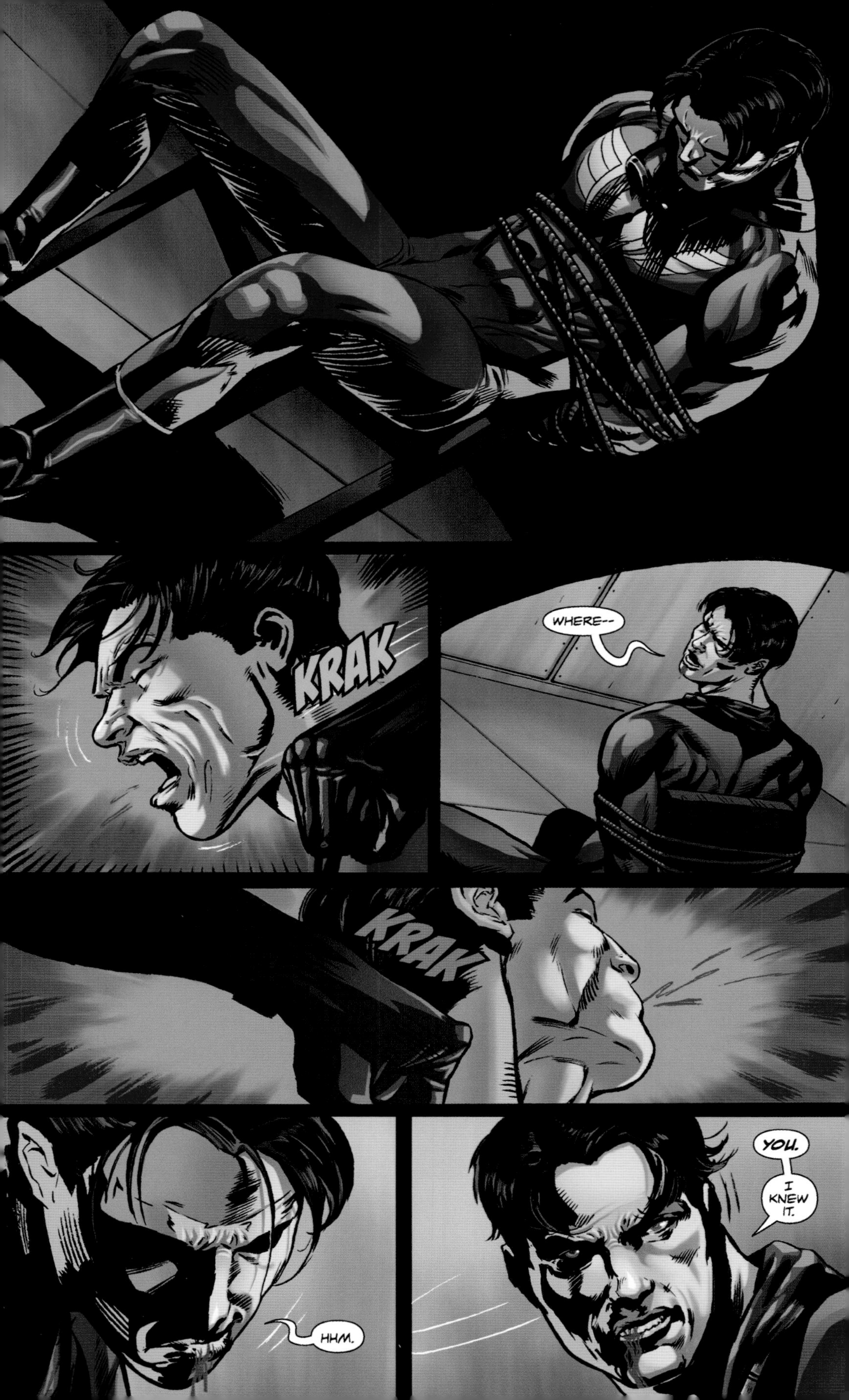
KRAK
WHERE--
KRAK
HHM.
YOU.
I KNEW IT.

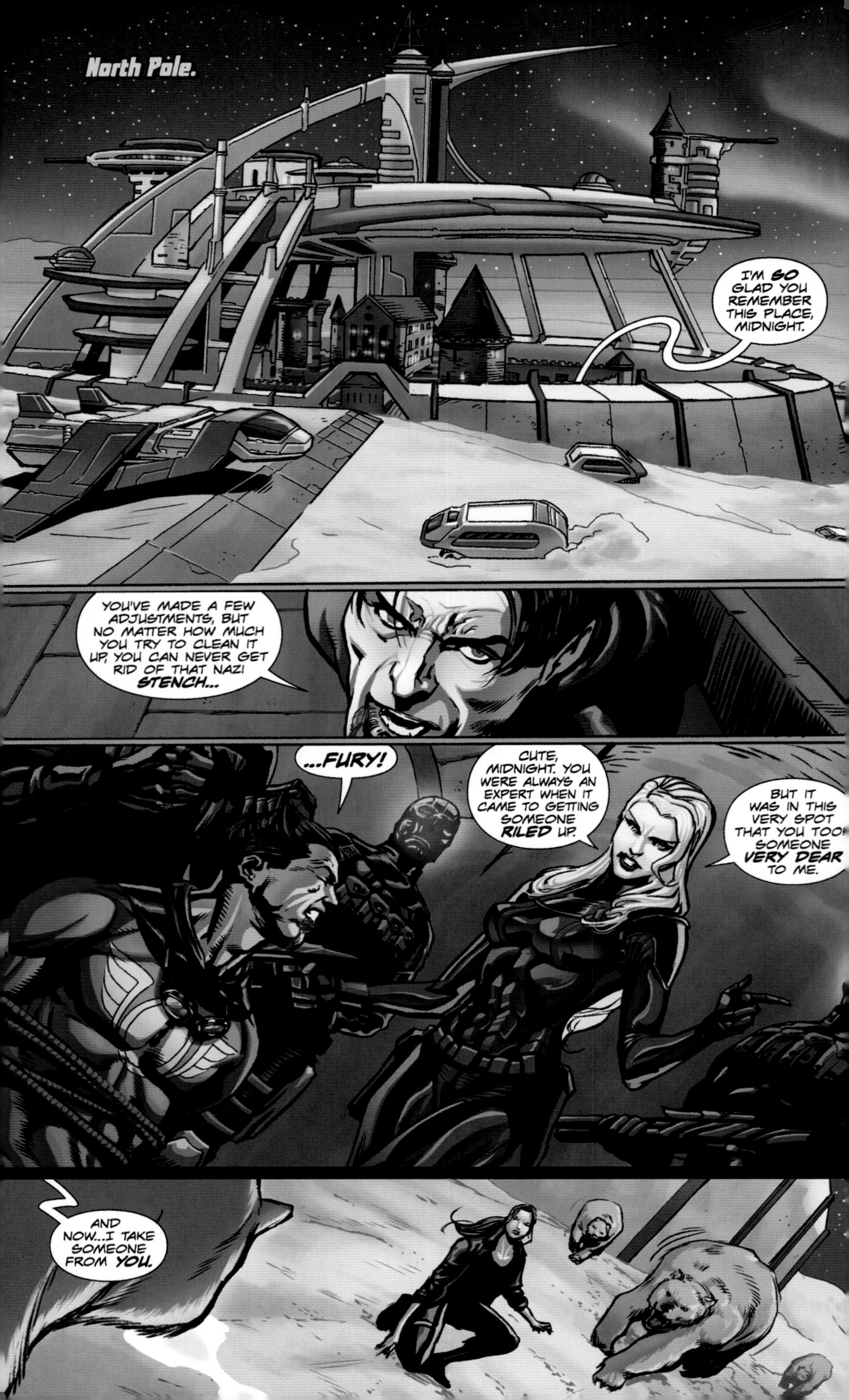
North Pole.
I'M SO GLAD YOU REMEMBER THIS PLACE, MIDNIGHT.
YOU'VE MADE A FEW ADJUSTMENTS, BUT NO MATTER HOW MUCH YOU TRY TO CLEAN IT UP, YOU CAN NEVER GET RID OF THAT NAZI STENCH...
...FURY!
CUTE, MIDNIGHT. YOU WERE ALWAYS AN EXPERT WHEN IT CAME TO GETTING SOMEONE RILED UP.
BUT IT WAS IN THIS VERY SPOT THAT YOU TOOK SOMEONE VERY DEAR TO ME.
AND NOW...I TAKE SOMEONE FROM YOU.

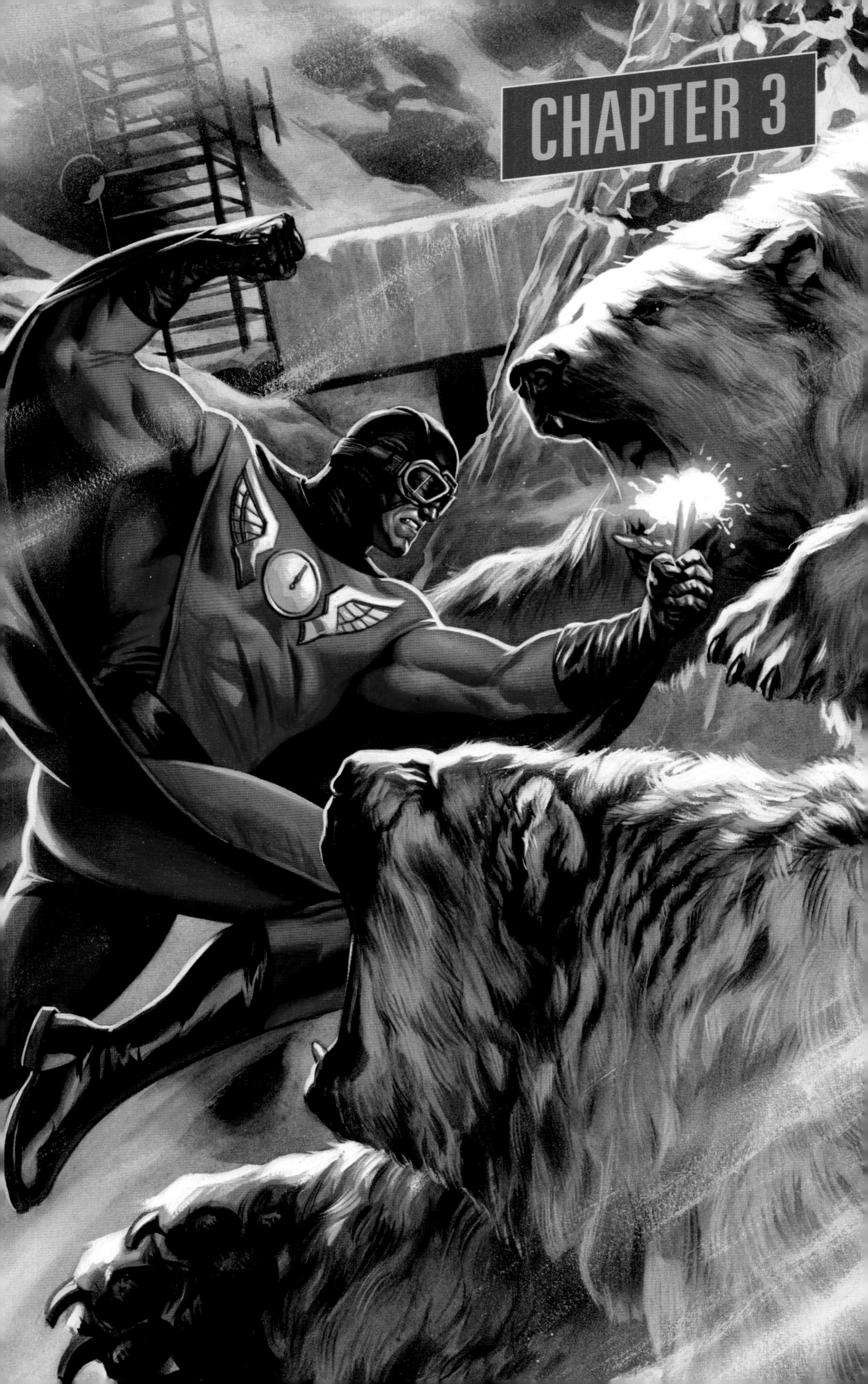
CHAPTER 3

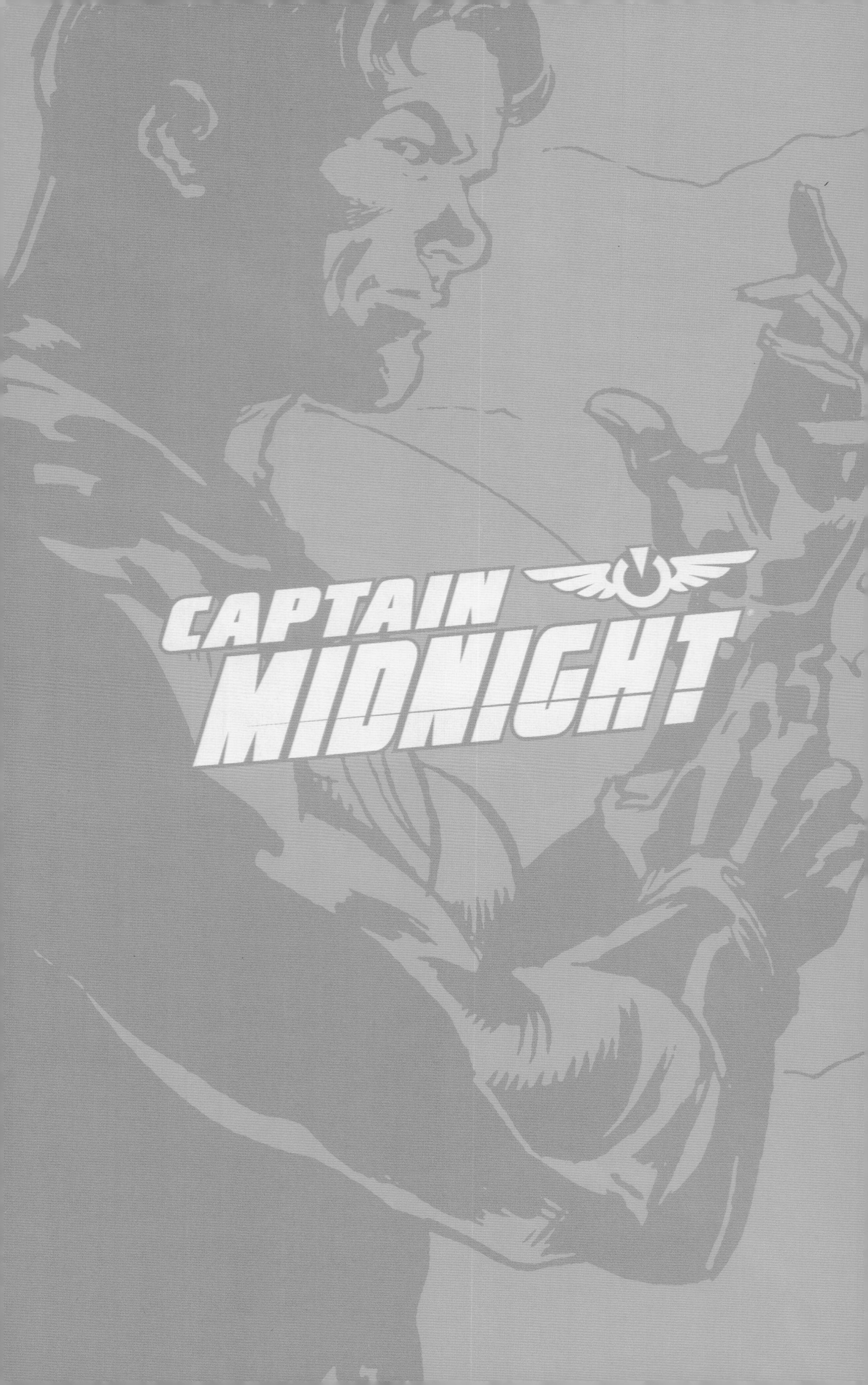
CAPTAIN
MIDNIGHT

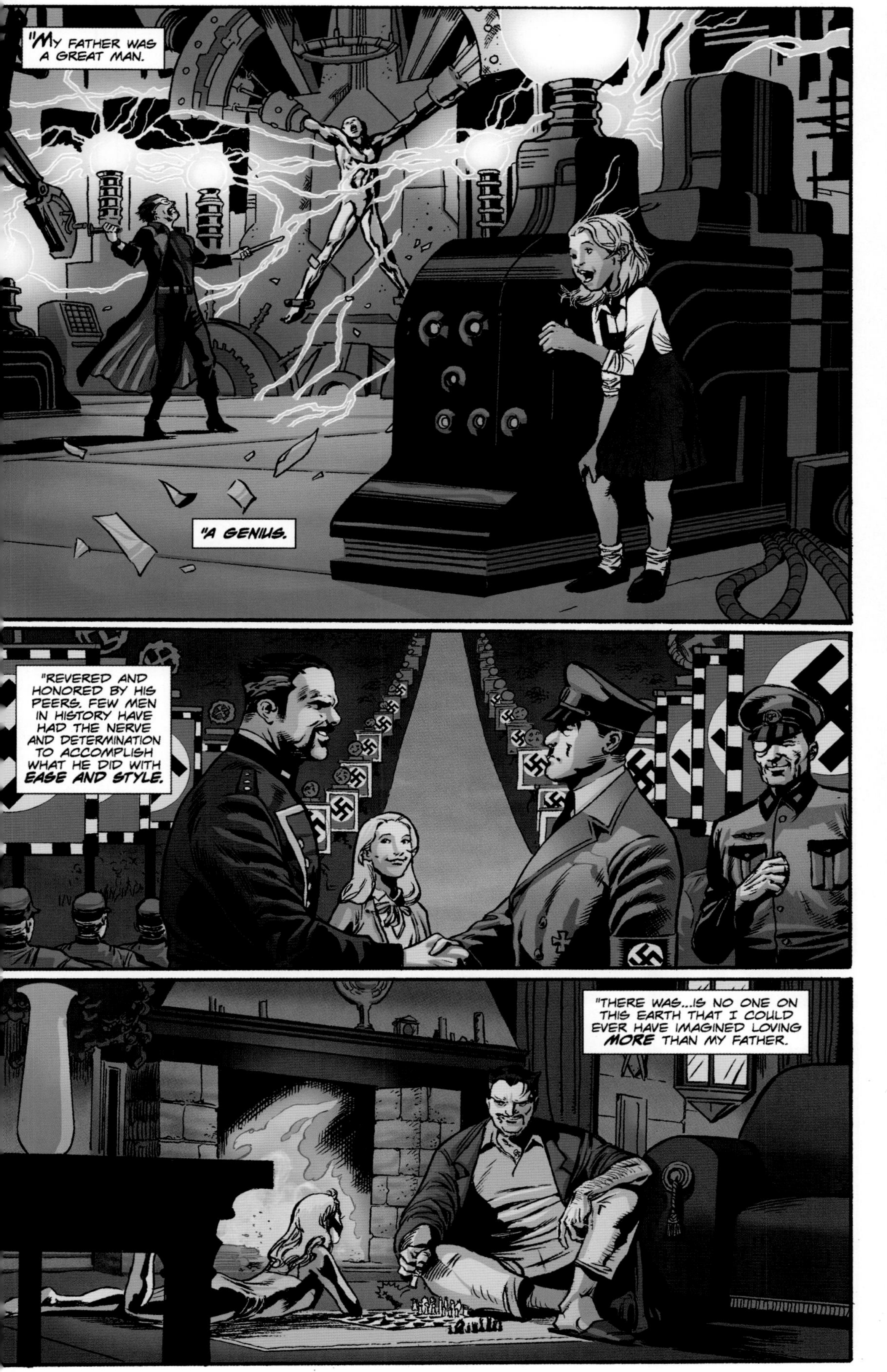
"MY FATHER WAS A GREAT MAN.
"A GENIUS.
"REVERED AND HONORED BY HIS PEERS. FEW MEN IN HISTORY HAVE HAD THE NERVE AND DETERMINATION TO ACCOMPLISH WHAT HE DID WITH EASE AND STYLE.
"THERE WAS...IS NO ONE ON THIS EARTH THAT I COULD EVER HAVE IMAGINED LOVING MORE THAN MY FATHER.

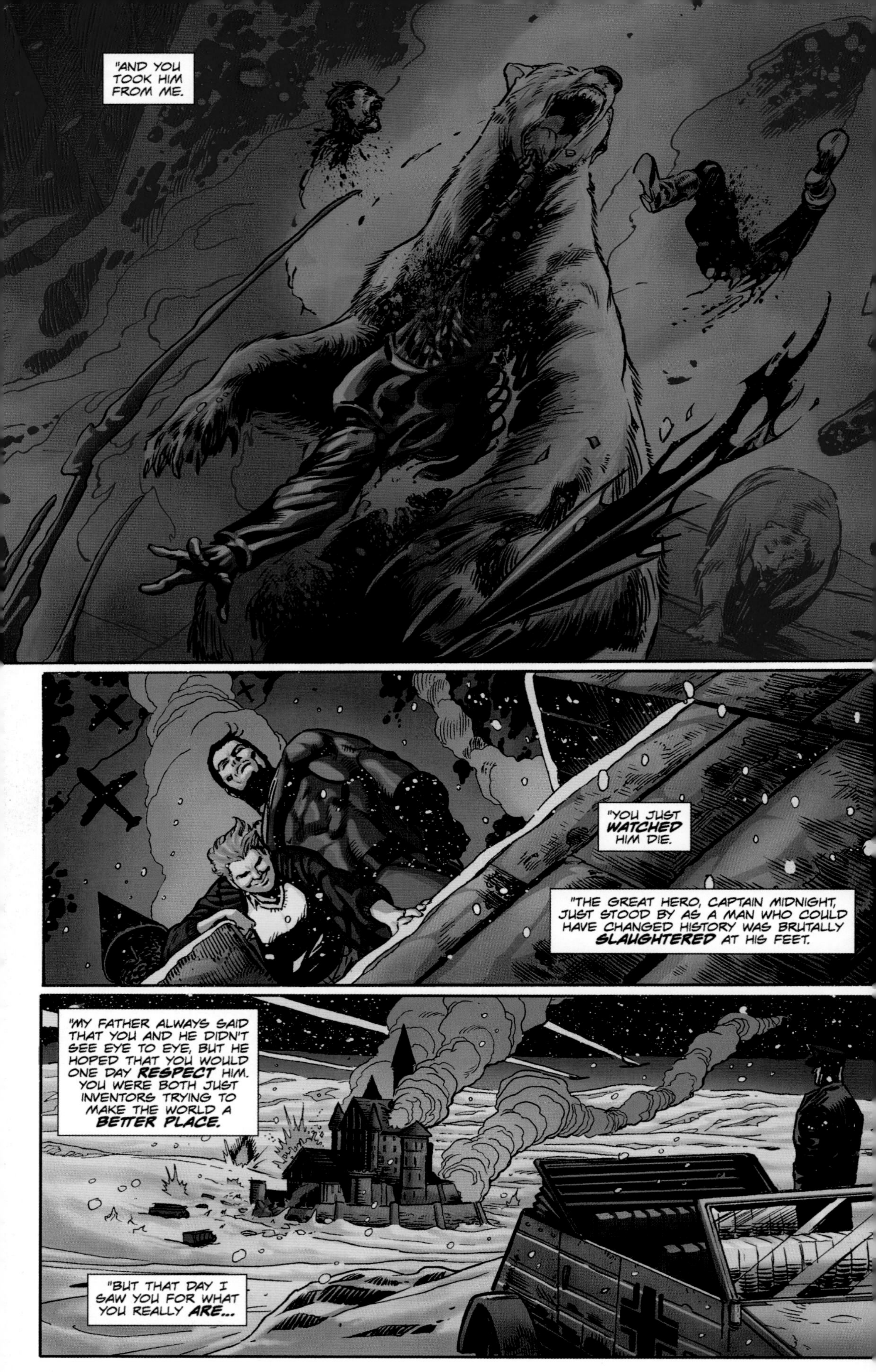
"AND YOU TOOK HIM FROM ME.
"YOU JUST WATCHED HIM DIE.
"THE GREAT HERO, CAPTAIN MIDNIGHT, JUST STOOD BY AS A MAN WHO COULD HAVE CHANGED HISTORY WAS BRUTALLY SLAUGHTERED AT HIS FEET.
"MY FATHER ALWAYS SAID THAT YOU AND HE DIDN'T SEE EYE TO EYE, BUT HE HOPED THAT YOU WOULD ONE DAY RESPECT HIM. YOU WERE BOTH JUST INVENTORS TRYING TO MAKE THE WORLD A BETTER PLACE.
"BUT THAT DAY I SAW YOU FOR WHAT YOU REALLY ARE...

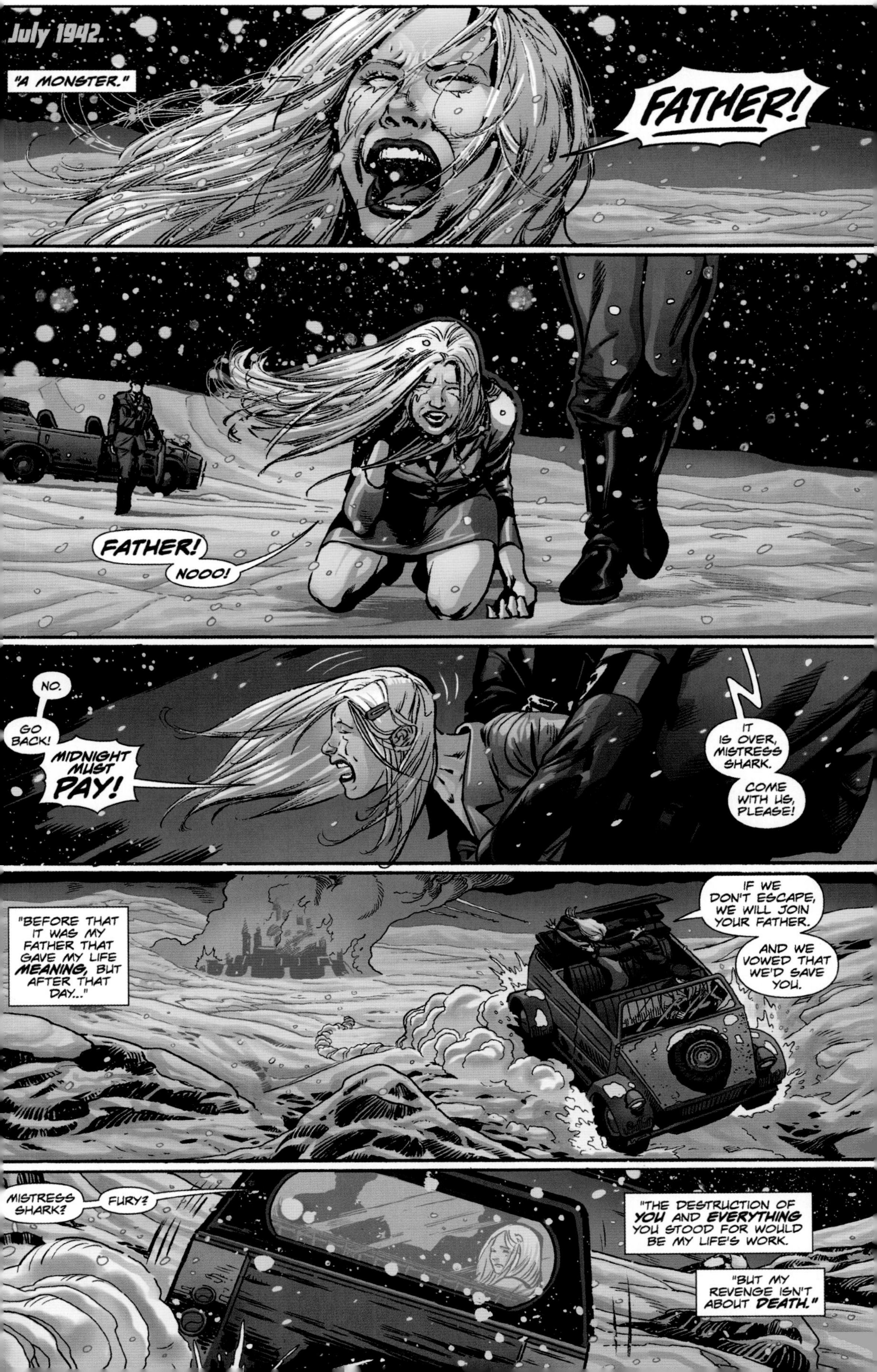

July 1942.
"A MONSTER."
FATHER!
FATHER!
NOOO!
NO.
GO BACK!
MIDNIGHT MUST PAY!
IT IS OVER, MISTRESS SHARK.
COME WITH US, PLEASE!
"BEFORE THAT IT WAS MY FATHER THAT GAVE MY LIFE MEANING, BUT AFTER THAT DAY..."
IF WE DON'T ESCAPE, WE WILL JOIN YOUR FATHER.
AND WE VOWED THAT WE'D SAVE YOU.
MISTRESS SHARK?
FURY?
"THE DESTRUCTION OF YOU AND EVERYTHING YOU STOOD FOR WOULD BE MY LIFE'S WORK.
"BUT MY REVENGE ISN'T ABOUT DEATH."

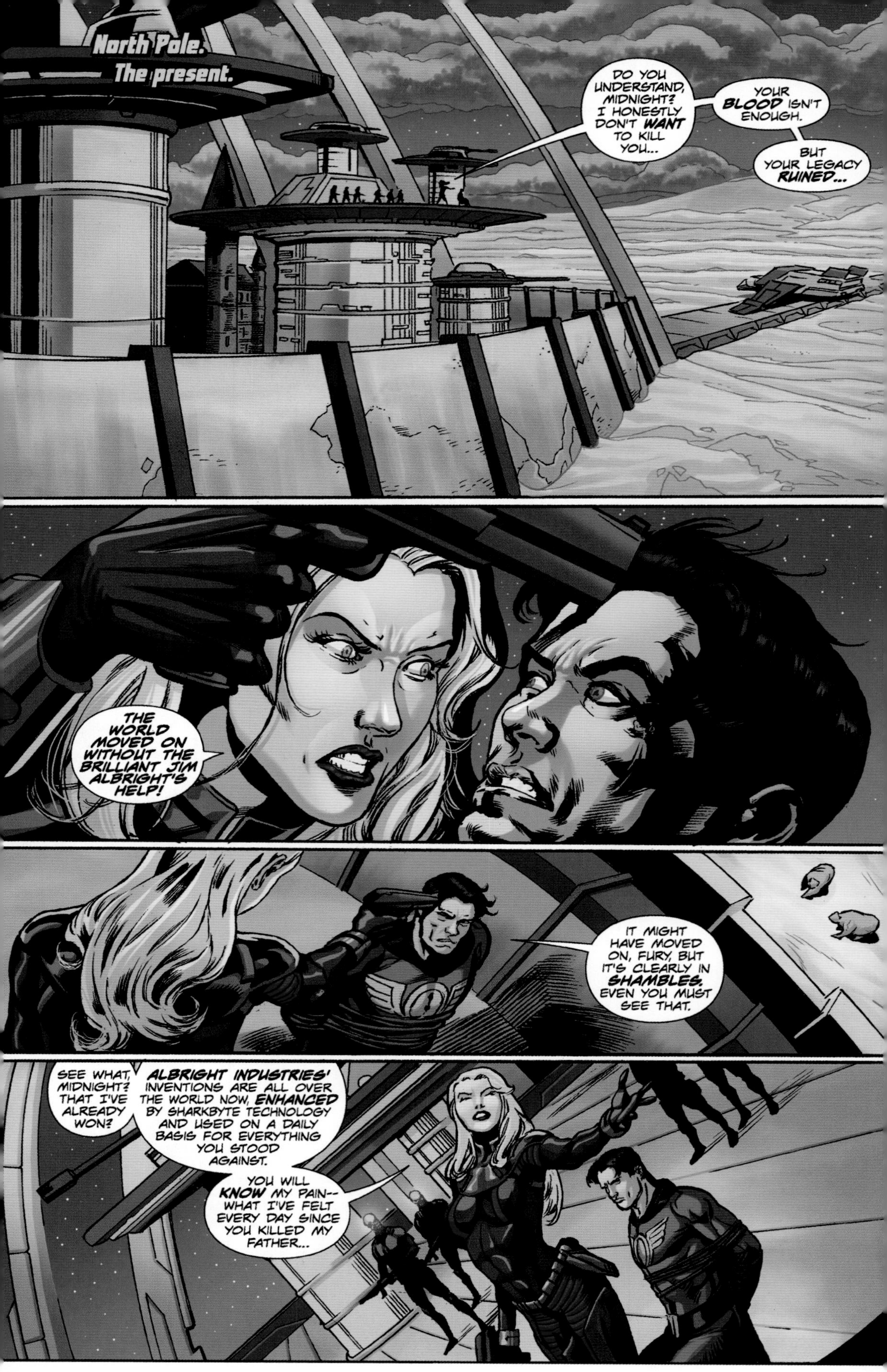
North Pole.
The present.
DO YOU UNDERSTAND, MIDNIGHT? I HONESTLY DON'T WANT TO KILL YOU...
YOUR BLOOD ISN'T ENOUGH.
BUT YOUR LEGACY RUINED...
THE WORLD MOVED ON WITHOUT THE BRILLIANT JIM ALBRIGHT'S HELP!
IT MIGHT HAVE MOVED ON, FURY, BUT IT'S CLEARLY IN SHAMBLES. EVEN YOU MUST SEE THAT.
SEE WHAT, MIDNIGHT? THAT I'VE ALREADY WON?
ALBRIGHT INDUSTRIES' INVENTIONS ARE ALL OVER THE WORLD NOW, ENHANCED BY SHARKBYTE TECHNOLOGY AND USED ON A DAILY BASIS FOR EVERYTHING YOU STOOD AGAINST.
YOU WILL KNOW MY PAIN-- WHAT I'VE FELT EVERY DAY SINCE YOU KILLED MY FATHER...

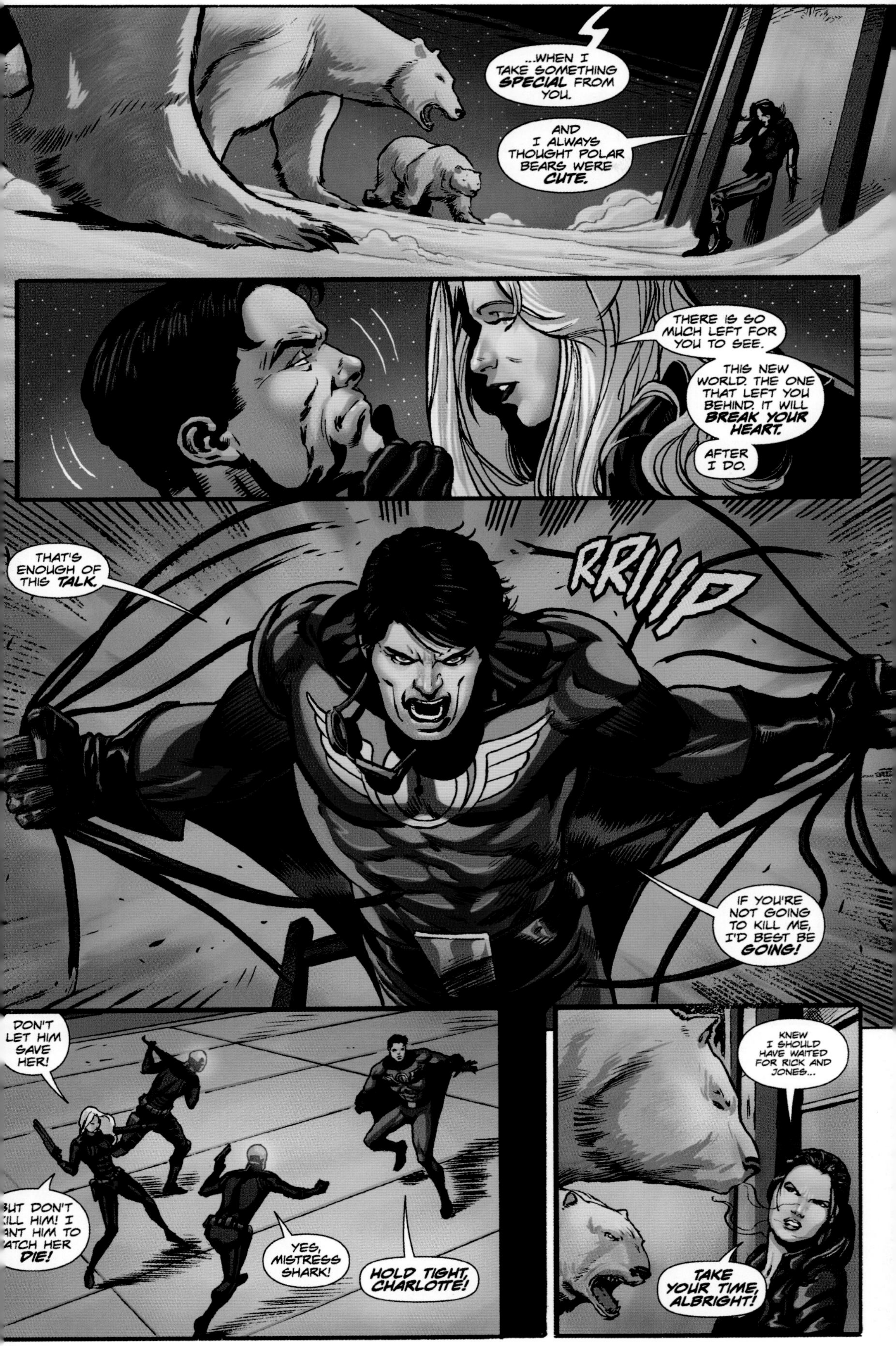
...WHEN I TAKE SOMETHING SPECIAL FROM YOU.
AND I ALWAYS THOUGHT POLAR BEARS WERE CUTE.
THERE IS SO MUCH LEFT FOR YOU TO SEE.
THIS NEW WORLD. THE ONE THAT LEFT YOU BEHIND. IT WILL BREAK YOUR HEART.
AFTER I DO.
THAT'S ENOUGH OF THIS TALK.
RRIIIP
IF YOU'RE NOT GOING TO KILL ME, I'D BEST BE GOING!
DON'T LET HIM SAVE HER!
BUT DON'T KILL HIM! I WANT HIM TO WATCH HER DIE!
YES, MISTRESS SHARK!
HOLD TIGHT, CHARLOTTE!
KNEW I SHOULD HAVE WAITED FOR RICK AND JONES...
TAKE YOUR TIME, ALBRIGHT!

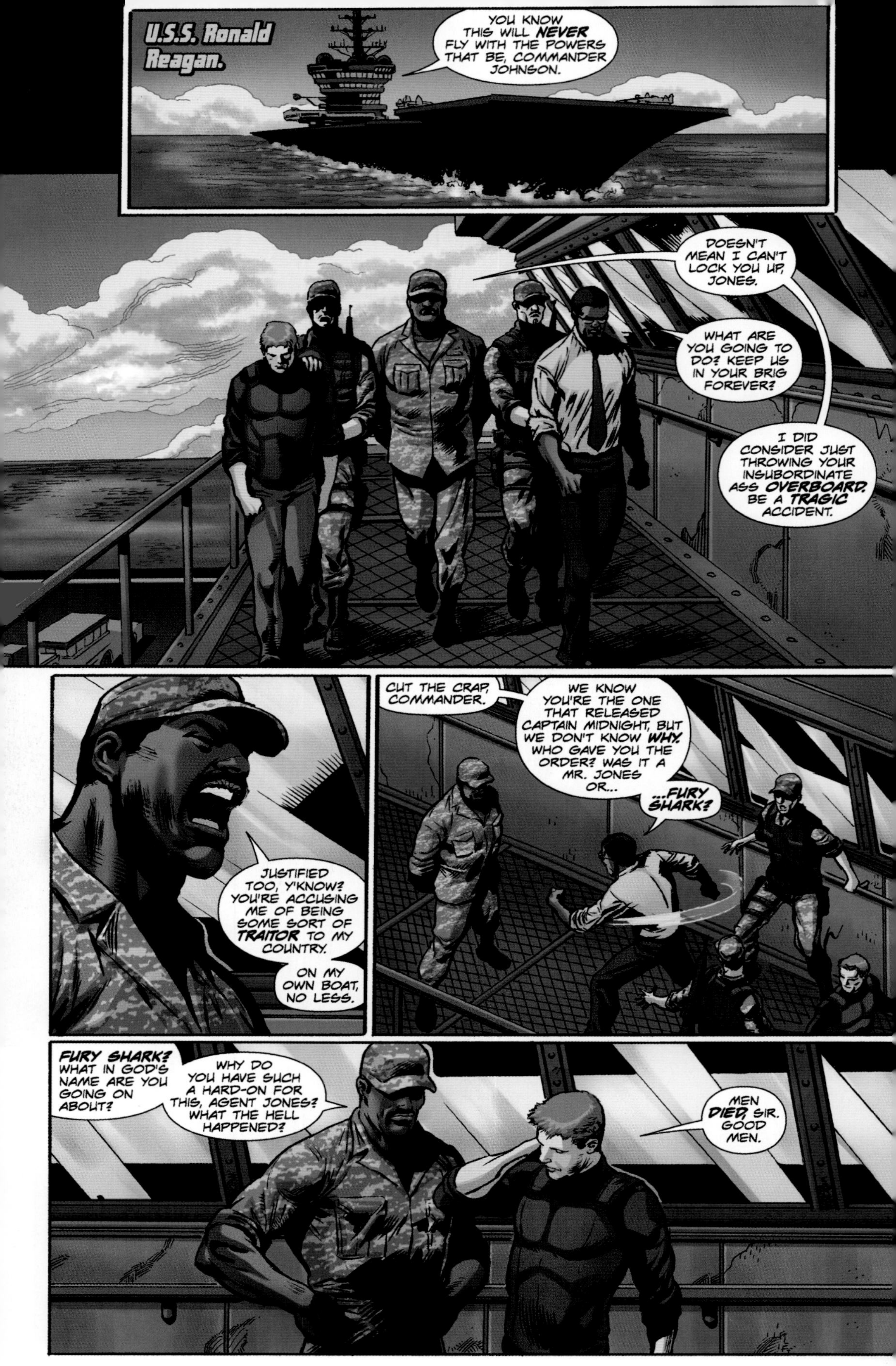
U.S.S. Ronald Reagan.
YOU KNOW THIS WILL NEVER FLY WITH THE POWERS THAT BE, COMMANDER JOHNSON.
DOESN'T MEAN I CAN'T LOCK YOU UP, JONES.
WHAT ARE YOU GOING TO DO? KEEP US IN YOUR BRIG FOREVER?
I DID CONSIDER JUST THROWING YOUR INSUBORDINATE ASS OVERBOARD. BE A TRAGIC ACCIDENT.
JUSTIFIED TOO, Y'KNOW? YOU'RE ACCUSING ME OF BEING SOME SORT OF TRAITOR TO MY COUNTRY.
ON MY OWN BOAT, NO LESS.
CUT THE CRAP, COMMANDER.
WE KNOW YOU'RE THE ONE THAT RELEASED CAPTAIN MIDNIGHT, BUT WE DON'T KNOW WHY. WHO GAVE YOU THE ORDER? WAS IT A MR. JONES OR...
...FURY SHARK?
FURY SHARK? WHAT IN GOD'S NAME ARE YOU GOING ON ABOUT?
WHY DO YOU HAVE SUCH A HARD-ON FOR THIS, AGENT JONES? WHAT THE HELL HAPPENED?
MEN DIED, SIR. GOOD MEN.

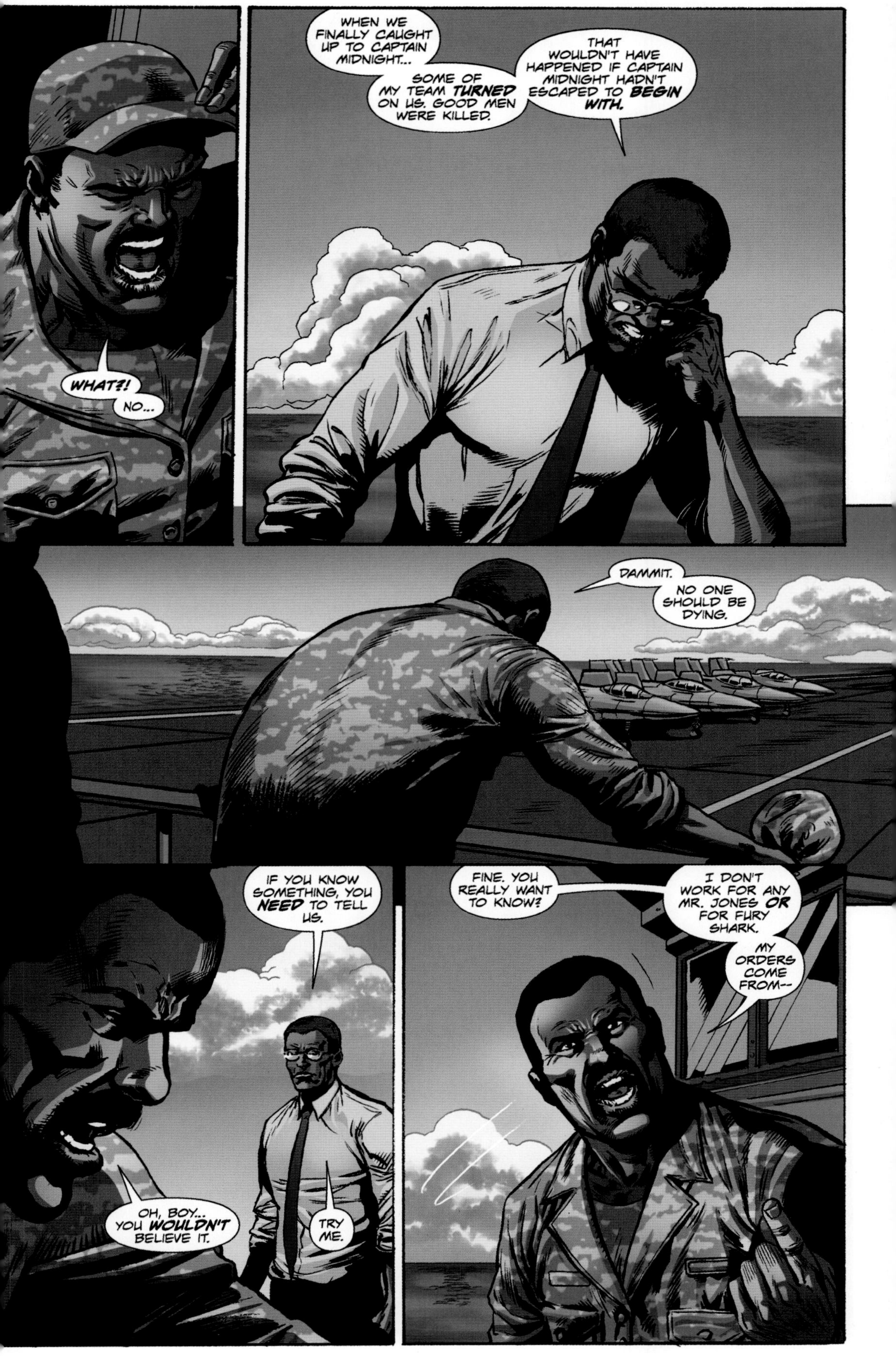
WHEN WE FINALLY CAUGHT UP TO CAPTAIN MIDNIGHT...
SOME OF MY TEAM TURNED ON US. GOOD MEN WERE KILLED.
WHAT?! NO...
THAT WOULDN'T HAVE HAPPENED IF CAPTAIN MIDNIGHT HADN'T ESCAPED TO BEGIN WITH.
DAMMIT. NO ONE SHOULD BE DYING.
IF YOU KNOW SOMETHING, YOU NEED TO TELL US.
OH, BOY... YOU WOULDN'T BELIEVE IT.
TRY ME.
FINE. YOU REALLY WANT TO KNOW?
I DON'T WORK FOR ANY MR. JONES OR FOR FURY SHARK.
MY ORDERS COME FROM--

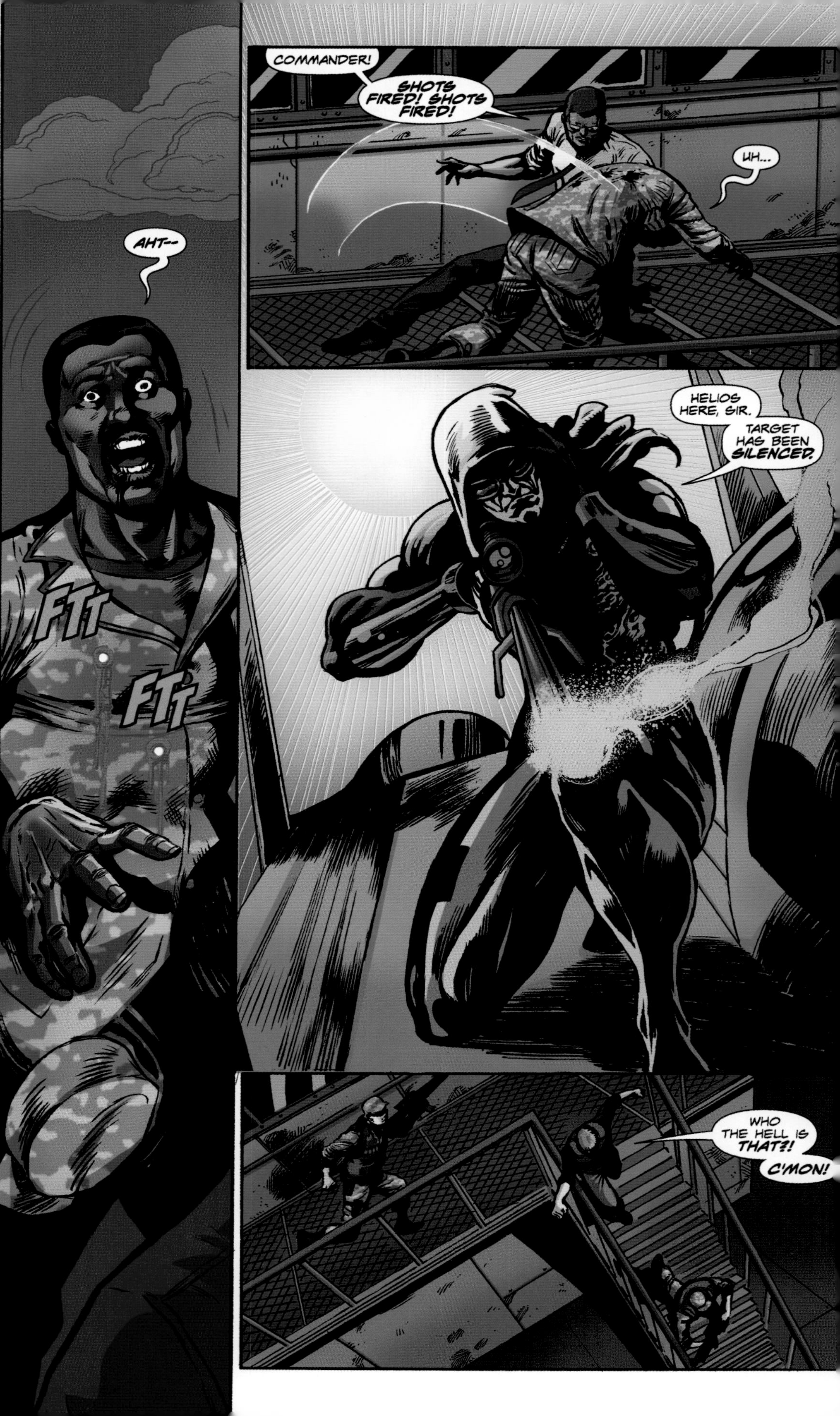
AHT--
FTT
FTT
COMMANDER!
SHOTS FIRED! SHOTS FIRED!
UH...
HELIOS HERE, SIR.
TARGET HAS BEEN SILENCED.
WHO THE HELL IS THAT?!
C'MON!

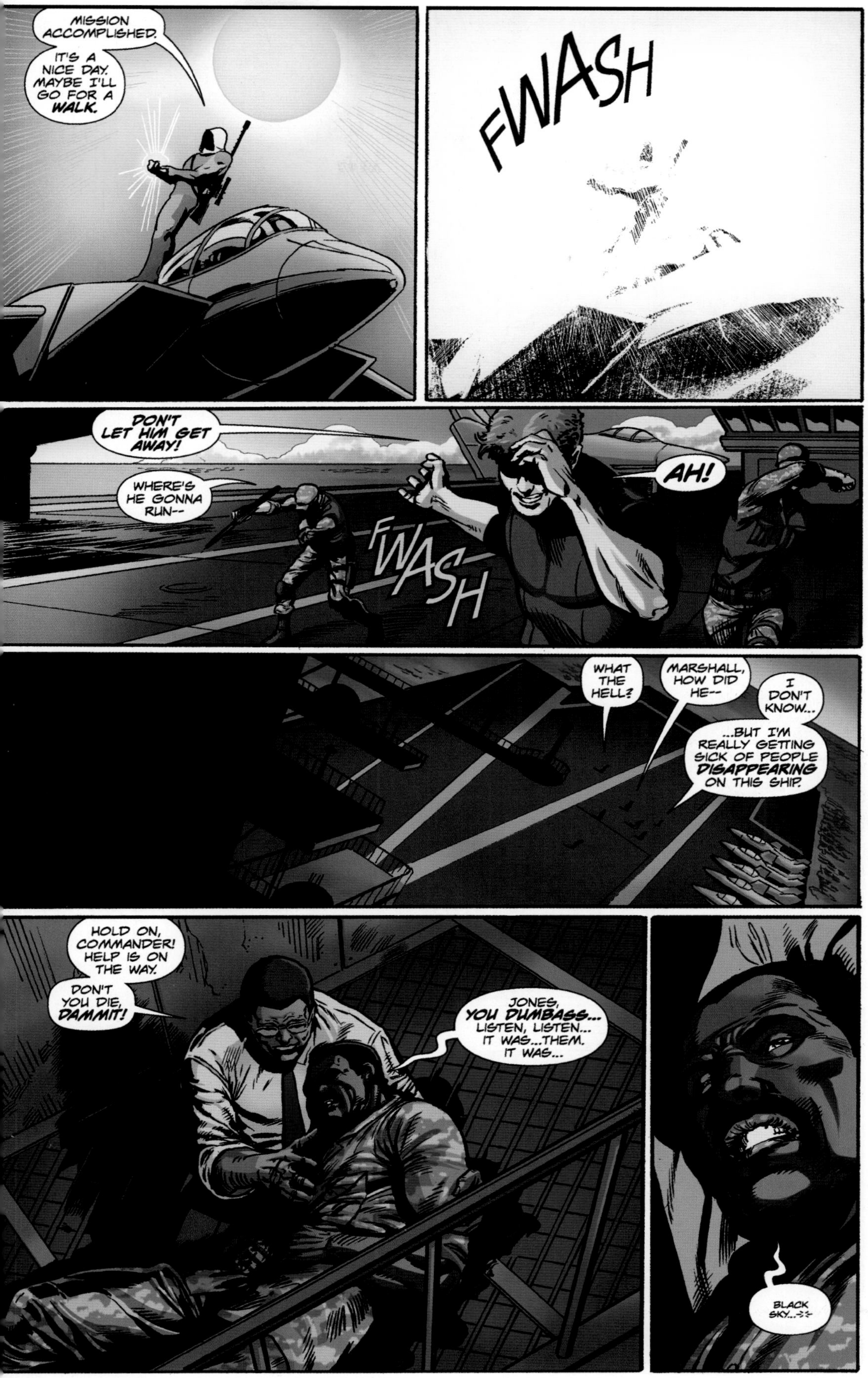
MISSION ACCOMPLISHED.
IT'S A NICE DAY. MAYBE I'LL GO FOR A WALK.
FWASH
DON'T LET HIM GET AWAY!
WHERE'S HE GONNA RUN--
AH!
FWASH
WHAT THE HELL?
MARSHALL, HOW DID HE--
I DON'T KNOW...
...BUT I'M REALLY GETTING SICK OF PEOPLE DISAPPEARING ON THIS SHIP.
HOLD ON, COMMANDER! HELP IS ON THE WAY.
DON'T YOU DIE, DAMMIT!
JONES, YOU DUMBASS... LISTEN, LISTEN... IT WAS...THEM. IT WAS...
BLACK SKY...

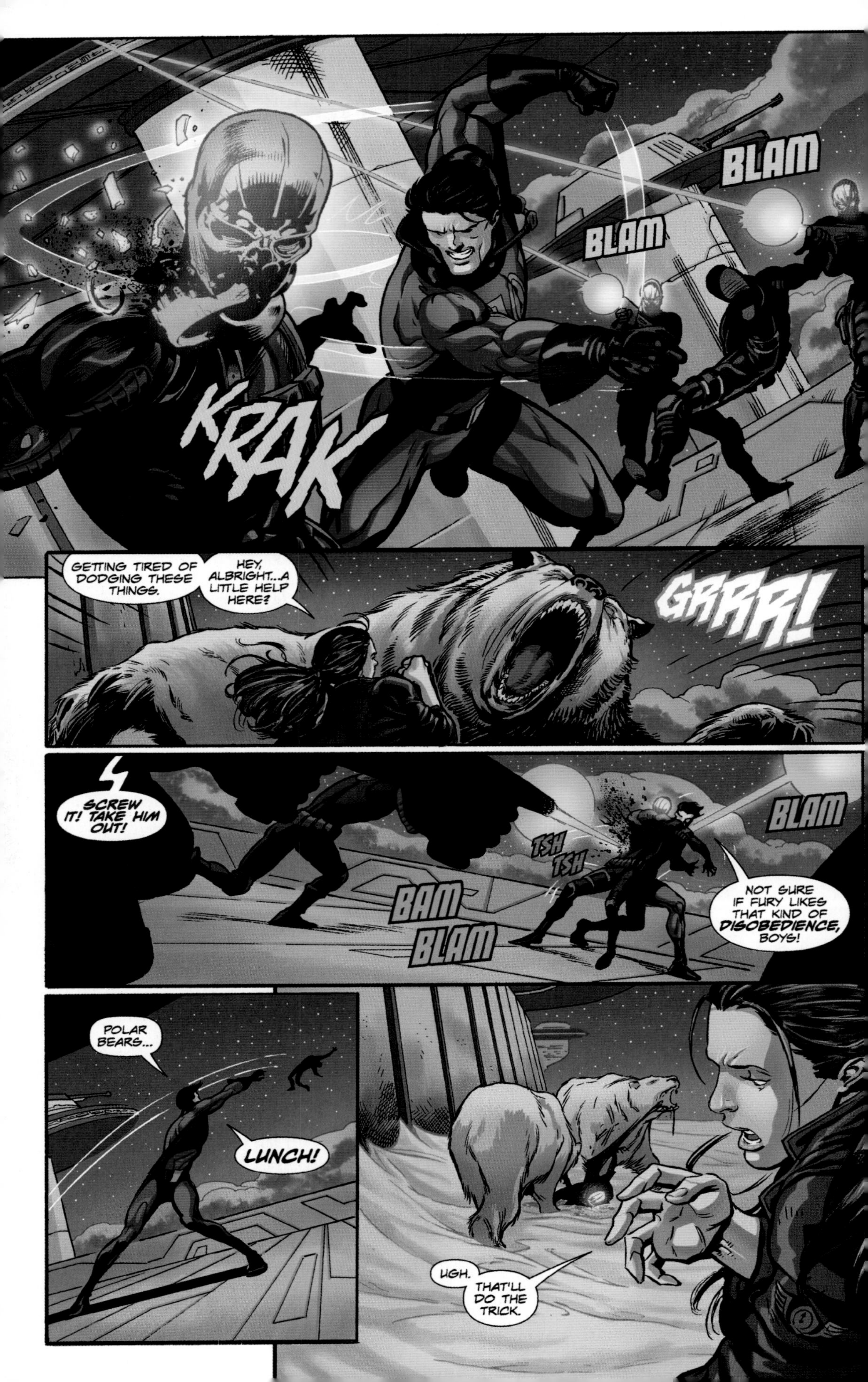
BLAM
BLAM
KRAK
GETTING TIRED OF DODGING THESE THINGS.
HEY, ALBRIGHT...A LITTLE HELP HERE?
GRRR!
SCREW IT! TAKE HIM OUT!
BLAM
TSH TSH
BAM BLAM
NOT SURE IF FURY LIKES THAT KIND OF DISOBEDIENCE, BOYS!
POLAR BEARS...
LUNCH!
UGH. THAT'LL DO THE TRICK.

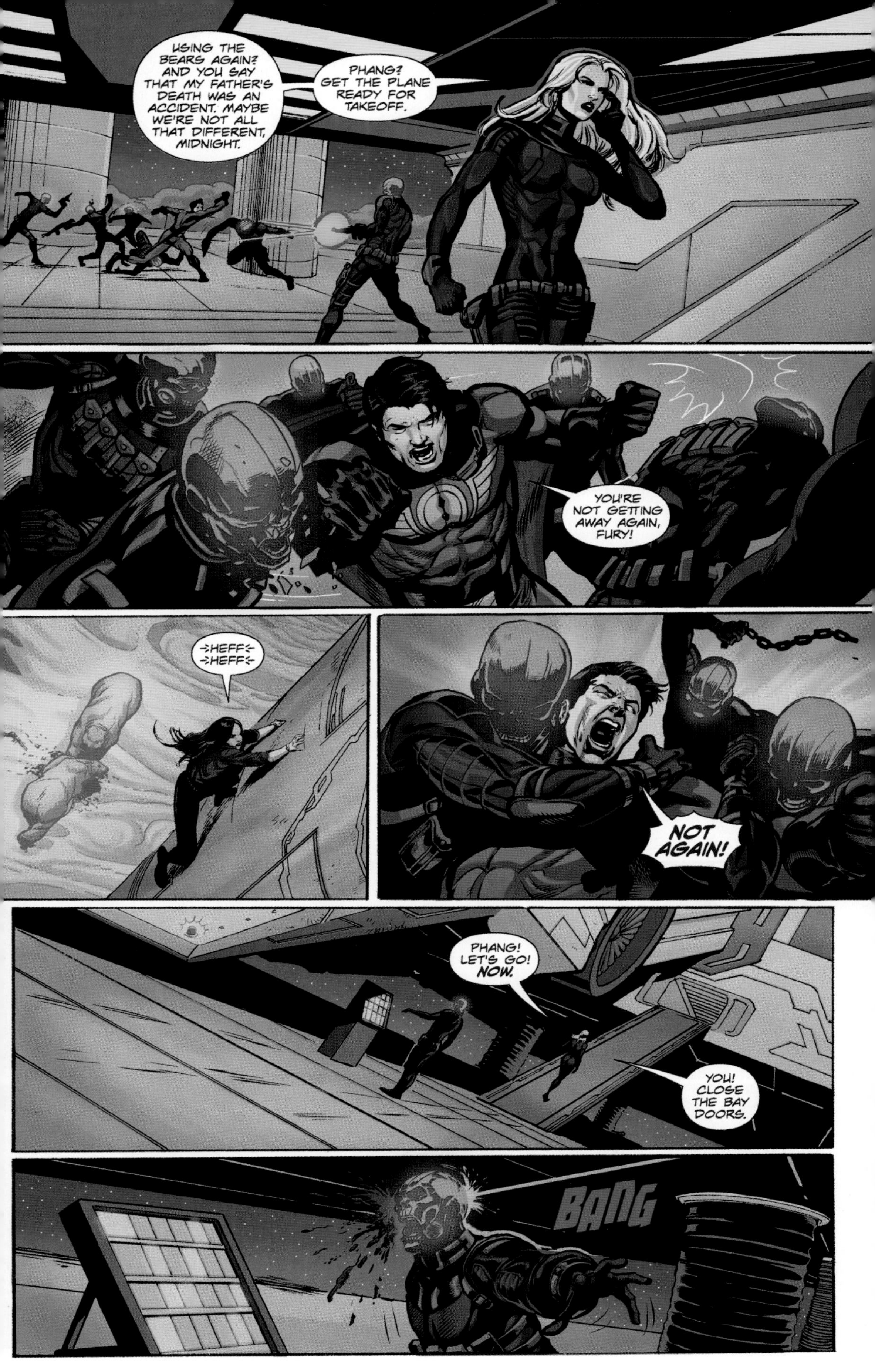
USING THE BEARS AGAIN? AND YOU SAY THAT MY FATHER'S DEATH WAS AN ACCIDENT. MAYBE WE'RE NOT ALL THAT DIFFERENT, MIDNIGHT.
PHANG? GET THE PLANE READY FOR TAKEOFF.
YOU'RE NOT GETTING AWAY AGAIN, FURY!
HEFF HEFF
NOT AGAIN!
PHANG! LET'S GO! NOW.
YOU! CLOSE THE BAY DOORS.
BANG

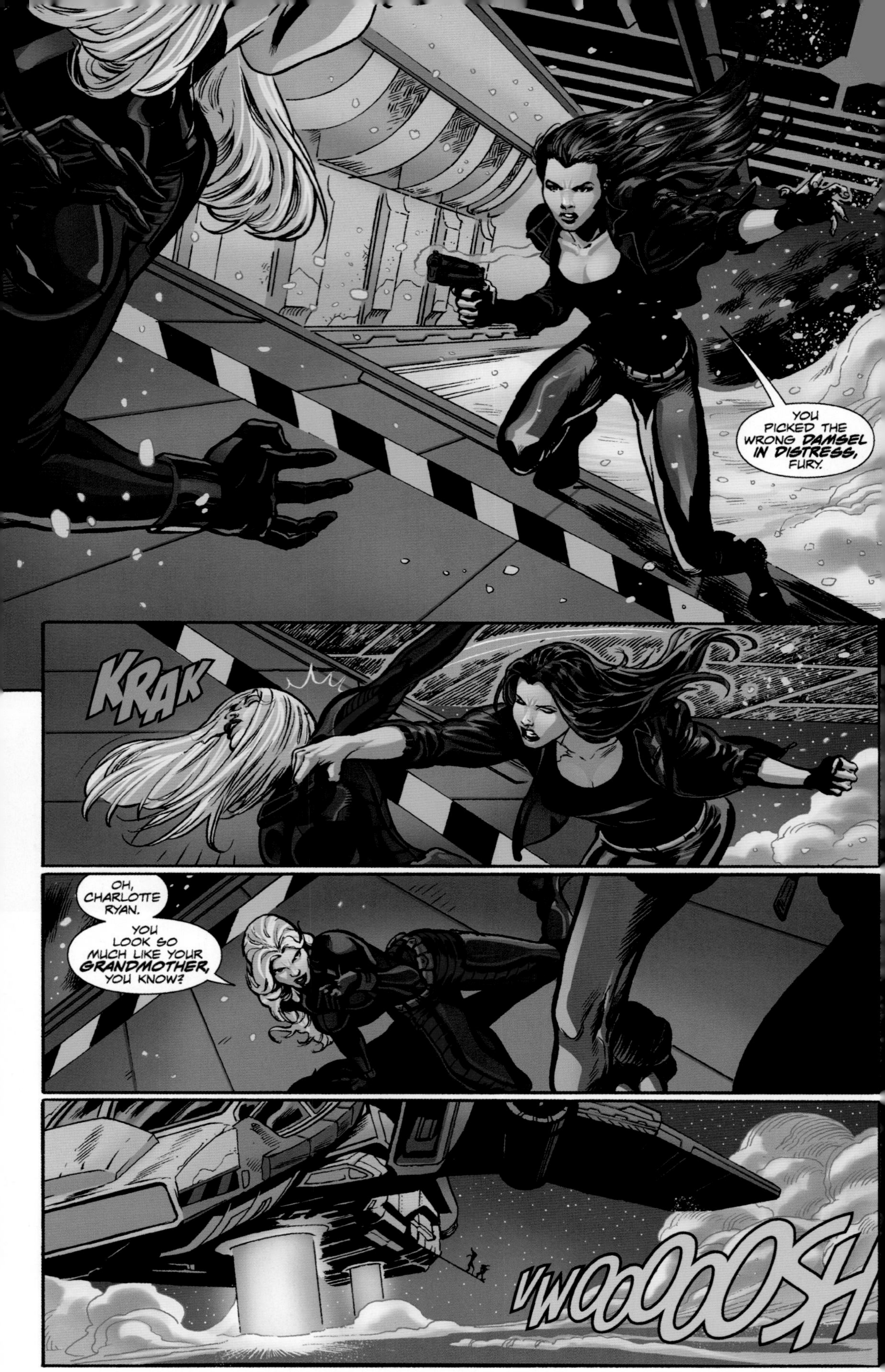
YOU PICKED THE WRONG DAMSEL IN DISTRESS, FURY.
KRAK
OH, CHARLOTTE RYAN.
YOU LOOK SO MUCH LIKE YOUR GRANDMOTHER, YOU KNOW?
VWOOOOOOSH

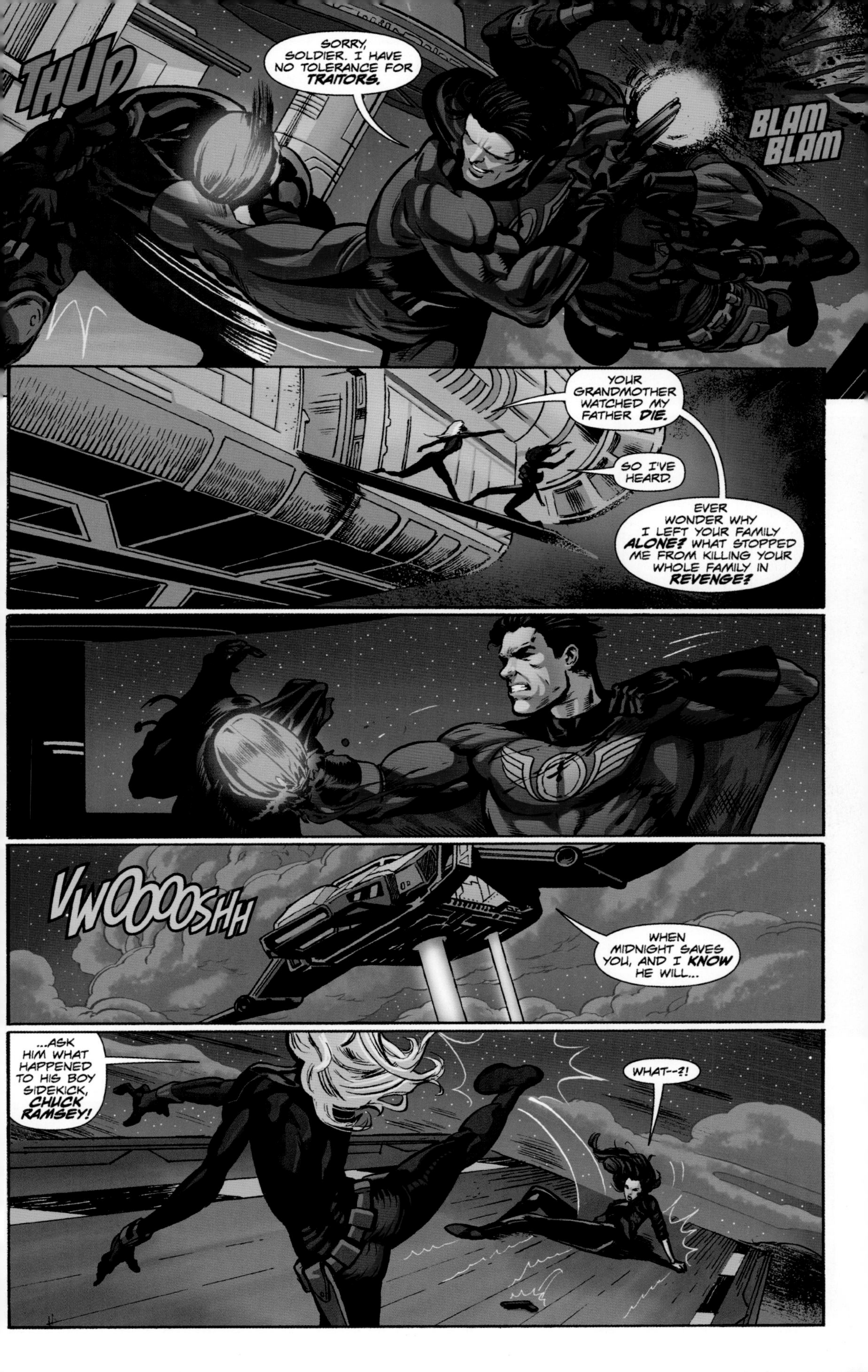
THUD
SORRY, SOLDIER. I HAVE NO TOLERANCE FOR TRAITORS.
BLAM BLAM
YOUR GRANDMOTHER WATCHED MY FATHER DIE.
SO I'VE HEARD.
EVER WONDER WHY I LEFT YOUR FAMILY ALONE? WHAT STOPPED ME FROM KILLING YOUR WHOLE FAMILY IN REVENGE?
VWOOOOSHH
WHEN MIDNIGHT SAVES YOU, AND I KNOW HE WILL...
...ASK HIM WHAT HAPPENED TO HIS BOY SIDEKICK, CHUCK RAMSEY!
WHAT--?!

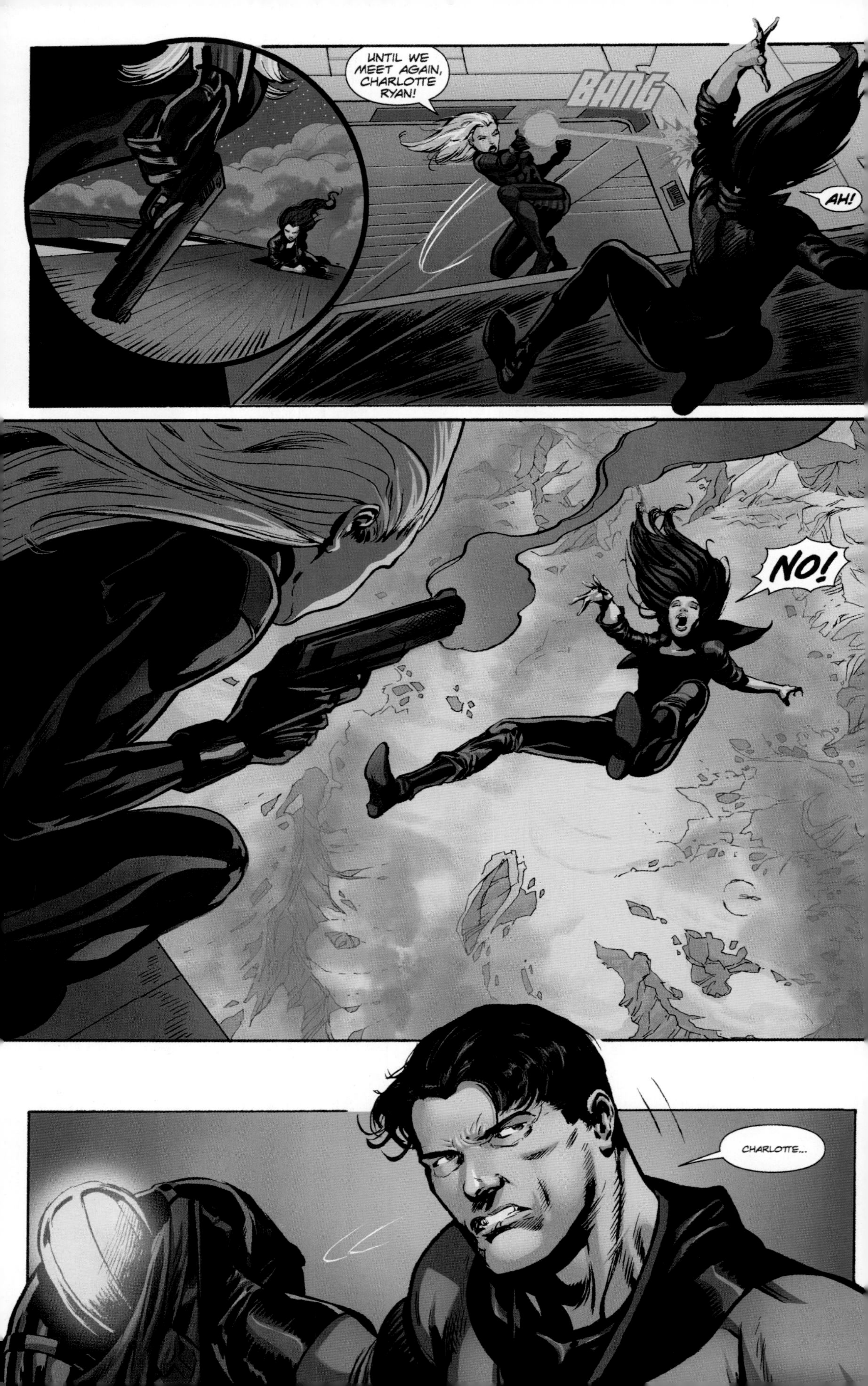

UNTIL WE MEET AGAIN, CHARLOTTE RYAN!
BANG
AH!
NO!
CHARLOTTE...

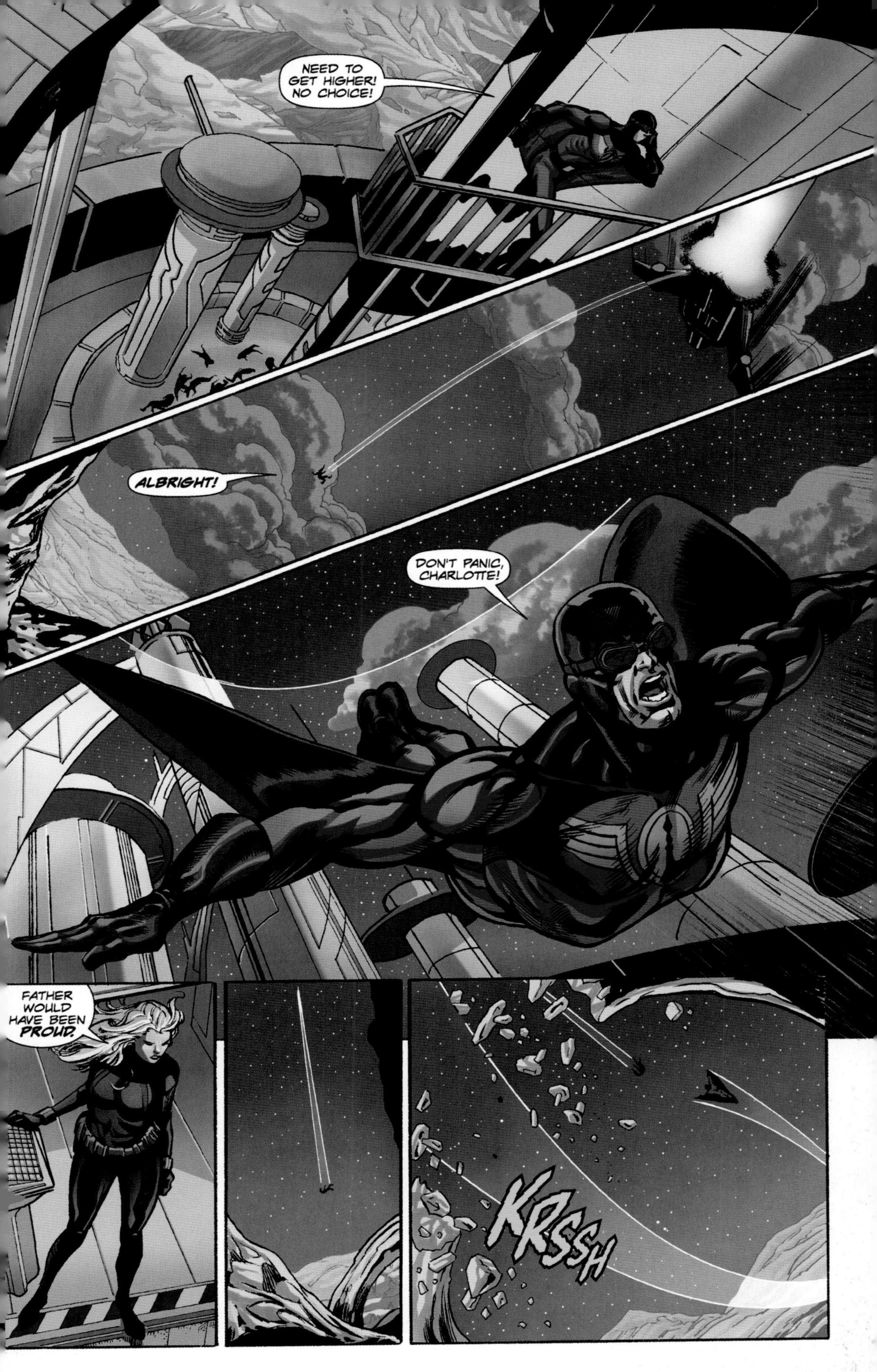
NEED TO GET HIGHER! NO CHOICE!
ALBRIGHT!
DON'T PANIC, CHARLOTTE!
FATHER WOULD HAVE BEEN PROUD.
KRSSH

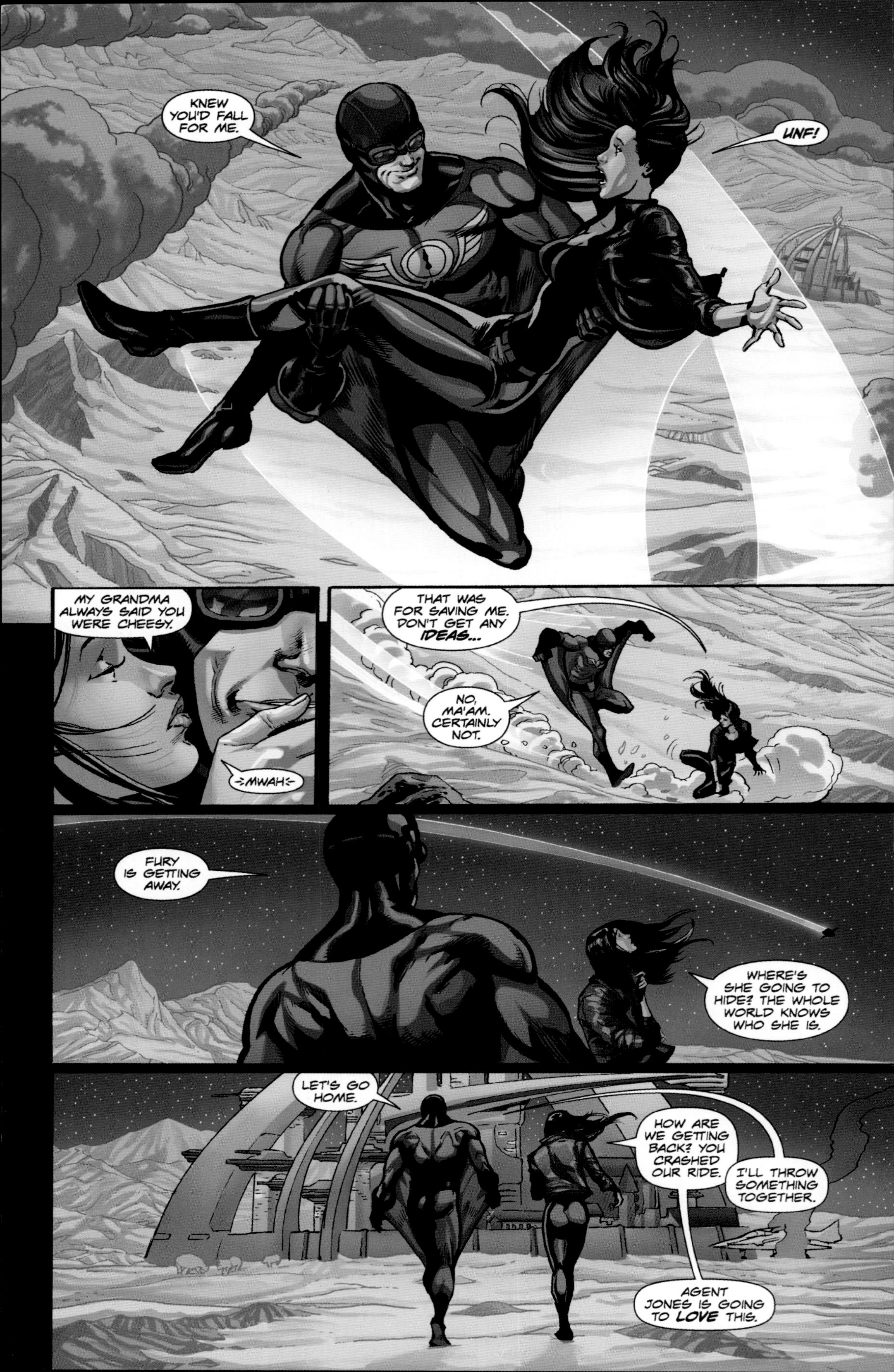
KNEW YOU'D FALL FOR ME.
UNF!
MY GRANDMA ALWAYS SAID YOU WERE CHEESY.
MWAH
THAT WAS FOR SAVING ME. DON'T GET ANY IDEAS...
NO, MA'AM. CERTAINLY NOT.
FURY IS GETTING AWAY.
WHERE'S SHE GOING TO HIDE? THE WHOLE WORLD KNOWS WHO SHE IS.
LET'S GO HOME.
HOW ARE WE GETTING BACK? YOU CRASHED OUR RIDE.
I'LL THROW SOMETHING TOGETHER.
AGENT JONES IS GOING TO LOVE THIS.

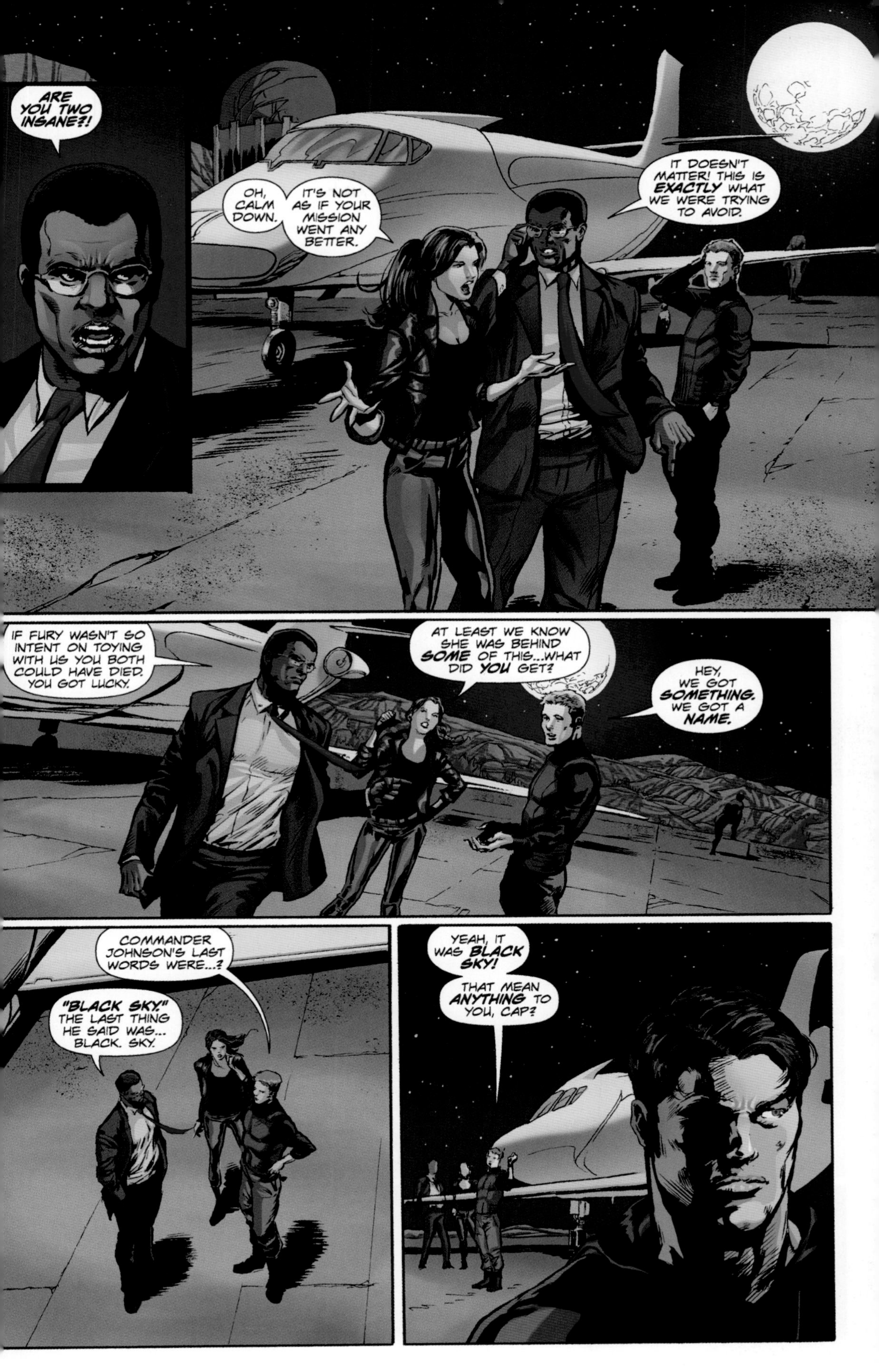
ARE YOU TWO INSANE?!
OH, CALM DOWN.
IT'S NOT AS IF YOUR MISSION WENT ANY BETTER.
IT DOESN'T MATTER! THIS IS EXACTLY WHAT WE WERE TRYING TO AVOID.
IF FURY WASN'T SO INTENT ON TOYING WITH US YOU BOTH COULD HAVE DIED. YOU GOT LUCKY.
AT LEAST WE KNOW SHE WAS BEHIND SOME OF THIS...WHAT DID YOU GET?
HEY, WE GOT SOMETHING. WE GOT A NAME.
COMMANDER JOHNSON'S LAST WORDS WERE...?
"BLACK SKY." THE LAST THING HE SAID WAS... BLACK. SKY.
YEAH, IT WAS BLACK SKY!
THAT MEAN ANYTHING TO YOU, CAP?

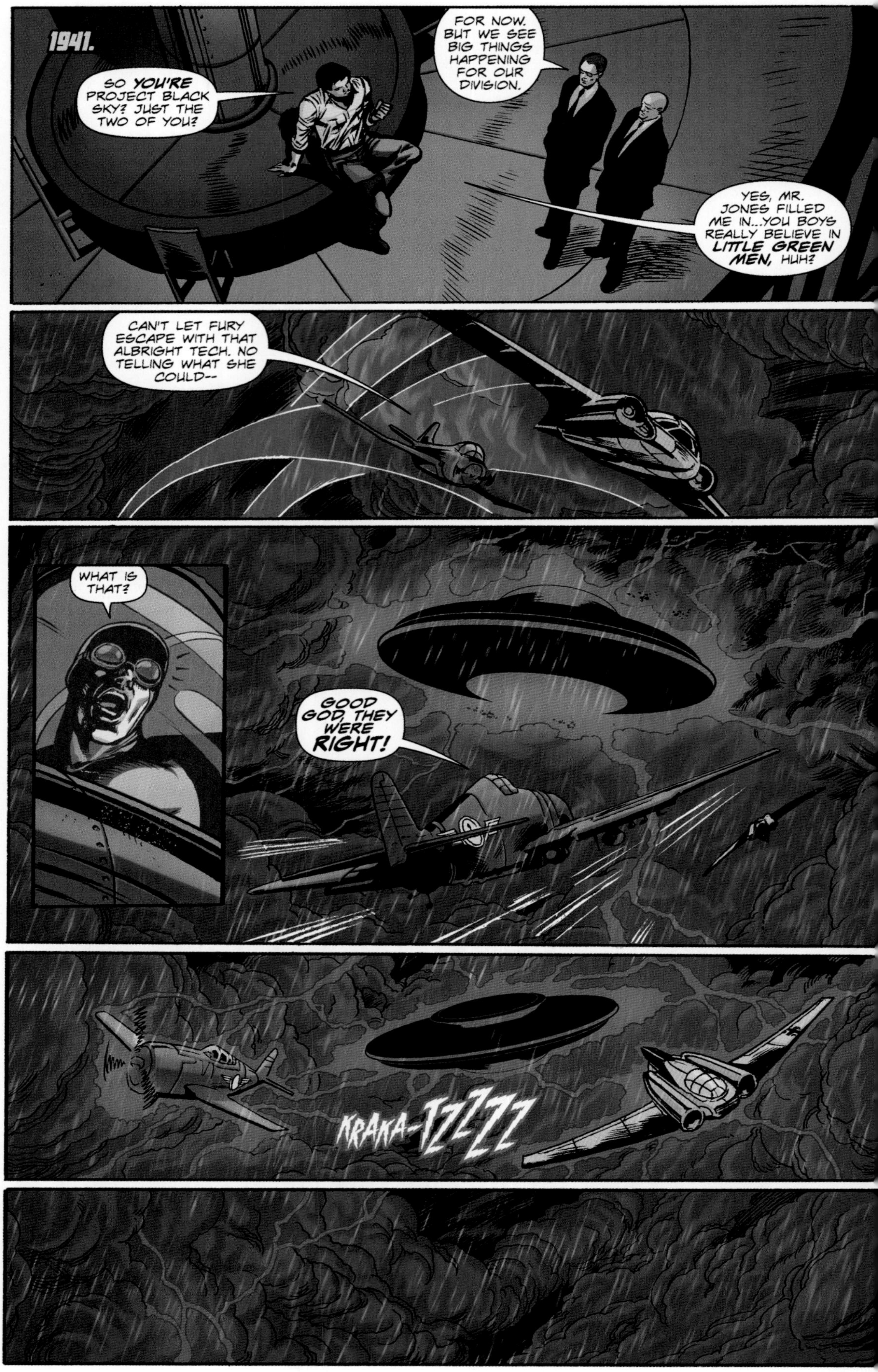
1941.
SO YOU'RE PROJECT BLACK SKY? JUST THE TWO OF YOU?
FOR NOW. BUT WE SEE BIG THINGS HAPPENING FOR OUR DIVISION.
YES, MR. JONES FILLED ME IN...YOU BOYS REALLY BELIEVE IN LITTLE GREEN MEN, HUH?
CAN'T LET FURY ESCAPE WITH THAT ALBRIGHT TECH. NO TELLING WHAT SHE COULD--
WHAT IS THAT?
GOOD GOD, THEY WERE RIGHT!
KRAKA-TZZZZZ

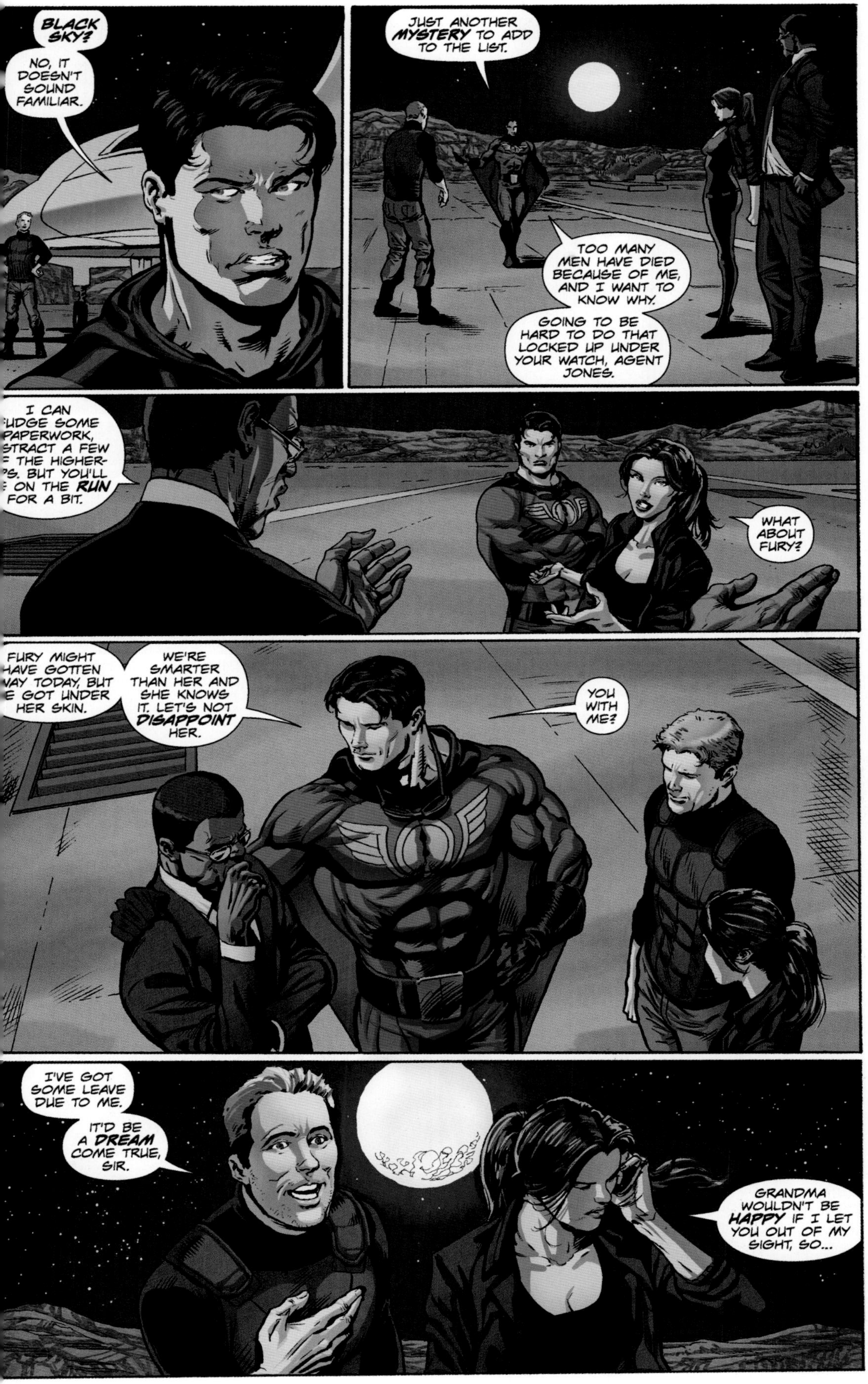
BLACK SKY?
NO, IT DOESN'T SOUND FAMILIAR.
JUST ANOTHER MYSTERY TO ADD TO THE LIST.
TOO MANY MEN HAVE DIED BECAUSE OF ME, AND I WANT TO KNOW WHY.
GOING TO BE HARD TO DO THAT LOCKED UP UNDER YOUR WATCH, AGENT JONES.
I CAN FUDGE SOME PAPERWORK, STRACT A FEW F THE HIGHER- PS. BUT YOU'LL E ON THE RUN FOR A BIT.
WHAT ABOUT FURY?
FURY MIGHT HAVE GOTTEN WAY TODAY, BUT E GOT UNDER HER SKIN.
WE'RE SMARTER THAN HER AND SHE KNOWS IT. LET'S NOT DISAPPOINT HER.
YOU WITH ME?
I'VE GOT SOME LEAVE DUE TO ME.
IT'D BE A DREAM COME TRUE, SIR.
GRANDMA WOULDN'T BE HAPPY IF I LET YOU OUT OF MY SIGHT, SO...

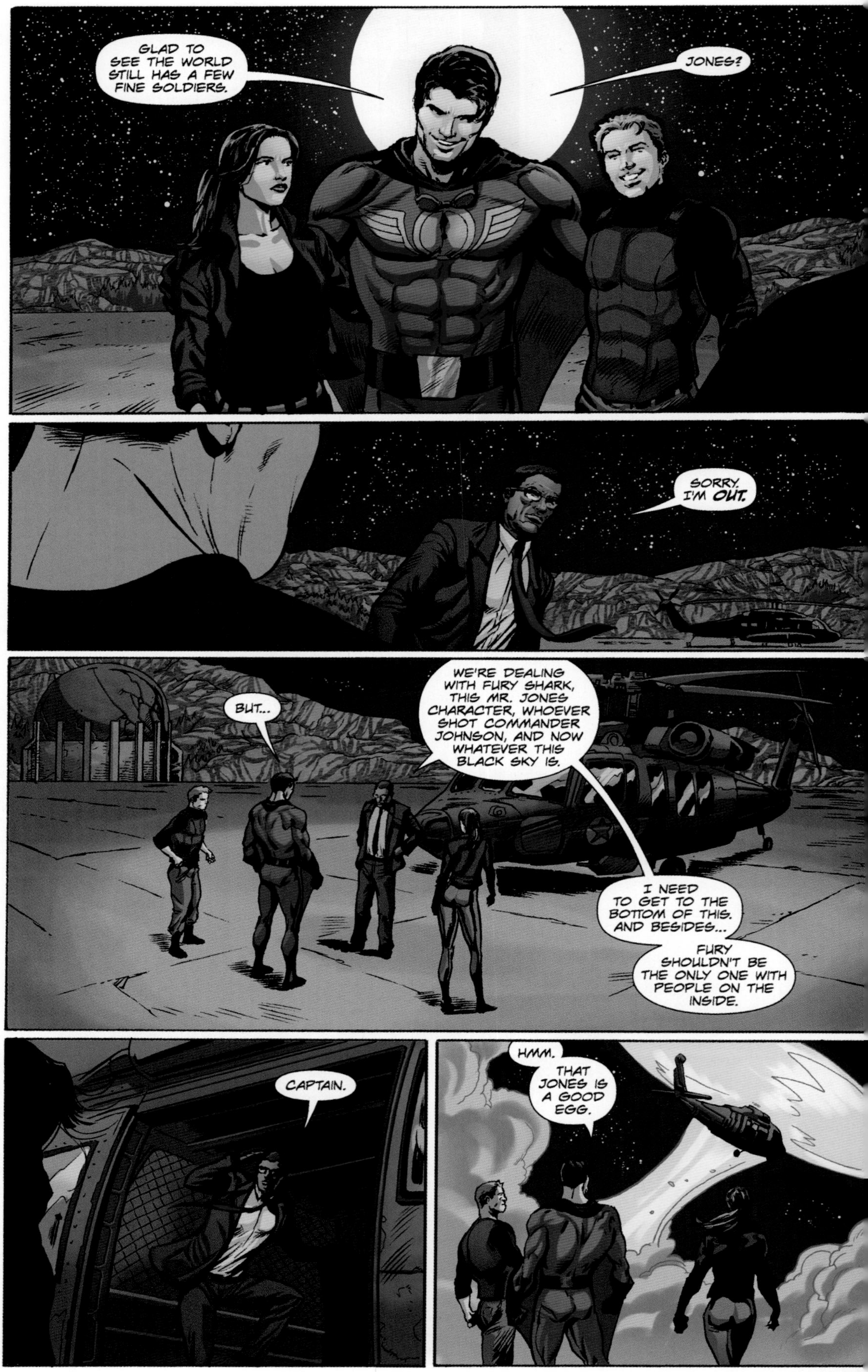

GLAD TO SEE THE WORLD STILL HAS A FEW FINE SOLDIERS.
JONES?
SORRY. I'M OUT.
BUT...
WE'RE DEALING WITH FURY SHARK, THIS MR. JONES CHARACTER, WHOEVER SHOT COMMANDER JOHNSON, AND NOW WHATEVER THIS BLACK SKY IS.
I NEED TO GET TO THE BOTTOM OF THIS. AND BESIDES...
FURY SHOULDN'T BE THE ONLY ONE WITH PEOPLE ON THE INSIDE.
CAPTAIN.
HMM.
THAT JONES IS A GOOD EGG.

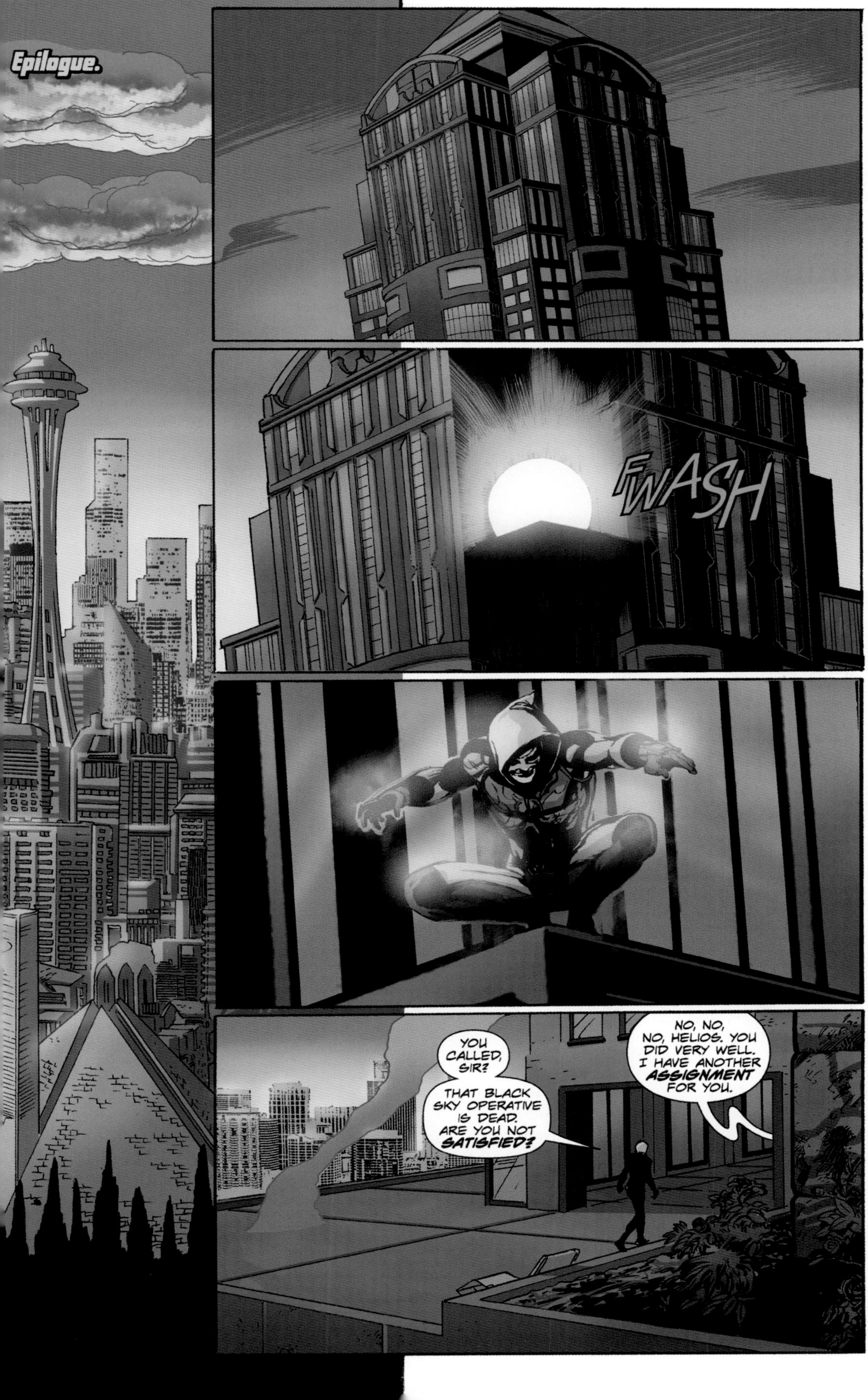
Epilogue.
FWASH
YOU CALLED, SIR?
THAT BLACK SKY OPERATIVE IS DEAD. ARE YOU NOT SATISFIED?
NO, NO, NO, HELIOS. YOU DID VERY WELL. I HAVE ANOTHER ASSIGNMENT FOR YOU.

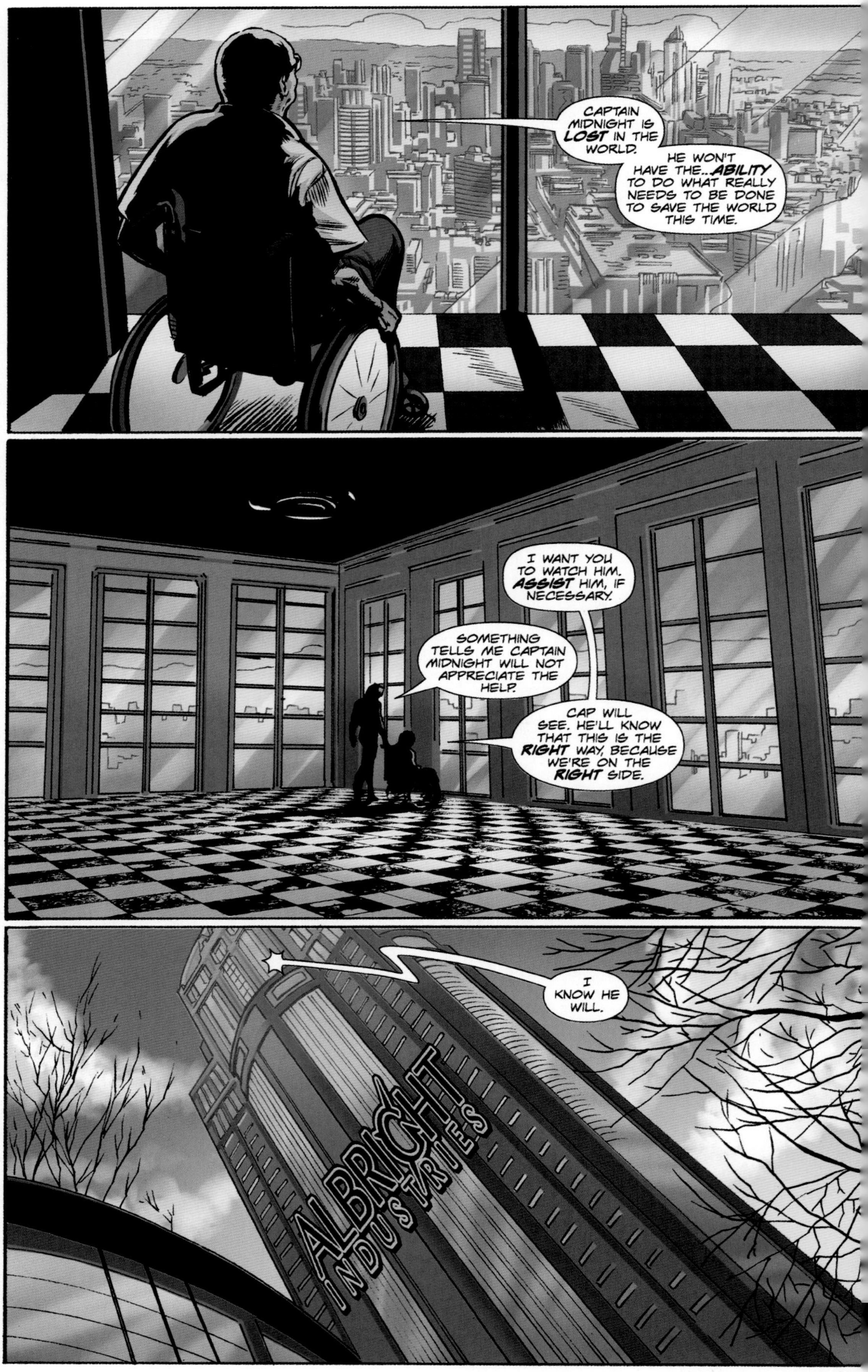
CAPTAIN MIDNIGHT IS **LOST** IN THE WORLD.
HE WON'T HAVE THE... **ABILITY** TO DO WHAT REALLY NEEDS TO BE DONE TO SAVE THE WORLD THIS TIME.
I WANT YOU TO WATCH HIM. **ASSIST** HIM, IF NECESSARY.
SOMETHING TELLS ME CAPTAIN MIDNIGHT WILL NOT APPRECIATE THE HELP.
CAP WILL SEE. HE'LL KNOW THAT THIS IS THE **RIGHT** WAY, BECAUSE WE'RE ON THE **RIGHT** SIDE.
I KNOW HE WILL.
ALBRIGHT INDUSTRIES

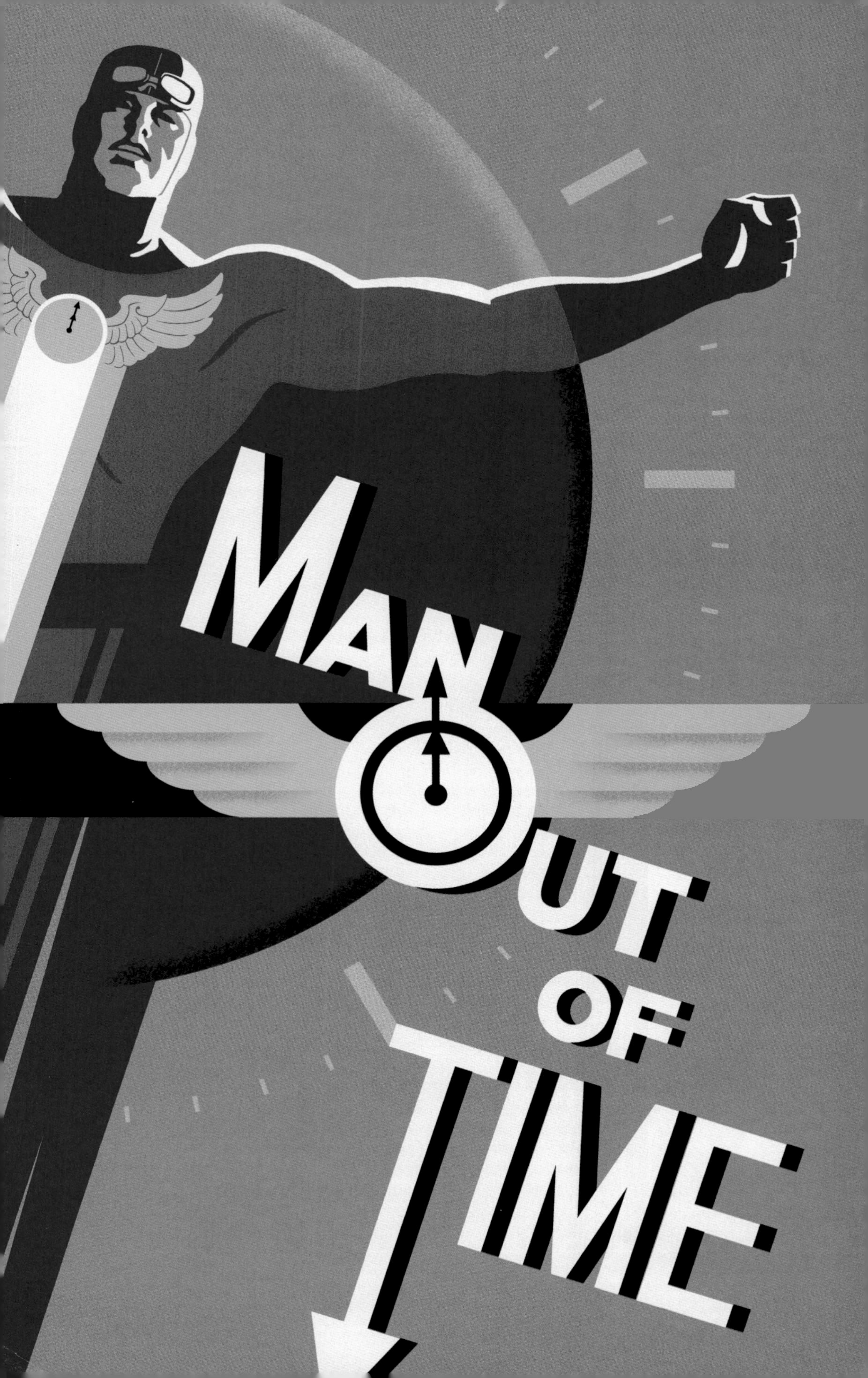
MAN
OUT
OF
TIME

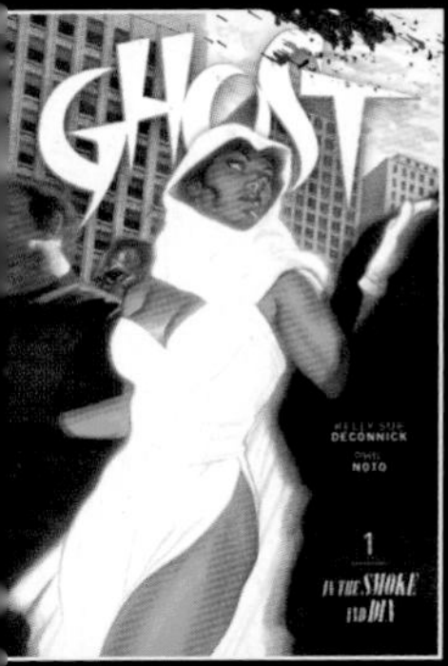
GHOST
DECONNICK
NOTO
1

X VOLUME 1: BIG BAD
Duane Swierczynski and Eric Nguyen
A masked vigilante dispenses justice without mercy to the criminals of the decaying city of Arcadia. Nonsto
visceral action, with Dark Horse's most brutal and exciting character—X!
978-1-61655-241-1 | $14.99

GHOST VOLUME 1: IN THE SMOKE AND DIN
Kelly Sue DeConnick, Phil Noto, Alex Ross, and Jenny Frison
Paranormal investigators accidentally summon a ghostly woman. The search for her identity uncover a deadly alliance between political corruption and demonic science! In the middle stands a woma trapped between two worlds!
978-1-61655-121-6 | $14.99

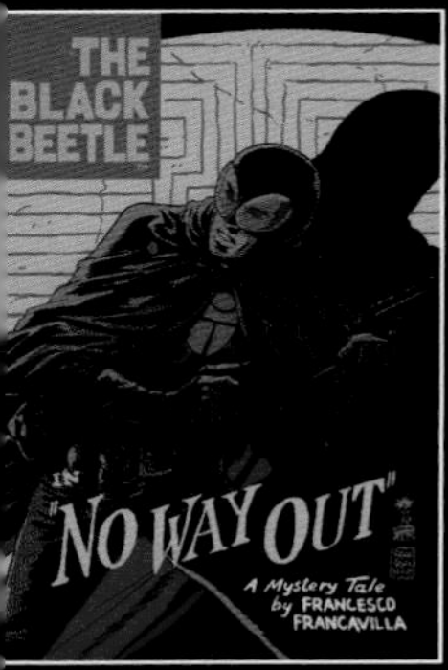
THE BLACK BEETLE
IN
'NO WAY OUT'
A Mystery Tale by FRANCESCO FRANCAVILLA

THE BLACK BEETLE VOLUME 1: NO WAY OUT
Francesco Francavilla
After witnessing an explosion that decimates the city's organized crime community, the Black Beetle—Colt City's sleuthing sentinel—is on the hunt for answers and justice in Francesco Francavilla's critical acclaimed series.
978-1-61655-202-2 | $19.99

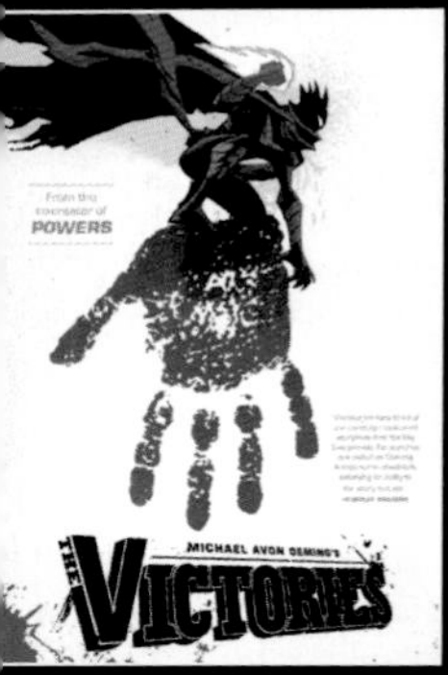
POWERS
MICHAEL AVON OEMING'S
VICTORIES

MICHAEL AVON OEMING'S THE VICTORIES
Michael Avon Oeming
From the cocreator of *Powers*! The Victories: a team of heroes sworn to protect us from crime, corruption, and the bizarre designer drug known as Float.

VOLUME 1:
978-1-61655-100-1 | $9.99

VOLUME 2: TRANSHUMAN
978-1-61655-214-5 | $17.99

THE OCCULTIST VOLUME 1
Mike Richardson, Tim Seeley, Victor Drujiniu, Jason Gorder, Andrew Dalhouse, and Steve Morris
With a team of hit mages hired by a powerful sorcerer after him, it's trial by fire for the new Occultist, as he learns to handle his powerful magical tome, or suffer at the hands of deadly enemies. From the mind of Dark Horse founder Mike Richardson (*The Secret*, *Cut*, *The Mask*)!
978-1-59582-745-6 | $16.99

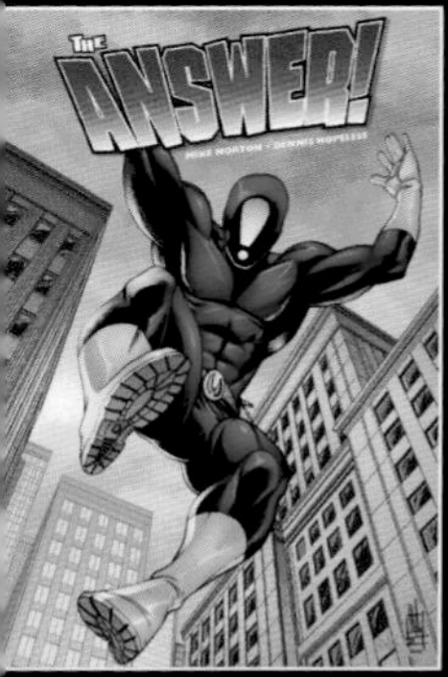
THE ANSWER!
MIKE NORTON · DENNIS HOPELESS

BLOODHOUND VOLUME 1: BRASS KNUCKLE PSYCHOLOGY
Dan Jolley, Leonard Kirk, and Robin Riggs
Criminals don't stand a chance when the FBI unleashes the Bloodhound! Offered a reduced sentenc in exchange for helping the FBI capture a superpowered serial killer, ex-cop Travis Clevenger agree when he learns that the killer's next intended victim is his dead partner's daughter. Can the disgrace hero redeem himself, and can the FBI control him once they've let him loose?
978-1-61655-125-4 | $19.99

THE ANSWER!
Mike Norton and Dennis Hopeless
Insomniac librarian Devin MacKenzie is yanked into mayhem and mystery by the punctuation-face crime fighter known as the Answer! Can this unlikely team take on the sinister BRAIN TRUST? A thoroughly original superhero adventure packed with thrills, intrigue, and a hilarious sense of humor
978-1-61655-197-1 | $12.99